Religion and Identity in the South Asian Diaspora

Religious identity constitutes a key element in the formation, development and sustenance of South Asian diasporic communities. Through studies of South Asian communities situated in multiple locales, this book explores the role of religious identity in the social and political organization of the diaspora. It accounts for the factors that underlie the modification of ritual practice in the process of resettlement, and considers how multicultural policies in the adopted state, trans-generational changes and the proliferation of transnational media has impacted the development of these identities in the diaspora. Also crucial is the gender dimension, in terms of how religion and caste affect women's roles in the South Asian diaspora. What emerges then from the way separate communities in the diaspora negotiate religion are diverse patterns that are strategic and contingent. Yet, paradoxically, the dynamic and evolving relationship between religion and diaspora becomes necessary, even imperative, for sustaining a cohesive collective identity in these communities.

This book was published as a special issue of *South Asian Diaspora*.

Rajesh Rai is Assistant Professor in the South Asian Studies Programme at the National University of Singapore. Co-editor of *The Encyclopedia of the Sri Lankan Diaspora* (2013), *The South Asian Diaspora: Transnational Networks and Changing Identities* (2009), *Nationalism in South Asia* (2009), he was also Assistant Editor for *The Encyclopedia of the Indian Diaspora* (2006), which has received considerable acclaim. His articles have been published in *Modern Asian Studies*, *South Asia: Journal of South Asian Studies*, *Journal of Southeast Asian Studies*, *South Asian Diaspora* and elsewhere. His research interests are in the fields of diaspora studies and transnational identities, nationalism and the post-colonial history and politics of South Asia.

Chitra Sankaran is Associate Professor in the Department of English Language and Literature at the National University of Singapore. She has published monographs, books, edited volumes and chapters in books. Her articles have been published in *The Journal of Commonwealth Literature*, *ARIEL*, *World Literatures Written in English*, *Journal of South Asian Literatures* and elsewhere. Her research interests include South Asian Fictions and Comparative Literatures.

Religion and Identity in the South Asian Diaspora

Edited by
Rajesh Rai and Chitra Sankaran

Routledge
Taylor & Francis Group
LONDON AND NEW YORK

First published 2014 by Routledge

2 Park Square, Milton Park, Abingdon, Oxfordshire OX14 4RN
711 Third Avenue, New York, NY 10017

Routledge is an imprint of the Taylor & Francis Group, an informa business

First issued in paperback 2018

British Library Cataloguing in Publication Data
A catalogue record for this book is available from the British Library

ISBN13: 978-0-415-70815-9 (hbk)
ISBN13: 978-1-138-37737-0 (pbk)

Typeset in Times New Roman
by Taylor & Francis Books

Publisher's Note
The publisher accepts responsibility for any inconsistencies that may have arisen during the conversion of this book from journal articles to book chapters, namely the possible inclusion of journal terminology.

Contents

Citation Information

The chapters in this book were originally published in *South Asian Diaspora*, volumes 1 and 3, issue 1 (March 2011). When citing this material, please use the original page numbering for each article, as follows:

Preface
Editorial
P. Pratap Kumar
South Asian Diaspora, volume 3, issue 1 (March 2011) pp. 1–4

Chapter 1
Religion and the South Asian diaspora
Rajesh Rai and Chitra Sankaran
South Asian Diaspora, volume 3, issue 1 (March 2011) pp. 5–14

Chapter 2
Homogenisation and fragmentation, inclusivism and exclusion in the development of Hinduism in Singapore
Rajesh Rai
South Asian Diaspora, volume 1, issue 1 (March 2011) pp. 3–17

Chapter 3
The dynamics of preserving cultural heritage: the case of Durban's Kathiawad Hindu Seva Samaj, 1943–1960 and beyond
Surendra Bhana and Kusum K. Bhoola
South Asian Diaspora, volume 3, issue 1 (March 2011) pp. 15–36

Chapter 4
Religion and gender: the Hindu diaspora in Portugal
Inês Lourenço
South Asian Diaspora, volume 3, issue 1 (March 2011) pp. 37–52

Chapter 5
Talking 'gender superiority' in virtual spaces: web-based discourses of Hindu student groups in the US and UK
Anjana Narayan and Bandana Purkayastha
South Asian Diaspora, volume 3, issue 1 (March 2011) pp. 53–70

Chapter 6

From the fringes of the diasporic garment: creative pageants of Indian Christian identity from Malaysia and Singapore
Shanthini Pillai and Sharenee Philomena Paramasivam
South Asian Diaspora, volume 3, issue 1 (March 2011) pp. 71–88

Chapter 7

Celebrating 'the sons of Jats': the return of tribes in the global village
Anjali Gera Roy
South Asian Diaspora, volume 3, issue 1 (March 2011) pp. 89–102

Chapter 8

Multiple modernities and the Tibetan diaspora
John Whalen-Bridge
South Asian Diaspora, volume 3, issue 1 (March 2011) pp. 103–116

Chapter 9

'Forget not your old country': absence, identity, and marginalization in the practice and development of Sri Lankan Buddhism in Malaysia
Jeffrey Samuels
South Asian Diaspora, volume 3, issue 1 (March 2011) pp. 117–132

Please direct any queries you may have about the citations to clsuk.permissions@cengage.com

PREFACE

There is a growing interest in the role that religion plays in the diaspora in promoting identity and providing an avenue for social networking. In many diasporic contexts, religious organizations have provided much needed moral and social support to immigrant communities and often facilitated the process of immigration. Recent scholarship in this area is significant. It is in this context that the essays in this Special Issue deal with a range of issues associated with religion in the diaspora.

There is significant evidence to suggest that most religious organizations that were started by the Indian diaspora also offered educational facilities for the community. It is through them that language and religious education was pursued. In doing so, such organizations also provided an identity to the community. Such identity came to be constructed both along the lines of general Indian-ness as well as in the sense of a specific ethnic identity. In the context of transnationalism and globalization, religious communities, through their various religious institutions, have more often than not, also entrenched narrower ethnic identities. A good example is the Swaminarayan community in the UK and USA where they have perpetuated through their institutional approach a unique Gujarati linguistic or ethnic identity. Another example is evident in the experience of the Sikh community which illustrates how religious communities entrench ethnic identities within the context of globalization through their transnational networks that run along ethnic lines rather than along broader national lines. Therefore, it is not sufficient to approach transnational identities through broad categories of nationalities, but rather, there is a need also to look at the transnational networks along ethnic lines.

Gender issues have also become more complex and nuanced in the context of the South Asian diaspora. Especially in the first generation immigrant communities in UK, USA and elsewhere, both within the community as well as in the host societies, the issue of readjustment of gender roles has come to the forefront of scholarly attention. The diasporic community may strategize to challenge the preconceived perceptions of the host communities about the place of women in traditional societies of the immigrant communities. At the same time there is evidence to suggest that women may take up new roles as ritual specialists, and play a significant role in reproducing traditional society in the host country.

Another area where religion has played a key role in the context of the diaspora is in creating or challenging modern identities. In doing so, religious communities recreate not only their conventional identity that they bring to the host society, but also produce new identities through assimilation and adaptations. For example, in the case of Islam, new strategies and structures are produced to teach Islam in the European context. Some universities in Europe (e.g. in the Netherlands) are putting in place in a secular context, training of religious specialists for Islam. Such new strategies compel Muslim communities to adopt new identities that are compatible with local communities. Yet another example is how the Tibetan diasporic community is compelled to adjust to modern society's demands, and this is expressed by the inclusion of science subjects in their monastic training curriculum. By doing so, the Tibetan diaspora is likely to adopt multiple identities as both Tibetan monks and as citizens in a modern society.

One of the problems in constructing religious identities within the diasporic communities is to focus mainly on the dominant religious communities, e.g. Hindu or Muslim. The peripheral communities often receive no significant attention which skews the theoretical understanding of the role of religion in the diaspora. A number of essays in this issue provide a correction to such one-sided engagement in scholarship. Marginal communities such as Christians in the diaspora, starting with a disadvantage of being a minority in their country of origin, are doubly disadvantaged as minorities in their host country. Studies of these communities can add significantly to the overall understanding of the broader Indian self-hood.

In this Special Issue, several essays also deal with the place of religion and caste both in India as well as in the diaspora. The intrinsic relationship between Hinduism and caste has been enunciated since the first census reporting during the colonial era both by sociologists, cultural anthropologists, historians and religionists as well as politicians, Hindu reform leaders and lay people. From Max Weber to Louis Dumont scholars of South Asia have engaged in the role that caste plays in social stratification of South Asia. As many social scientists have noted, the role that caste plays in the context of Hindu ritual seems to have given it the most dominant place in conceptualizing South Asian society.

However, this endemic relationship between caste and Hindu ritual tends to obfuscate the most fundamental features of caste as an instrument of social stratification. Whether it is in the context of ritual or in social relations in general, caste is fundamentally about two important sociologically significant relationships – first, who can have inter-dining relationship with whom, and who can exchange bodily fluids with whom. These are the guiding principles of caste which fundamentally presuppose endogamous social ordering. Having understood the intrinsic nature of these two principles for the practice of caste, the question then needs to be asked whether caste operates only within Hindu society or outside of it as well. What seems to have happened is that the two fundamental principles of caste became a general practice in South Asian society in creating social hierarchy independent of Hinduism. In other words, who eats with whom and who marries who has gone beyond Hindu religious practice and has become a determining factor across religions. It is in this sense, that caste is not distinctive to Hindu society but runs right through the South Asian society across religious distinctions. Therefore, one finds the operations of caste in Christian communities, Muslim communities, the Sikh, the Jain and in others. Even though Buddhism rejected such distinctions, the association of Indian Buddhist community predominantly with the historically 'untouchable castes' is not unduly surprising. Despite rejection of caste, Sikh religious groups are also distinguished along caste lines such as the Valmikis and the Ravidasis and so on. The South Asian diaspora is no exception in certain cases, especially among first generation South Asian immigrants, but in places like South Africa, although caste as an organizing social institution could not survive due to the absence of traditional structures, the caste consciousness of people is evidently present if one takes note of the predominance of caste names as last/surnames among most South African Indians. In the absence of traditional caste structures, some castes obtained cognate caste status rather arbitrarily based on which marriage alliances tended to be carried out.

This Special Issue, with interesting essays on the overarching place of religion and issues of caste, ethnicity, gender, modernity, and minority status as well as transnationalism, illuminates the various issues embedded in these discourses.

P. Pratap Kumar
University of KwaZulu-Natal, South Africa

Introduction: Religion and the South Asian diaspora

Rajesh Rai[a] and Chitra Sankaran[b]

[a]South Asian Studies Programme, National University of Singapore, Singapore; [b]English Language and Literature, National University of Singapore, Singapore

In the expansive manner in which 'diaspora' has come to be employed, the centrality of religion in the 'classical' understanding of the concept has been subsumed under categories such as 'ethnicity' and 'culture'. Yet even as religious practices and beliefs undergo transformation in the diaspora, studies of South Asian emigrant groups show that religion remains a key marker of community identity – its pivotal role invigorated by the contemporary precipitation in global connections. By scrutinising the specific experiences, practices and contentions of a wide-array of diasporic communities, the articles in this Special Issue reveal the renewed power of religion in the South Asian diaspora.

'Diaspora' is an ancient notion, although its contemporary acclaim is the outcome of an extensive interest in examining the experience of large numbers of ethnic collectivities that have moved to territories beyond what is identified as their 'ancestral homeland' and 'whose social, economic and political networks cross the borders of nation-states or, indeed, span the globe' (Vertovec 1997, p. 277). Today a wide spectrum of emigrant groups appropriate the term. Indeed 'diaspora' – whatever its original delineations – has been willingly embraced as a self-descriptive category even by recent migrants and short-term dwellers in foreign lands, sometimes if only because of the notion's perceived quixotic aestheticism:

> Diaspora is one of the buzz words of the post modern age; it has the virtue of sounding exotic while rolling sibilantly off the English tongue; it whispers the promise of hidden depths of meaning yet assimilates them to the shape of a wave breaking gently on native shores … it offers a desirable feminine ending, and much versatility. (Cohen 1993, p. 3, cited in Baumann 2000, pp. 325–326)

Bolstered by the continued precipitation in international migration, neither the cessation of the appropriation of the term as a marker of identity, nor moderation in the interest in studying diasporas is likely in the near future. Yet, while there is no denying the growing pervasiveness in the use and study of 'diaspora', concerns have been articulated over the 'journalistic free-for-all' (Cohen 2008, p. 4) employment of the term for a vast array of differentiated experiences of movement and settlement away from an 'ancestral homeland'. In response, scholars in the field have attempted to define contours of the notion through painstaking studies of the changing etymology of the term and delineations that have sought to mark out the conditions and typologies of diaspora(s) (Baumann 2000, Chaliand and Rageau 1995, pp. xiii–xxi, Cohen

2008). For collectivities 'to shelter under the increasingly broader circumference of the diasporic umbrella' (Cohen 2008, p. 5) without completely damaging the notions 'descriptive usefulness' (Vertovec 1997, p. 277), these studies have tended to employ the following logic:

> [a] need *both* to draw generalized inferences from the Jewish tradition *and* to be sensitive to the inevitable dilutions, changes and expansions of the meaning of the term diaspora as it comes to be more widely applied. (Cohen 2008, p. 5, italics in original)

Within this coterie, Baumann's (2000) study of the 'genealogies of the semantics' of diaspora has been particularly useful in underlining the centrality of religion to the notion, especially in the way it was employed in the classical period. Going beyond the 'spiritual and soteriological' implications of Diaspora in its application for dispersed Jewish communities 'far from the promised land', Baumann drawing on Arowele's doctoral thesis, points out that Christians 'adopted' the term from the first century CE (Baumann 2000, pp. 316–319). In biblical stories, he notes that the early Church was construed 'as a pilgrim, sojourning and dispersed community' and that

> Christians living in dispersion would function as the 'seed' to disseminate the message of Jesus. The Christians' real home, however, was the 'heavenly city of Jerusalem', the goal of Christian pilgrimage. (p. 319)

By the time of the Reformation, diaspora had come to denote a 'geographic–sociological signifier', although the umbilical connection to religion remained intact as the term was used for 'Protestant minorities … in Roman Catholic environments' and vice-versa for Roman Catholics in 'Protestant dominated countries'. Even in the early nineteenth century, diaspora continued to be bound to religion as was evident in the employment of the term for a 'confessional church residing in a confessionally different environment' (p. 320).

In the expanded usage of diaspora from the 1960s, the notion has been used well beyond the confines of the Jewish and Christian traditions. Vertovec informs us that in 1998, seven years after the launch of the journal *Diaspora*, 'no less than thirty-six communities … had been identified by academics as, or who have called themselves, "diasporas"' (Vertovec 2004, p. 277). In that article, Vertovec's AltaVista search on the Internet uncovered 102,435 web pages for the term (p. 277). That number has grown exponentially – while writing this piece, a search via Google generated a mind-boggling 16,100,000 hits of web-pages where the term was employed. It would probably not be an exaggeration to suggest that millions of these would not meet even the most nominal conditions of diaspora as set out by scholars in the field.

A comprehensive discussion of contemporary criteria *vis-à-vis* the initial condition of diaspora has been oft repeated and is tangential to the focus of this article. What is pertinent, however, is that in the expansive manner in which diaspora has come to be employed since the 1960s, the tie with religion – crucial in the classical understanding of the notion – has been subverted. This is not simply a matter of popular usage. Contemporary theoretical delineations of the notion primarily underscore 'ethnicity' as the operative category for diaspora. The usual trans-ethnic character of religions, alongside the tendency, 'in the case of faiths widely spread around the globe … [to] not seek to return to, or to recreate, a homeland' (Vertovec 2000, p. 2) has rendered it problematic to 'theorize the connection between religion and diaspora' (Cohen 2008, p. 153).

Notwithstanding the theoretical quagmire, scholars recognize that there are exceptions especially in cases where religion and ethnicity are closely intertwined, and correspondingly fundamental to the diasporas' connection to an 'ancestral homeland'. This is evident most clearly in the Jewish and Sikh cases where the 'ancestral homeland' is also 'holy-land'. Among such diasporas, affiliation to that distant geographical territory extends well beyond the confines of ethnicity *per se*. In the case of Parsis, while ties to the original homeland have come to be attenuated, nevertheless 'Bombay has effectively become a displaced homeland because of the many religious sites located there' (Cohen 2008, p. 153). Vertovec posits adding Hindus to this select group because Hinduism is 'generally non-proselytising' and that among 'committed Hindus, the tie to India goes beyond ethnic … origins' (Vertovec 2000, p. 3). To this list we propose that dispersed groups who may constitute part of widely-spread global religions may also be considered, especially where specific traditions developed that were tied exclusively to the 'ancestral homeland' – as in the case, for example, of dispersed Saint Thomas Christians from the Malabar Coast.

Even if scholars disagree with notions of 'religious diaspora' or of 'diaspora religion' – on the grounds that these typologies are precarious – even inoperable – without an ethnic base – it does not follow that the argument invalidates Baumann's definition that underscores the religious implications of the notion by maintaining that the constitution of diaspora involves 'a *perpetual recollecting identification with a fictitious or far away existent geographic territory and its cultural–religious traditions*' (Baumann 2000, p. 327, italics in original). Granted that this definition may perturb those who identify themselves as a diaspora but for whom the affiliation to the 'ancestral homeland' may lack a religious underpinning, yet even the most ardent proponents of a more inclusive definition of diaspora, would find it difficult not to concede that religion does effectively provide an 'additional cement to bind a diasporic consciousness' (Cohen, cited in Vertovec 2000, p. 3). In his effort to cognize the usefulness of religion in the life of transnational migrants, Thomas Tweed believes that religions involve two spatial practices – 'dwelling and crossing'. Since religions are concerned with making sense of human joys and sufferings in both 'everyday' and 'cosmic' terms, he argues that they can be characterized by both 're-orientation, constraint and boundary marking' as well as 'exchange, mixture and transformation' in diasporas (2006, p. 7).

Religion and the South Asian diaspora

The 'cementing' role of religion in diaspora was the starting point for our interest as guest editors in working towards a Special Issue on *Religion and the South Asian Diaspora*. Beyond the religious myth-symbol complexes that informed the nostalgia for an 'ancestral homeland' among emigrants, historical records show that in many, if not most locations where stable South Asian diasporas developed, the archetypal institutions directly produced through the agency of these emigrants were typically religious. In the case of the 'old' diaspora born out of colonial capital (Mishra 2007, p. 70), the initial structures of these places of worship may have been unassuming – a banyan tree housing a Hindu deity, or simple thatched huts with a corrugated iron roof, but that did not in itself limit their role as important building blocks for organizing and mobilizing incipient diasporan communities. In Singapore for example, soon after the advent of South Asian emigration, Hindus of differentiated regional and caste backgrounds came together to build the Mariamman Temple. In parallel, Tamil

Muslims from the Coromandel Coast, who comprised some of the wealthiest South Asians at the early settlement, established the Jamae Chulia Mosque, the Nagore Dargah and Kuchu Palli (also known as Masjid Al-Abrar). For the early Tamil Muslim emigrants, their shrines, beyond performing a religious function, also acted as markers of their ethnic difference *vis-à-vis* local Malay-Muslims.

Shrines may have been the most overt personification of diasporic religious identities, but possibly more salient were day-to-day ritual practices. Divine symbols and icons revered at home; daily *puja* – in the sacred language of the 'ancestral homeland' (even if not fully understood by adherents); and alongside these of religious taboos and notions of 'purity' and 'pollution', sustained albeit in a modified form, in the diaspora. At different times of the year, religious festivals and processions – *Diwali*, *Dusshera*, *Thaipusam* and *Vaisakhi* for example – would take centre-stage, re-invoking memories and re-affirming their collective connection to a remembered 'ancestral homeland'. For transported convicts from the subcontinent in the nineteenth century for example, historical records show that these were the most cherished days of their lives in banishment. Threatened with a ban on their religious processions, in 1856, the prisoners' plea to the Governor of the Straits Settlements was informative of their sentiments:

> [The convicts] prostrate at your Honor's feet to forgive them if they have any crime for the sake of Heavenly Father and for the act of charity .... Your Hindu and Mussulman Petitioners humbly prays your Honor will have compassion on their hard case, and grant them the privilege of their approaching Festival and will remember your Honor's generosity for their everlasting life and gratitude .... (*The Straits Times*, 14 October 1856, p. 5)

Stories from the age-old religious epics – the *Ramayana* and the *Mahabharata* – particularly the former – resonated in the new communities that were born out of exile. In his testament, Totaram Sanadhya observes that in Fiji it was commonplace for the Tulsidas *Ramayana* to be read collectively by indentured labourers (cited in Mishra 2006, p. 122). In the Caribbean theatrical re-enactments of the *Ramayana* became popular in the diaspora, as Nobel Laureate V.S. Naipaul remembers:

> One of the first big public things I was taken to was the Ramlila, the pageant-play based on the Ramayana, the epic about the banishment and later triumph of Rama, the Hindu hero-divinity .... Everything in that Ramlila has been transported from India in the memories of people. And although as theatre it was crude, and there was much that I would have missed in the story, I believe I understood more and felt more than I had done during The Prince and the Pauper ... at the local cinema .... The Ramayana was the essential Hindu story. (cited in Haraksingh 2006, p. 283)

The 'cementing' role of religion in the South Asian diaspora should not however be taken to imply that in the transnational context, religious beliefs and practices of these communities did not undergo major transformations. In the 'old' diaspora – characterized by fracture – religious traditions were formed out of 'a select subset of [an] ... original memory bank', and were often 'modified to fit the needs and the imaginations of the early generations living in ... [the] new setting' (Younger 2010, p. 8). Granted that within the 'new' diaspora of South Asians in the USA or in Europe no equivalent fracture from the 'homeland' may have been evident, yet even here, veritably religion has adapted [or modified] in response to these 'new cultural settings' and accordingly 'the development of diasporic religious communities and their exposure to foreign influences, [have transformed] ... the organization, practices and beliefs of the religion as a whole' (Cohen 2008, p. 153). Indeed, Stuart Hall has suggested that contemporary cultural identities oscillate between two opposing movements – reactive attempts to reinstate boundaries that reify the groups' collective identity, affirming their difference from mainstream belief-systems, yet also, contrarily, as an outcome of globalization, inculcating greater cultural hybridity (Hall 1992, p. 304).

It is at this site – focused on processes of change and development – that a rich corpus of literature has been produced in the study of religion in the South Asian diaspora. One way to categorize these works is in terms of 'stages' in the formation and development of the diaspora – with the caveat that there exist overlaps between categories and as well differences in the experiences of both the 'old' and 'new' South Asian diaspora. As mentioned above, at the early stage of movement and incipient diasporic formation, the development of religious institutions was a crucial imperative for emigrants. Studies of religious institutions show, however, that often beyond simply drawing from 'pre-migration social and cultural factors' they were also subject to 'residential patterns in the new setting' (Vertovec 2004, p. 283). In diasporas, characterized by fracture from the homeland, modifications or even the 'invention' of ritual practices and traditions have also been commonplace (Younger 2010) – in part stemming possibly from a pragmatic impulse of the need to dilute differences between different regional traditions.

As the diaspora becomes established, studies of religious institutions often show 'a high degree of conflict and contestation' (Vertovec 2004, p. 283) that may lead to intermittent periods of 'homogenization' and 'fragmentation' in community formation (Rai 2009). Religious expressions, impacted by state regulations in multi-cultural settings can effect the 'compartmentalization' of religious life (Babb 1976) even as attempts at resistance through mobilization for minority rights lead to a heightening of religious awareness (Lewis 1994, Fetzer and Soper 2005). Changes in gender roles are evident and women have been shown to undertake new functions in religious practice, even as heightened concerns of sexual transgression can render them subject to more conservative strictures. Caste identities come to be reconstituted – as in the case of North Indians in Mauritius where the label 'Chamar' is used to encompass 'many others of lower caste background who were not within the … landowning class of "Singhs"' (Younger 2010, p. 32) – rendered altogether obsolete, or re-emerge as important signifiers as recent developments in the case of Sikhs in contemporary Britain seem to show (Roy, this issue). As well in the diaspora, living in the midst of 'foreign' influences has often fostered the development of a questioning attitude *vis-à-vis* religious traditions and practices in the younger generation. Studies reveal myriad outcomes from these processes, possibly a rejection of tradition, or even a turn towards the perceived 'fundamentals' of a religion.

Notwithstanding these transformations, there is little evidence to suggest a decline in the salience of religion as a marker of community identity in the diaspora. On the contrary, as Gerd Baumann posits in the case of South Asian communities settled in Southall, 'religion continues to function as the local *community* marker *par excellence*' (cited in Vertovec 2000, p. 151). In the current 'stage' of the development of the South Asian diaspora – characterized by the precipitation of global interconnections that has led to '[diminishing] divergences between diaspora and home communities' (Smart 1999, p. 423) and 'blurred and multiplied' the 'master narrative of a diaspora's triangular relationship' (Baumann 2000, p. 331) – where advances in communications; heightened concerns over 'transnational religious terrorism'; and the agency of mobile religious teachers and religious political organizations have collectively raised an unprecedented 'awareness of global religious identities' (Vertovec 2004, p. 291), it would not be an exaggeration to suggest that Gerd Baumann's conclusion for Southall, holds true as well for many, if not most other South Asian diasporas.

This Special Issue

Developments in the contemporary world has meant that for good or ill, religion has become one of the main ways of identifying and classifying migrant groups and diasporas in modern societies. Hence a closer scrutiny of the experiences of South Asian religious diasporas, their practices and their contentions becomes not only important but imperative. The renewed power of religion as a marker of identity in the diaspora is an underlying theme that is central to this Special Issue entitled 'Religion and the South Asian Diaspora'. Examining the various ways through which disparate diasporic communities mark their identities, it emerges from the studies of the various contributors to this issue that the continuing pivotal role played by religion cannot be overlooked or even subsumed under other categories such as 'ethnicity' or 'culture' without losing something of value. As such, the articles in this issue explore the distinctive ways through which negotiations of power and their ramifications work in 'religious' diasporas as divergent as 'Indian Christians in Malaysia', or the Sikh diaspora in the UK. A closer examination of these communities reveals facts about just how, by whom and for what purposes religious discourse is deployed in a collective. In attempting this exploration, the articles move closer to the objectives of many scholars of religion who have 'problematised' the uncomplicated idea of 'religion' as a cross cultural and trans-historical phenomenon (McCutcheon 1997). To these scholars, the *nuances* that inform the distinctive natures of religious diasporas situated in different parts of the world as presented in this issue are what will emerge as deeply significant.

Diaspora studies have shown (McLoughlin 2010, p. 574) that huge moral and economic investments are made by diasporic communities to 'establish and sustain' autonomous associations that would enhance the profile of these communities. These investments are accelerated as the diaspora matures and new generations are born that need to be socialized and educated in the old ways while adjusting to their new land. It is precisely this issue that is addressed by Surendra Bhana and Kusum K. Bhoola in their essay 'The dynamics of preserving cultural heritage'. The essay showcases an important aspect of diasporas that were formed on the basis of religious identity markers – namely, that in mobilizing their social and cultural 'capital' to mould the younger members of the diaspora, the earlier narrow, factional ethnic identities can expand to become more inclusive. Thus in this case, the religious identity marker (Hindu) was preserved while ethnic markers (Gujarati) proved too parochial to be sustained and all Hindus were embraced in the later endeavors of the group.

Envisioned as sacrosanct and beyond human intervention, religion functions to facilitate an imagined sense of continuity with a 'sacred' past. The role of religious ritual is particularly valuable in this regard in the diaspora. As previous studies reveal, these practices can be 'elaborated, standardized or reoriented' in the new space (McLoughlin 2010, p. 574). Discussing one such re-orientation of ritual in the Hindu diaspora in Portugal, Inês Lourenço in her essay 'Religion and gender' reveals that Hindu women in Portugal are assigned a new status through religion, thus replacing the traditional male *pujari* or priest. She asserts that this not only leads to the empowerment of women but also assures the perpetuation of conservative, nationalist ideologies within transnational networks. As has been noted in previous religion-in-diaspora studies (Goheen 1996, Tatla 1999), much is dependent on the age and gender profiles of members of a diasporic community. Often, dominant constituencies such as older men can marginalize the interests of younger men and women. This can lead to internal tensions within the diaspora, which can manifest themselves through the medium of newer technologies.

The focus of Anjana Narayan and Bandana Purkayastha's study is of web-based discourses of Hindu Student Groups (HSG) in the UK and in the USA. They assert that in the virtual spaces, one interesting phenomenon that can be observed is the HSGs' deployment of 'strong woman' imagery to assert their 'superior cultures'. These constructions of the strong Hindu women, they aver, while challenging the gendered/racialized construction of minorities in Western societies as traditional and non-modern, also works towards creating 'contemporary gender hierarchies' *vis-à-vis* other groups in the diaspora. Hence we note how, while co-operation among various minority groups and diasporic groups of same or similar ethnicities was a feature of early settlements, fissures and fragmentations can develop very quickly as these groups settle in the new spaces (McLoughlin 2010, p. 575). However, in both of the above studies, one trajectory that emerges as fairly significant in religious diasporas is 'gender' and how it is deployed in various ways to invent or reify certain collective identities.

Often, however, these kinds of negotiations between groups in the diaspora can be contentious, marked by dissension and infighting, causing deep anxieties, both ideological and actual. Shanthini Pillai and Sharenee Philomena Paramasivam, while pointing out the inventiveness of the diasporic imaginary to reterritorialize Indian culture-scapes into local contexts in their study entitled 'From the fringes of the diasporic garment' raise the question: would there be different modulations to the tones, inflections of the diasporic experience when the creative imaginary intersects and negotiates with the Christian, the Indian as well as the Malaysian and Singaporean experience? This article raises our awareness of how, very often, when the focus is on ethnicity, culture or race as the overarching criteria for delineating the identity of a diasporic group, the finer differences that arise in smaller groups distinguished by their religious differences tend to be overlooked, leading to a marginalization of these groups. If the needs of these 'fringe' groups are neglected, it can produce counter movements that lead to fragmentation. Thus questions regarding hierarchy and power need to be sensitively handled.

Indeed, questions about power and hierarchy are the central concerns of Anjali Gera Roy's article 'Celebrating "the sons of Jats"' which marks a movement in the Sikh diaspora countering the homogenizing wave of globalization by 'a return to the tribes' mentality that is marked by a reinforcement of primary boundaries. These borders, Roy notes, converge on core identity markers such as linguistic, regional and caste based affiliations. This could well be a reactionary move by younger generations to protest against the threat of their erasure of identities when confronted by the more powerful mainstream culture or it could be a means of constructing hierarchies within the diasporic community itself. It revolves around the action by some members of the group to impress on the larger group, regulatory norms based on their specific notions of identity. The tendency for groups in the diaspora to reify their culture, not recognizing its dynamic, evolving, nature has been theorized. As McLoughlin (2010, p. 575) observes:

> ... earlier anthropological theories of culture did tend to essentialise it as something unified and undivided ... today culture is understood more dynamically by anthropologists as a practice, something all people are in the continuous process of *making* and *remaking*. (emphasis in original)

One interesting feature that emerges from Roy's and other contributors' studies is the discrepancy between theory and practice in the self-imaging of these communities. Rather than identifying their practices as that of a 'travelling' culture, to use Clifford's term (Clifford 1994) wherein self-identification is continually modified contextually and dialectically in relation to the ascriptions of others, the reactionary tendency of many members of the community is to invoke a unitary and sealed identity.

In many instances, however, this propensity to essentialize 'identity' proves very valuable to communities. Both John Whalen-Bridge in his article 'Multiple modernities and the Tibetan diaspora' and Jeffrey Samuels in his study of Sri Lankan Buddhism in Malaysia demonstrate how diasporic communities seek a context and purpose through means of such essentialized identities. Jeffrey discusses how the Sri Lankan community in Malaysia compulsively imagines and re-imagines its 'Sinhalese-ness' through revisiting particular sites of memory—Buddhist institutions, rituals and cemeteries. Whalen Bridge reveals through his interviews with three Tibetan 'patriarchs' how enabling the construction of a unified identity is in helping the community to embrace 'modernity' without losing its traditions and in negotiating such binaries in novel ways that were hitherto not conceived of in the community, either through a lack of necessity or because newer ways of self conception have emerged in the diaspora.

One of the interesting facts that emerge out of this exploration of religious diasporas of South Asian origin is that more often than not, most categories and frameworks that are used to deploy power in the diaspora are strategic and contingent. These however, paradoxically, work towards hypostatizing the collective identity of the community. What emerges then is that no set pattern can be identified in the way separate communities in the diaspora negotiate religion. Rather, a dynamic and evolving relationship between the two becomes necessary, even imperative, for sustaining a cohesive cultural identity in these communities.

Acknowledgements

We were heartened by the great number of research papers we received for this Special Issue. We would like to take this opportunity to acknowledge all contributors and express our sincere gratitude to the anonymous reviewers whose thorough reports and constructive comments were instrumental in raising the quality of the articles. Special thanks are due to Professor Pratap Kumar for his editorial that has embellished this Special Issue. Finally, we are indebted to Dr Ajaya Sahoo, the editor of *South Asian Diaspora*, for his support throughout this process. Without his expertise and goodwill, this Special Issue would not have been possible.

Notes on contributors

Rajesh Rai is Assistant Professor in the South Asian Studies Programme at the National University of Singapore. He has published several scholarly articles and book chapters on the South Asian diaspora. Co-editor of *The South Asian Diaspora: Transnational Networks and Changing Identities* (2009) and *Nationalism in South Asia* (2009), he was also Assistant Editor for *The Encyclopedia of the Indian Diaspora* (2006) which has received considerable acclaim. His research interests are in the fields of diaspora studies and transnational identities, nationalism and the post-colonial history and politics of South Asia.

Chitra Sankaran is Associate Professor in the Department of English Language & Literature at the National University of Singapore. She has published monographs, books, edited volumes and chapters in books. Her articles have been published in *The Journal of Commonwealth Literature, ARIEL, World Literatures Written in English, Journal of South Asian Literatures* and elsewhere. She is an Invited Member of the Editorial Committees for the journals *The Post-colonial Text* and *Asiatic: IIUM Journal of English Language and Literature*. Her research interests include South Asian Fictions and Comparative Literatures. She is currently editing a volume on Amitav Ghosh for SUNY Press.

References

Babb, L., 1976. Patterns of Hinduism. *In*: R. Hassan, ed. *Singapore: society in transition.* New York: Oxford University Press, 189–204.

Baumann, M., 2000. Diaspora: genealogies of semantics and transcultural comparison. *Numen,* 47 (3), 313–337.

Chaliand, G. and Rageau, J., 1995. *The Penguin Atlas of diasporas.* New York: Viking.

Cohen, R., 2008. Global diasporas: an introduction. New ed. London: Routledge.

Fetzer, J.S. and Soper, J.C., 2005. *Muslims and the state in Britain, France and Germany.* New York: Cambridge University Press.

Goheen, M., 1996. *Men own the fields, women own the crops: gender and power in the Cameroon grassfields.* Madison, WI: Wisconsin University Press.

Hall, S., 1992. The question of cultural identity. *In*: S. Hall, D. Held and T. McGrew, eds. *Modernity and its futures.* Cambridge: Polity Press (in association with Blackwell Publishers, Oxford and The Open University), 273–325.

Haraksingh, K., 2006. Trinidad and Tobago. *In*: B.V. Lal, P. Reeves and R. Rai, eds. *The encyclopedia of the Indian diaspora.* Singapore: Editions Didier Millet, 278–286.

Lewis, P., 1994. Being Muslim and being British: the dynamics of Islamic reconstruction in Bradford. *In*: R. Ballard, ed. *Desh Pardesh: the South Asian presence in Britain.* London: Hurst, 58–87.

McCutcheon, R.T., 1997. *Manufacturing religion.* New York: Oxford University Press.

McLoughlin, S., 2010. Religion and diaspora. *In*: J.R. Hinnels, ed. *The Routledge companion to the study of religion.* London: Routledge, 558–580.

Mishra, V., 2006. Voices from the diaspora. *In*: B.V. Lal, P. Reeves and R. Rai, eds. *The encyclopedia of the Indian diaspora.* Singapore: Editions Didier Millet, 120–139.

Mishra, V., 2007. *The literature of the Indian diaspora: theorizing the diasporic imaginary.* London: Routledge.

Rai, R., 2009. Homogeneisation and fragmentation, inclusivism and exclusivism in the development of Hinduism in Singapore. *South Asian Diaspora,* 1 (1), 3–17.

Smart, N., 1999. The importance of diasporas. *In*: S. Vertovec and R. Cohen, eds. *Migration, diasporas and transnationalism.* Aldershot: Edward Elgar.

Tatla, D.S., 1999. *The Sikh diasporas: the search for statehood.* London: University College London Press.

The Straits Times, 14 October 1856, Singapore.

Tweed, T., 2006. *Our lady of the exile: diaspora religion at a Cuban Catholic Church in Miami.* New York: Oxford University Press.

Vertovec, S., 1997. Three meanings of 'diaspora', exemplified among South Asian religions. *Diaspora,* 6 (3), 277–299.

Vertovec, S., 2000. *The Hindu diaspora: comparative patterns.* London: Routledge.

Vertovec, S., 2004. Religion and diaspora. *In*: P. Antes, A.W. Geertz and R.R. Warne, eds. *New approaches to the study of religion: volume two: textual, comparative, sociological and cognitive approaches.* Berlin: Walter de Gruyter, 275–304.

Younger, P., 2010. *New homelands: Hindu communities in Mauritius, Guyana, Trinidad, South Africa, Fiji and East Africa.* Oxford: Oxford University Press.

Addendum

Scholars of religion in the diaspora have been attentive to the adaptation of religious beliefs, practices and institutions in the diasporic context. State policies, tensions that arise from living in the new multi-religious setting, and the influence of wider transnational social and religious currents, are some of the many variables that can potentially transform religion in the diaspora. Rajesh Rai's article, which examines the development of Hinduism in Singapore, emphasizes the need to contextualise such changes historically. His study reveals how early Hindu immigrants in Singapore, because of their small number and resource limitations, displayed a tendency to exercise flexibility, setting aside traditional differences in the establishment of their religious institutions. Interestingly, as Hindu numbers increased and the diaspora became more settled, a turn towards conservatism was manifest, so that regional and caste-based boundaries 're-emerged' as important markers of difference. In the postcolonial period, Rai investigates how state initiatives created pressures towards homogenizing Hinduism. These, however, have met only partial success, in part because of the arrival of new migrants and the proliferation of global 'Hindu-oriented' movements that have added to the diversity of Hinduism(s) in Singapore.

Homogenisation and fragmentation, inclusivism and exclusivism in the development of Hinduism in Singapore

Rajesh Rai

South Asian Studies Programme, National University of Singapore, Singapore

Even as scholars question the efficacy of the term Hinduism to denote a single world religion, there is widespread acknowledgement that the label Hindu and Hinduism hold considerable resonance in the diaspora. Alongside identification with these categories, scholars have provided evidence of the advance of a 'homogenised Hinduism', which has underplayed differences between groups. Through a study of the historical development of Hinduism in Singapore, this article posits that evolving tensions between exclusive and inclusive community structures have had reverberations that problematise the notion of a simplistic linear move from plurality to homogenisation. In addition to differences in region, caste and sect, at various points in time this process has been punctuated by the influence of socio-religious and political currents from the subcontinent. In recent decades the advent of new transnational Hindu-oriented religious movements and the arrival of migrant professionals, have reconfigured earlier patterns, even as they have added to the diversity of Hinduism(s) existent in the island-city.

Introduction

The use of the term 'Hinduism' to denote a religion in the same way as Islam or Christianity has been subjected to considerable criticism by historians and anthropologists of South Asia. Drawing on the writings of Orientalists and Indian reformers, many have argued that 'Hinduism' as a unitary religion was a nineteenth century construction that fundamentally altered a term used initially as an ethnic category to refer to inhabitants of the subcontinent, into a 'catch-all' phrase for the vast array of religious and cultural rituals, beliefs and philosophies of Indians who were not Muslim, Christian, Jewish or Zoroastrian (Dalmia 1995; Fuller 2004; King 1999, p. 146; Sinha 2006, pp.145–146; von Stietencron 1995). These claims have not gone uncontested. Citing evidence from pre-nineteenth century Indian and European sources Lorenzen (2005, p.77) provides a scathing critique of this position, arguing that:

> ...during the centuries of rule by dynasties of Muslim sultans and emperors... Hindus developed a consciousness of a shared religious identity based on the loose family resemblance among the variegated beliefs and practices of Hindus, whatever their sect, caste, chosen deity, or theological school.

Regardless of the debate on dating the construction of Hinduism and it's problematic use when employed to refer to a single world religion, scholars nevertheless recognise that both in India and in the diaspora, the labels Hindu and Hinduism have grown increasingly salient and are now 'embraced and internalised among practitioners' (Sinha 2006, p. 146). What is more, in addition to the considerable resonance of these labels, there is strong evidence to suggest that amongst various Hindu diasporic communities 'differences in social and religious practice have been underplayed in the course of a long-term historical process in which a homogeneous Hindu community has been constructed' (van der Veer and Vertovec 1991, p. 149). While the agents of change have varied according to location, the key structural factors put forth to explain the advance of a 'homogenised Hinduism' in the diaspora include: a growing self-consciousness of beliefs and practices in the context of ethnic and religiously plural societies; the development of congregational modes of worship; and the lack of salience for divisive institutions such as caste (van der Veer and Vertovec 1991, p. 153).

Notwithstanding the existence of these conditions in diasporic locations, the advance of 'homogenised Hinduism' in the diaspora raises a number of questions. Can the development of Hinduism(s) in different diasporic locations be seen as a linear historical move from diversity to homogenisation? Who/what are the key agents of change, and are there other structural factors that need to be accounted for? Have there been attempts to resist homogenisation, and if so how has this impacted on the development of Hinduism(s) in the diaspora? Has the growth of transnational linkages across different diasporic locations, and between the diaspora and the homeland strengthened the possibility of a global 'homogenised Hinduism' or has this ushered in greater diversity?

Through a study of the historical development of Hinduism in Singapore, this article is an attempt to deal with some of the questions outlined above. It posits the view that tensions between exclusive and inclusive community structures have been an important feature in the development of Hinduism in Singapore, which in turn has had reverberations on the process of homogenisation. Comprising traditions divided by region, caste and sect, Hinduism in Singapore provides a rich case-study of the negotiation of multiple identities in close proximity. Unlike the movement of Indians to the Caribbean, Fiji, South Africa and Mauritius, which were formed overwhelmingly through the experience of indenture, Hindu religious life in Singapore, since its formation in the early nineteenth century, has been punctuated by different trajectories of migration that along with a continuous flow of socio-religious currents from the subcontinent have added to its complexity. In the postcolonial period, even as the state has emerged as an important player in shaping religious identities, the advent of new transnational Hindu-oriented religious movements and the arrival of migrant professionals from India from the 1990s have continued to reconfigure the development of Hinduism in the island-city.

Overview of Indian religious communities in Singapore

All the major religious communities of the sub-continent are represented in the Indian diaspora in Singapore. Table 1 provides a breakdown of the religious affiliations of the approximately 195,500 Indian residents (aged 15 and over) enumerated in the 2000 census. The percentage of Hindus as a proportion of the Indian resident population (aged 15 and over) declined from 56.5% to 53.1% from 1980 to 1990

Table 1. Religious affiliations of the Indian resident population aged 15 years and over (%) (1980–2000)[3].

Religion (Aged 15 Years & Over)	1980 (%)	1990 (%)	2000 No. (%)
Hinduism	56.5	53.1	55.4
Islam	21.8	26.5	25.6
Christianity	12.4	12.2	12.1
Other religions	8.0	7.1	6.3
No religion	1.2	1.2	0.6

Source: Department of Statistics, Singapore. Available at: http://internet-stg1.singstat.gov.sg/pubn/ papers/people/religiousaff.html (accessed 10 October 2008).

before increasing to 55.4% in 2000. This increase can largely be explained by the arrival of Indian professionals who have taken up residency in Singapore since 1990, amongst whom the proportion of Hindus has been greater than the erstwhile resident Indian population.[1] The percentage of Muslims as a proportion of the Indian resident population increased from 21.8% to 26.5% between 1980 and 1990 before showing a slight decline to 25.6% in 2000, while that of Christians has remained constant at just over 12% between 1980 and 2000. Sikhs formed the vast majority of Indian residents aged 15 and over labelled in the category 'other religions' in Table 1, although this figure cannot be relied upon to represent the total number of Sikhs in Singapore.[2]

Early Hindu institutions – a collaborative enterprise

Even at the earliest stage of Singapore's development, Hindu migrants comprised a diversity of region, caste and sect. These included high caste sepoys linked to the British militia both from the Bengal and Madras armies, traders and migrant labourers arriving mainly from the Madras Presidency, and a motley mix of convict-labourers who represented: 'Almost every strata [sic] of Indian society… including Benares *brahmanas*,… Dogra *kshatriyas*, Chettiar, Bengali… financiers and *ryots* and untouchables from various parts of the subcontinent' (McNair 1899, p. 73). We know little of the total numbers of Hindus in Singapore since that category did not exist in early enumeration exercises, though the total number of Indian residents (excluding those linked to the British militia) was estimated at 756 in 1824 growing to some 11,500 by the time of the first official census in 1871, the majority of whom were Tamil (Turnbull 1989, p. 27; Shantakumar 1993, p. 867). While there exists limited information in official and non-official records on the religious practices of the early Hindus, the richest source comes from the early temples that the Hindus established soon after their arrival.

Interestingly, the oldest Hindu shrine in Singapore, the Sri Mariamman temple established in 1827, showed numerous inclusive characteristics which lend support to Lorenzen's (2005) position of the need to account for a longer history of a shared Hindu religious identity. Clothey (2006, p. 63) notes that the formation of the temple was a collaborative effort involving *pillais* from the Tanjore district 'with harbour workers, drawn from castes such as *tevars*, *kauntars*, and others from Tanjore; …in construction they used the help of convicts brought by the colonial government from all over India; and Telugus [who] participated in the temple life, as did Vaisnavas'.

This inclusive character was reflected not only in the heterogeneity of backgrounds of devotees at the shrine but also in the addition of subsidiary shrines at the temple, most distinctly manifest in the inclusion in a position of prominence, of the non-Saivite deity – Sri Rama – soon after the formation of the temple.

Similarly the Sivan temple, which can be counted amongst the oldest Hindu shrines in Singapore, also reflected the collaboration of various regional groups. While a temple structure was first built at the original site in 1850, the Sivalinga there was said to have been worshipped well before that date (Hindu Endowments Board 2008). The initial site of the temple, situated at the start of Orchard Road (marked today by the Dhoby Ghaut MRT station), was in the vicinity of the Indian convict colony and the Stamford Canal occupied by Indian washermen at the time. Benefactors included the money-lending Nattukottai Chettiars, while temple records inform that a significant shrine in the temple housed the goddess Visalatchi, which is the name associated with Siva's spouse in Benares, in contemporary Uttar Pradesh (Clothey 2006, p. 67). In its contemporary form, situated now on a site in Geylang East, the temple has maintained an inclusive outlook in its architecture and ritual calendar that shows a combination of both South and North Indian features:

> …the ritual calendar includes elements to be found in many Tamil Saiva temples: the months bear Tamil names, and the Skanda Sasthi and Brahmotsavam festival held are common in South Indian Saivagamic temples. Yet festivals such as the Vasantha Navarattiri… and Vinayakar Caturti are more popular in North India. (Clothey 2006, pp. 67–68)

Notwithstanding the scarcity of information available on the early Hindus, numerous factors suggest that they may have been willing to collaborate in the formation of the early Hindu shrines in spite of their differences. The foremost would have been the pragmatic needs of the new environment. Collaboration was necessary for the formation and development of initial structures, their maintenance, the procurement and payment of priests, and the organisation of public festivals. An inclusive approach enabled benefactors and a fellowship that extended beyond regional or caste-based differences. A further factor, encouraging such a collaborative approach was the fact that the early Hindus were not a settled community, but mainly made up of men who viewed their stay in Singapore as temporary. Their outlook was reflected in the makeshift structure of the early shrines:

> …many of these early Indians understood themselves to be in Singapore (and in the Malay Peninsula alike) only temporarily. The shrines were seldom more than a space and a picture or simple (usually portable) representation of the deity. That these early shrines were temporary suggests the status of many… as "sojourners", living and working, usually without families, away from home. These early shrines suggest also something of the liminal character of the migrants' lives in the nineteenth century. (Clothey 2006, p. 59)

The fact that the early Hindus were overwhelmingly transient men enabled flexibility in setting aside boundaries or shedding particular inhibitions, which were viewed as temporary arrangements until the men's return to the 'homeland'. In the study of diasporas, such flexibility amongst the early pioneers was not uncommon, as Roger Ballard (1996a) points out in the case of the early British Sikhs, 'In terms of caste… since overall numbers were so small, such differences were then of less significance than they are today' (p. 94).

From transients to settlers – the (re)emergence of regional, ethnic and caste boundaries

The late nineteenth and early twentieth century saw a further expansion in the size of the Hindu population in Singapore. In addition to the influx of labourers from the Madras Presidency, the period was marked by the arrival of Malayali and Sri Lankan Tamil administrators and skilled workers, and growing numbers of traders from various parts of India (Rai 2006, p. 178). This expansion was reflected in a growth in the number of Hindu institutions, and the refurbishment of many of the existing makeshift shrines. Yet, while the earliest Hindu shrines were formed out of collaboration of differentiated groups, increasingly Hindu institutions came to reflect the exclusive regional, ethnic and caste identities. A turn towards conservatism as the number of kinsmen increased has also been found to be the case amongst South Asians in the United Kingdom after the 1960s:

> As the inflow continued, chain migration brought kinsmen and fellow villagers together in ever larger residential and occupational clusters… they began to reconstruct a familiar social order around themselves, complete with all its associated cultural norms. All of a sudden conformity mattered. (Ballard 1996b, p. 15)

In the Singapore context, this movement paralleled the greater social roles that temples began to assume. Always an important gathering place for new migrants, the temple became a place where ceremonies were conducted, meetings held and cultural events organised (Clothey 2006, p. 72). This was evident in the case of the Thandayuthapani temple built by the Chettiars as early as 1859. The temple would come to play a wider business function, as a bank from which the Chettiars could borrow money to facilitate their money-lending business, and would go on to house the headquarters of the Chettiar Chamber of Commerce when it was founded in 1931 (Evers and Pavadarayan 1993, p. 856). Similarly the increase in Malayali and Sri Lankan Tamil administrators and skilled workers led to the development of their own temples and associations such the Sri Senpaga Vinayagar temple, consecrated in 1930, through the efforts of the Singapore Ceylon Tamils' Association (Sri Senpaga Vinayagar Temple, 2008).

While the wealthier groups were in a position to form their own exclusive institutions, even in the case of more broad-based Hindu temples, there was a shift to cater to the needs and traditions of the larger regional communities. For example, in the case of the Krishna temple at Waterloo Street that was initially 'built' by a North Indian (Rai 2004b, p. 16), its devotees and administration came to be increasingly made up of Tamils and Telugus. Accordingly, in part because of concerns about being displaced, North Indian Hindus began to form their own exclusive associations, the first of which was the North Indian Hindu Funeral Association (later renamed the North Indian Hindu Association), which was founded in 1921 (Rai 2004b, p. 18).

Alongside regional/ethnic boundaries, the period also saw the strengthening of caste-based divisions within the Hindu community, in part due to the influx, through the indenture and *kangani*[4] systems, of low caste and Adi Dravida ('untouchable') Tamil labourers from the second half of the nineteenth century onwards. Mani (1978) points out that, in addition to caste influencing occupational patterns, it was also practiced in terms of 'distance maintenance' in settlement. Where there were sizeable numbers of Hindus, enclaves were marked out for Adi-Dravidas. For example, Serangoon Road

> ...[was] peopled by caste-Hindus, whilst the area between Jalan Besar and the Rochore Canal was the *Adi-Dravida* area... 'Lorong Lalat' in the Adi-Dravida zone was termed the 'core' of this zone. Even today (sic), many Hindus refer to 'Lorong Lalat' as the Street of *Pariahs* (untouchables). (Mani 1978, p. 19)

Restrictions were also placed on the entry of lower castes and untouchables to the homes of caste-Hindus and '[untouchables] could [not] enter the "mainstream" temples' (Clothey 2006, p. 71). This in part explained the proliferation, at this time, and in the areas settled by untouchables, of makeshift shrines dedicated to their own deities. Boundaries of exclusion were not limited to 'mainstream' temples, but also for shrines constructed by untouchable groups. Mani (1978, p. 24) found that:

> The *Adi-Dravidas* seemed to have maintained their internal differences within their own enclaves. In the case of the Jalan Besar area, where the greatest number was concentrated, a clear division seemed to have existed amongst the *Adi-Dravidas*. They were divided into *Pallars* and *Paraiyans*. This was ritually expressed in their spatial separation of their worship sites. The *Pallans* being of higher category than their counterparts had their own shrine at French Road, whilst the *Paraiyans* had their shrine at Jalan Berseh.

While the increase in the number of Indian women from the 1920s encouraged permanent settlement, at the same time there were concerns over sexual transgression along caste lines and often 'widowed women were just "kept" by members of her [sic] caste, so that she would not be "polluted" by other castes' (Mani 1978, p. 23).

The impact of 'homeland' reform movements in the early twentieth century

Given the proximity of the island to the subcontinent and the constant movement of migrants to these parts, socio-religious and political developments in the 'homeland' had reverberations on the diaspora in Singapore. The late nineteenth century saw a number of Hindu reform movements in India that sought to modernise Hinduism through an intellectual reassessment of Hindu traditions. Although these movements were in themselves diverse, they were largely aimed at creating a sense of pride in the Hindu heritage by propagating models of Hinduism that could meet the 'rational-scientific' challenges of the colonial era. Often with a penchant for an intellectual approach towards Hinduism, they sought to transform Hindu society by advocating reform of institutions such as caste, by preaching egalitarianism, by encouraging women's education and by emphasising social work. Both the Arya Samaj founded in 1875 by Swami Dayanand Saraswati, and the Ramakrishna Mission founded by Swami Vivekananda in 1897 actively sought to reach out to the diaspora and were able to set up a base in Singapore in 1927 and 1928 respectively (Arya Samaj Singapore 2003, p. 14; Rahman 2004).

These missions met with limited success in the Singaporean context. The popularity of the Arya Samaj in Singapore, like the movement in India, was confined to North Indian Hindus, primarily those from the Punjab and Uttar Pradesh alongside some Gujaratis. The Ramakrishna Mission proved more successful in bridging regional divisions, aided by its efforts in providing service to the community through a Tamil school for boys and girls in 1932. Saying that, however, there was a clear class dimension, with membership largely comprising the educated elite who had an 'intellectual-orientation' towards Hinduism. Similarly, the Sree Narayana mission based on the Advaita *math* and advocating egalitarianism also came to be established in Singapore prior to the Second World War. However, its members were predominantly drawn from the Malayali Hindu community, many of whom worked at the British Naval Base.

Of greater consequence than the above-mentioned reformist organisations was the Tamil Nadu-based 'Self-Respect' movement, which sought the moral, social and religious upliftment of Tamil society. With an anti-Brahmin bent, opposing the caste system and emphasising monogamy – the 'Self-Respect' movement grew in popularity especially following the visit of Ramasamy Naicker to Malaya in 1929. Spearheaded by the Tamil Reform Association in Malaya and Singapore, the movement influenced many within the Tamil intelligentsia, especially teachers and journalists. Ironically, the movement did not have a religious orientation and its founders and leaders in Tamil Nadu tended to advocate atheism.

Despite that, however, the movement had strong reverberations in the religious arena. One of the main achievements of the 'Self-Respect' movement in Singapore was to institute a challenge to the discrimination meted out to the Tamil lower castes and untouchables. Mani (1978) highlights numerous instances of how lower caste and untouchable groups began to challenge erstwhile norms vis-à-vis distance maintenance and demanding access to upper caste shrines and the Hindu crematorium (p. 29). The movement's call for an end to practices such as self-immolation in religious festivals like *Thaipusam* and *Timiti*, were, however, less successful (Sinha 1993, p. 829).

While the advent of the Japanese occupation of Singapore (1942–1945) did mark a diversion from the social reformist zeal of the 'Self-Respect' movement, the difficult conditions of the war period, nevertheless continued the process of breaking-down discrimination based on caste lines. Mani (1978) noted that 'the war period appears to have been instrumental in the disappearance of "distance maintenance" imposed by the caste Hindus' and that 'all temples were opened to Adi-Dravidas, without their asking' (p. 29). Participation in the Indian National Army (INA) also played a role. One respondent, a retiree who was a former conscript in the INA recounts that while he was undergoing training:

> …there were problems initially, particularly on issues related to food. Some Hindus were concerned about who was preparing the food and did not like eating with the lower castes or Muslims. When the officers heard of it, they were furious, and told us that that it was because of such disunity that the British were able to conquer India. Seeing the example of the officers of different castes and religions eating together, the higher caste Hindus stopped making a fuss on the issue. (Interview with Ram Prasad; 12 October 2003)

Following the Japanese occupation, the Tamil reform movement re-emerged in Singapore, supported by the arrival of young Tamil workers affected by the popular Dravida Munnetra Kazagham (DMK) party in Tamil Nadu. Given that the more overt bases for discrimination on grounds of caste had come to be significantly challenged, the focus of the movement turned towards emphasising the unity of 'Dravidian' groups. As far as Hindus were concerned this had the effect of sharpening region-based divisions and strengthened the process of the 'Tamilisation' of Hindu institutions.

Post-independence developments

As far as regionalism was concerned, independence did not mark a major shift in patterns of Hinduism with the continued division of Hindu temples and associations according to Southern and Northern lines (Babb 1976, p. 191).[5] The augmentation in the number of Tamils moving from Malaysia to Singapore in the late 1950s and 1960s (Department of Statistics 1973, Table 13.11) possibly resulted in some North Indian Hindu groups undertaking safeguards to reduce the possibility of being 'taken over' by others. For example, the constitution of the Shree Lakshmi Narayan Temple, formed in 1969, limited official positions at the temple to North Indians (Shree Lakshmi Narayan Temple 1969, Article 19a). As far as participation in worship was concerned, while some North Indian Hindus continued to visit South Indian shrines in their neighbourhoods or those with which they had a long-standing association, few, if any, South Indians, participated in the activities of North Indian temples and organisations. This division was manifest as well in the celebration of religious festivals. In spite of overlap in the festive calendar of both groups – in the celebration of pan-Indian festivals such as *Deepavali*, *Navarathri* and *Maha Shivrathri* for example – these tended to be tied to their respective regional temples and organisations. Where festivals were specific to a region, participation was limited to that regional community, the exception being a small number of North Indians participating in *Timiti* and *Thaipusam*. In addition to regional divisions, amongst Tamil groups, there continued to exist differences between those who participated in Sanskritic traditions at 'mainstream' South Indian temples, and those, particularly from the lower castes and former untouchables, who practiced 'folk' Hinduism at smaller temples dedicated to village deities, which employed non-Brahmin priests, non-Sanskritic rituals, non-vegetarian offerings and the use of spirit-mediums (Babb 1976).

State-led initiatives in post-independence Singapore

Given these diversities, there is little evidence to argue for the prevalence of a homogenised Hinduism in Singapore in the early years after independence. Official policies, however, did act as a spur for homogenisation. Following independence, the state designated four 'racial' categories, Chinese, Malays, Indians and 'Others' (CMIO) as fundamental building blocks of Singapore's multiracial society. The CMIO categories in effect essentialised 'race', obscuring the heterogeneity that existed within them. Through the CMIO model of multiracialism, Chua (1996, p. 56) notes that:

> ...race is essentialized as an unchanging feature of the population so as to ground various specific ways of disciplining the social body... one's race supposedly determined one's culture (multiculturalism); this race-culture is assumed to be embedded in the language of the race... In this set of discursive processes which constitute individuals as members of distinct racial groups, differences among the population are radically reduced.

Measures taken to 'iron out' differences within racial categories extended to the religious arena. Accordingly, two statutory bodies, the Hindu Endowments Board (HEB) and the Hindu Advisory Board (HAB) were set up to advise the government on policy decisions vis-à-vis 'Hinduism'. The regulatory role of these official bodies, in effect meant that they could potentially deem what was and wasn't 'correct' Hindu practice at least as far as the government was concerned. Given the diversity existent in the Hindu community, this regulatory role, from time to time, has given rise to controversy. Sinha (1993) has cited the case of *Thaipusam* where, in spite of protests by some participants, the HEB justified a ban on musical accompaniments at the public festival on the grounds that 'the sanctity of the festival has [sic] to be preserved' (p. 833). Beyond public displays, the following example by a respondent, an office-bearer of a local Hindu temple further illustrates how this can extend to individual Hindus:

> A 15-year old Hindu boy informed me that his school principal had asked him to shave his moustache. He argued that this went against his religious traditions which required that he not shave his moustache so long as his father was alive. Since his father was a member of the temple, we wrote a letter to the school informing that this was indeed a tradition practiced by some Hindus in Uttar Pradesh and requesting that the boy be allowed to keep his moustache. The school however rejected our request saying that on matters concerning Hinduism they would turn to the Hindu Endowments Board. (Interview with Jai[6]; 16 September 2006)

In the 1980s the HEB attempted to gain control of other Hindu shrines, arguing that 'these temples, if not supported by established families, communities, or individuals face financial and management difficulties' (Sinha 1993, p. 833). While the initiative was couched in terms of arguments for better management and financial stability, it was viewed with scepticism by temple committees and devotees who were concerned that a 'takeover' by the HEB would result in the temple either losing its regional character, or resulting in a direct 'influence [on] the content and direction of Hindu ritual and belief' (Sinha 1993, p. 834). North Indian Hindu temples and associations were concerned that this would lead to the 'Tamilisation' of their institutions, while Tamils who practiced 'folk' Hinduism were concerned that the move would accelerate the process of 'Sanskritisation'. These attempts were largely unsuccessful and to date, the HEB has direct control over only four of the 24 registered Hindu shrines (Sinha 2005, p. 93).

Following their formation, Hindu statutory bodies have also initiated moves 'to present a particular image of Hinduism in the public domain… that Hinduism is not a backward, superstitious, and stagnant religion; rather it is solemn, progressive, and disciplined' (Sinha 1993, p. 833). Beyond the need to keep religious practices and values relevant to modernity, the change was ushered in by concerns of a decline in the number of young Hindus participating in the activities of Hindu temples and associations; and of conversion to Christianity. Some attributed this trend to a sense of alienation amongst young Hindus to patterns of religious socialisation that did not provide explanation for their beliefs and practices, a necessity especially in the context of a multicultural, multi-religious society:

> There are many instances when non-Hindus and outsiders ask Hindus about their faith… to explain idol-worship, polytheism, the persistence of the caste system, the purpose of self-immolation and injury to the body (in Thaipusam and Timiti), amongst other aspects of Hinduism. (Sinha 1993, p. 837)

Consequently, the statutory bodies, the Hindu Centre (founded in 1977) and some religious institutions began drawing in part from 'models' adopted by other religious groups, to encourage a greater social, cultural and educational role for Hindu religious bodies. The attempt to 'educate' Hindus in their religion was aided by the Ministry of Education's initiative to introduce Religious Knowledge classes in secondary schools in 1984. The government's 'concern over the maintenance of "traditional cultural values" against the onslaught of modernization and undesirable "Western" influences' (Tan 1997, p. 607) led to the introduction of Buddhist Studies, Bible Knowledge,

Confucian Ethics, Hindu Studies, Islamic Religious Knowledge and Sikh Studies as examinable subjects for upper secondary students. For the purpose of setting up the curriculum for 'Hindu Studies' and providing training for teachers, the Ministry of Education turned to the Hindu statutory bodies. The Hindu Studies initiative was however subject to criticism by some Tamil Hindus who viewed the curriculum as a 'Brahmin conspiracy' because its syllabus (Sinha 1993, p. 840) drew mainly from 'Sankritised sources' – Vedas, Upanishads, Bhagavad Gita, Puranas and the Epics – without sufficient representation of Tamil 'folk' traditions. The critique was, however, short-lived. In 1989, the Ministry of Education did away with the study of Religious Knowledge as an examinable subject altogether. The turnaround stemmed from concerns that the introduction of Religious Knowledge in schools had in fact resulted in an intensification of revivalist and evangelistic activities amongst Christian and Buddhist groups (Tan 1997, p. 616).

The proliferation of global 'Hindu-oriented' movements[7]

In recent decades, the proliferation of global 'Hindu-oriented' movements has been particularly influential in adding to and reconfiguring existent patterns of Hinduism in postcolonial Singapore. While the expansion of Hindu-oriented movements has been particularly remarkable from the 1980s, the advent of such phenomena can be dated to an earlier period where the Ramakrishna Mission and the Arya Samaj, formed in Singapore in the early twentieth century, can be seen as preliminary forms. Amongst the first to establish a presence in Singapore in the post-independence period were the Sri Sathya Sai Association (officially registered in 1975) and the Hare Krishna movement, although the latter's attempt to officially register with the Registry of Societies (ROS) was denied (Sebastian and Parameswaran 2008, p. 67). The 1990s, however, saw a rapid increase in the number of these groups. Sinha (2008) notes at least 18 such organisations officially registered after 1965, although this does not constitute an exhaustive list. A comprehensive list of all such organisations functioning in Singapore is difficult to determine since many are fledgling, may not have their own premises, operate in the homes of devotees or in temple halls, and may seek to keep out of the eyes of the government especially where they have not gained official approval from the ROS, a requirement for them to function legally in Singapore. Amongst the larger groups with wide-ranging and regular activities include the Sri Sathya Sai Association, Mata Amritananda Mayi, Brahma Kumari, the Art of Living Foundation, and the Hare Krishna movement. In some cases crowds in excess of 5000 have been known to gather during the visitation of their respective gurus to Singapore, such as for example during Sri Sri Ravishankar's visit in April 2006.

While these groups have expanded in an age of growing transnational connections between Singapore and India, and with other diasporic locations, there are valid reasons to argue that these movements in Singapore should not necessarily be seen as a unitary phenomenon, nor as part of the process of the homogenisation of Hinduism. Vast differences exist amongst these groups as to whether, if, and the extent to which, they consider themselves as Hindu or for that matter even religious. Some are closely aligned to a particular deity, draw heavily from Hindu sources, and may follow an established Hindu *sampradaya*. Others desist altogether from associating with any deity or *sampradaya*, and the extent to which they draw from Hindu sources may be limited to emphasising breathing techniques such as *pranayama*, practicing certain yoga postures, and meditation.

Since many of these organisations seek to be inclusive of individuals regardless of their professed religion, they may not be comfortable in being characterised as Hindu organisations *per se*. Some are syncretistic, employing the teaching and symbols of other religions and thus may feel that the term Hindu is too exclusive. Given this outlook, it is not surprising to find that the activities of some groups are attended by a large number of non-Indians, particularly Chinese participants, who may even hold positions as office-bearers or form branches of the organisation in Singapore. This has been especially evident in the case of Sri Sathya Sai Association, where Mandarin bhajans have also been developed for Chinese devotees. Non-Indian participants usually do not identify with the terms Hindu or Hinduism but rather see themselves only as devotees of Sai Baba.

Some organisations may reject the term Hindu for precisely the opposite reason, i.e. its inclusive umbrella-like quality comprising beliefs, practices and traditions that may be deemed contrary to those emphasised by these organisations. They may prefer, as in the case of some Hare Krishna devotees, to be identified by the sectarian category of 'Vaishnavas' rather than Hindu. At the other end, some of these groups reject the label 'religious' altogether, characterising themselves as organisations seeking the moral, physical and spiritual upliftment of individuals and society through exercise (*yoga*), meditation and service amongst other such activities. The Art of Living Foundation, founded by Sri Sri Ravi Shankar, stands out as a particularly good example of the latter, and its inclusive character is represented in its large multi-racial, multi-religious fellowship.

Yet there exist a number of similarities, which are also important factors accounting for the popularity of these groups. Although they have roots in India, many of these groups arrived in Singapore after establishing a significant presence in North America. Consequently, their sophisticated discursive practices have been influenced by the experience they have gathered in various locations. Nearly all these groups are 'tech savvy' with an established presence in cyber-space, using a variety of tools such as VCDs and DVDs to package their discourse and practices. An important feature is that these groups have grown out of, and remain centred upon, the teachings of a particular, often still living, 'guru', who may be perceived by the devotees as divine or possessing god-like qualities, and capable of performing 'miracles'. Beyond esoteric reasons, the popularity of these groups stems from an emphasis on spiritual education, and a considerable portion of their discourse is driven by the need to provide explanations for their practices and beliefs. This has played an important role in their ability to reach out to an increasingly educated Hindu population discontented with more traditional ritual-oriented, temple-type Hinduism.

The growth of the Hindu-oriented groups can also be explained by the large increase in the number of Hindu migrant professionals who have arrived in Singapore since the 1990s. It is no coincidence that the proliferation of the Hindu groups has paralleled this influx. In addition to the factors cited above, the reasons why some migrant professionals have chosen to join these groups include their previous participation in the activities of similar groups in India, while others point to the fact that they have felt more welcome in these new Hindu-oriented groups when compared to traditional Hindu institutions dominated by the 'old' diaspora, where they felt like 'outsiders'.

In addition to migrant professionals, the ranks of many new Hindu-oriented groups have been swelled by younger generation Hindus of the 'old' diaspora seeking an escape from the norms, beliefs, and controls of their traditional sub-ethnic community-based institutions that are often characterised by multiple-levels of relationship based on ethnicity, kinship and possibly even caste. One respondent, a teacher in her 30s notes:

> I always had an interest in religion, but from my late teens I began to avoid going to our [sic.] temple. It was not a spiritual place for me. The older people seemed to be there not for religious purposes but only to gossip about others in the community. I felt I was constantly being watched - the clothes I wore, how I behaved, who I was talking to… (Interview with Poonam; 14 June 2008)

While this characterisation could be applied even to some of the new global Hindu-oriented organisations, for many individuals the multiracial, multicultural character of some of these groups may offer the possibility of 'anonymity', and the prospect of being able to 'consume' spirituality without necessarily being subjected to the social controls that they may feel in traditional institutions.

Conclusions

Even as the fellowship of the global Hindu-oriented movements has increased over the last two decades, it would be incorrect to view the more traditional Hindu institutions as remaining static. Increasingly, a number of formerly exclusive regional organisations have undertaken a more inclusive stance, in part to stem the decline in their membership, but also to reach out to the growing numbers of Hindu migrant professionals. While they have only begun to come to terms with the 'tech savvy' methods employed by the new movements, they do hold some advantage in that many of the older organisations have their own properties. In an island-city where space comes at a premium, some older organisations have allowed new Hindu-oriented bodies to rent their premises. The funds generated have then been channelled to strengthen and support their own activities. At the same time, the attempt to forge unity amongst Hindu groups remains an ongoing project for some. For example, in recent years the Hindu Centre has brought together a variety of Hindu groups in the combined celebration of 'Raksha Bandhan'. In addition to fostering the aim of unity, the celebration of a predominantly North Indian festival has enabled the organisation to challenge possible aspersions that it is an exclusively South Indian Hindu body. The HEB also continues to play a coordinating role, seeking to gather support from various Hindu organisations either for charitable purposes, or in the celebration of major festivals such as the annual Deepavali 'light-up' in Serangoon Road.

Turning to some of the questions posed in the introduction, the development of Hinduism in Singapore challenges the notion that the homogenisation of Hinduism is a simple linear process. Although disparate Hindu groups reflected a semblance of shared religious identity in the early colonial period, the process vacillated from a pragmatism-driven collaborative impulse in a diaspora made-up largely of transient men before fragmenting according to caste and regional lines as these communities settled. Although caste-based divisions diluted by the end of the Second World War in part due to the activities of the Tamil reform association, the movement also had the effect of concretising segmentation amongst Hindus along roughly drawn North and South Indian lines. In the post-independence period, while organisations like the HEB and HAB and other state-led initiatives vis-à-vis religion did have a homogenising effect on Hinduism, these efforts faced resistance from practitioners of Tamil 'folk' Hinduism due to concerns that this would result in Sanskritisation, and amongst

Northern Indian groups that this would lead to the 'Tamilisation' of their institutions. Over the last two decades especially, a new set of imperatives has emerged with the arrival of Hindu migrant professionals and the proliferation of global 'Hindu-oriented' movements. The expansion in the interest in an 'intellectual' approach to Hinduism in a multicultural, multiracial society has to some extent been provided for by the advent of these global 'Hindu-oriented' movements whose discursive practices have been strongly influenced by their experience in the West, especially North America. Contrary to these being expressions of the homogenisation of Hinduism, they have, even as they have adopted an inclusive outlook, added to the diversity of the existent Hinduism(s) in the island-city.

Acknowledgments

I would like to thank Professor Peter Reeves, Dr Andrea Pinkney and Dr Sinderpal Singh for taking the time to read the piece and for their insightful comments.

Notes

1. The 2000 census informs that some 16,902 Hindu residents first arrived in Singapore between 1991 and 2000. While Hindus formed only 4% of the total resident population in Singapore aged 15 and over (2000), they numbered 13.67% of all residents (123,650) who first arrived in Singapore in the period 1991–2000. See Leow (2001, p. 119).
2. After the attack on the Golden Temple in India in 1984 and also because some Sikhs feel that in Singapore the 'Indian' category refers to Tamils, a number of Sikhs demanded that they not be identified as Indians in official documents.
3. The figures in 1980 and 1990 add to 99.9% and 100.1% as a result of the rounding off of percentages in these categories.
4. The term *kangani* is derived from the Tamil language meaning 'overseer'. *Kanganis* were employed both to recruit and supervise labourers. In Malaya and Singapore this system ran parallel to indenture throughout the late nineteenth and early twentieth century. Even after the end of indenture in 1910, the *kangani* system continued to function in these parts up to 1938 (Devadas 2006, p. 53).
5. For a detailed study of the division between North Indians and South Indians in Singapore, see Rai (2004a).
6. A pseudonym has been used as the respondent asked to remain anonymous.
7. In 2007–8 I attended two seminars by Professor Waghorne, the first entitled 'Global Gurus and the "De-ethnicization" of Hinduism in the United States and Singapore' (18/09/2007) at the Asia Research Institute and the second entitled 'Global Gurus in Motion: Re-linking public and person in a new space' (21/04/2008) at the South Asian Studies Programme. I am thankful for her insights that have influenced my ideas on the subject. I would also like to extend my appreciation to Mr. Rodney Sebastian, a graduate student at the department of Sociology at the National University of Singapore, who is working on the 'State's management of New Religious Movements in Singapore'.

Notes on Contributor

Rajesh Rai is Assistant Professor at the South Asian Studies Programme, National University of Singapore. He completed his Ph.D. at the School of Historical Studies at the University of Birmingham. His research interests are in the fields of diaspora studies and transnational identities, nationalism and the postcolonial history and politics of South Asia. He is the Editor (with Peter Reeves) of *The South Asian Diaspora: Transnational Networks and Changing Identities* (Routledge, 2008), and Assistant Editor of *The Encyclopedia of the Indian Diaspora* (Editions Didier Millet, 2006). He has published several articles on various aspects of the South Asian diaspora in Southeast Asia.

References

Arya Samaj Singapore, 2003. *75th Anniversary celebrations, souvenir magazine.* Singapore: Arya Samaj Singapore.

Babb, L., 1976. Patterns of Hinduism. *In:* R. Hassan, ed. *Singapore: society in transition.* New York: Oxford University Press, 189–204.

Ballard, R., 1996a. Differentiation and disjunction among the Sikhs. *In:* R. Ballard, ed. *Desh Pardesh: the South Asian presence in Britain.* Delhi: B.R. Publishing, 88–116.

Ballard, R., 1996b. Introduction: the emergence of Desh Pardesh. *In:* R. Ballard, ed. *Desh Pardesh: the South Asian presence in Britain.* Delhi: B.R. Publishing, 1–34.

Chua, B.H., 1996. Racial-Singaporeans: absence after the hyphen. *Social Scientist,* 24 (7/8), 51–68.

Clothey, F.W., 2006. *Ritualizing on the boundaries: continuity and innovation in the Tamil diaspora.* Columbia, S.C.: University of South Carolina Press.

Dalmia, V., 1995. The only real religion of the Hindus: Vaisnava self-representation in the late nineteenth century. *In:* V. Dalmia and H. von Stietencron, eds. *Representing Hinduism: the construction of religious traditions and national identity.* New Delhi: Sage, 176–210.

Devadas, V., 2006. The kangani and maistry system. *In:* B.V. Lal, P. Reeves and R. Rai, eds. *The encyclopedia of the Indian diaspora.* Singapore: Editions Didier Millet, 53–57.

Department of Statistics, 1973. *Report of the census of population Singapore 1970,* Vol. 1. Singapore: Department of Statistics.

Evers, H.-D. and Pavadarayan, J., 1993. Religious fervour and economic success: the Chettiars of Singapore. *In:* K.S. Sandhu and A. Mani, eds. *Indian communities in Southeast Asia.* Singapore: ISEAS and Times Academic Press, 847–861.

Fuller, C.J., 2004. *The camphor flame: popular Hinduism and society in India.* New Jersey: Princeton University Press.

Hindu Endowments Board, 2008. Sri Sivan Temple. Available at: http://www.heb.gov.sg/sst/main-sst.html (accessed 14 July 2008).

King, R., 1999. Orientalism and the modern myth of 'Hinduism'. *Numen,* 46 (2), 146–185.

Leow, B.G., 2001. *Census of population 2000: education, language and religion.* Singapore: Department of Statistics.

Lorenzen, D.N., 2005. Who invented Hinduism? *In:* J.E. Llewellyn, ed. *Defining Hinduism: a reader.* New York: Routledge, 52–80.

Mani, A., 1978. *The changing caste structure amongst the Singapore Indians.* Thesis (MA), National University of Singapore.

McNair, J.F.A., 1899. *Prisoners their own warders.* Westminster: A. Constable.

Rahman, N.-A.A., 2004. Sri Ramakrishna mission. *Singapore Infopedia,* Available at: http://infopedia.nl.sg/articles/SIP_410_2005-01–18.html (accessed 22 July 2008).

Rai, R., 2004a. Race and the construction of the north-south divide amongst Indians in colonial Malaya and Singapore. *South Asia: Journal of South Asian Studies,* 27 (2), 245–264.

Rai, R., 2004b. Sepoys, convicts and the 'bazaar' contingent: the emergence and exclusion of 'Hindustani' pioneers at the Singapore frontier. *Journal of Southeast Asian Studies,* 35 (1), 1–19.

Rai, R., 2006. Indians in Singapore. *In:* B.V. Lal, P. Reeves and R. Rai, eds. *The encyclopedia of the Indian diaspora.* Singapore: Editions Didier Millet, 176–188.

Sebastian, R. and Parameswaran, A., 2008. Hare Krishnas in Singapore: agency, state and Hare Krishna. *Sojourn,* 23 (1), 63–86.

Shantakumar, G., 1993. The Indian population of Singapore: some implications for development. *In:* K.S. Sandhu and A. Mani, eds. *Indian communities in Southeast Asia.* Singapore: ISEAS and Times Academic Press, 866–909.

Shree Lakshmi Narayan Temple, 1969. *Constitution of Shree Lakshmi Narayan Temple.* Singapore: Shree Lakshmi Narayan Temple.

Sinha, V., 1993. Hinduism in contemporary Singapore. *In:* K.S. Sandhu and A. Mani, eds. *Indian communities in Southeast Asia.* Singapore: ISEAS and Times Academic Press, 826–846.

Sinha, V., 2005. *A new god in the diaspora: Muneeswaran worship in contemporary Singapore.* Singapore: Singapore University Press.

Sinha, V., 2006. Constructing and contesting 'Singaporean Hinduism'. *In:* L.K. Fee, ed. *Race, ethnicity, and the state in Malaysia and Singapore.* Leiden: Brill, 145–168.

Sinha, V., 2008. 'Religiously-inspired', 'India derived' movements in Singapore. *In:* L.A. Eng, ed. *Religious diversity in Singapore.* Singapore: Institute of Southeast Asian Studies, 142–166.

Sri Senpaga Vinayagar Temple, 2008. Available from: http://www.senpaga.org.sg/history.asp [accessed 16 July 2008].

Tan, J., 1997. The rise and fall of religious knowledge in Singapore secondary schools. *Journal of Curriculum Studies,* 29 (5), 603–624.

Turnbull, C.M., 1989. *A history of Singapore, 1819–1988,* 2nd ed. Singapore: Oxford University Press.

van der Veer, P. and Vertovec, S., 1991. Brahmanism abroad: on Caribbean Hinduism as an ethnic religion. *Ethnology,* 30 (2), 149–166.

von Stietencron, H., 1995. Religious configurations in pre-Muslim India and the modern concept of Hinduism. *In:* V. Dalmia and H. von Stietencron, eds. *Representing Hinduism: the construction of religious traditions and national identity.* New Delhi: Sage, 51–81.

The dynamics of preserving cultural heritage: the case of Durban's Kathiawad Hindu Seva Samaj, 1943–1960 and beyond

Surendra Bhana[a] and Kusum K. Bhoola[b]

[a]*Department of History, University of Kansas, USA;* [b]*Independent Researcher, Durban, South Africa*

In 1943, the Kathiawad Hindu Seva Samaj brought together diverse castes of Gujarati-speaking Hindus to promote language and culture. In doing so, it linked itself to Kathiawad in India outside of South Africa. The Samaj expanded its objective to build much-needed English-medium schools open to all Indians regardless of their backgrounds. It used state patronage; and adopted an apolitical stance towards the apartheid regime. After 1970, it redirected its energies towards its primary goals, but expanded its horizons to accommodate new forms of South Africanism among Indians. It redefined 'Indianness' within a broader cultural framework even as individual members negotiated ambiguities relating to their identities.

The Kathiawad Hindu Seva Samaj (KHSS, hereafter referred to as Samaj) was established in 1943 by a group of leading Durban residents seeking to preserve traditional values associated with their ancestral region known today as Saurashtra. They called themselves 'Kathiawadis' from the term 'Kathis', the name originally given to Scythian migrants in the eighth and ninth centuries, although reference to 'Kathiawad' as a region occurred only in the eighteenth-century. Influenced by Mohandas K. Gandhi (1869–1948) and India's independence movement, Durban's Kathiawadis desired to move away from narrow caste-based affiliations. Creating an organization to promote such values gave the group a legitimate platform for its activities. What Brettel says about Asian Indians in the Dallas–Fort Worth complex is true of Kathiawadis in Durban.

To achieve their goals, they deployed 'social capital', a term that refers to ethnic, personal, and group networking. In this way they ensured the continued existence of themselves as a community in a 'deterritorialized' world in which Kathiawad served as a cultural point of reference (Brettell 2005). The Samaj's primary goal was to promote Gujarati as *matrubasha* (mother tongue) and the Hindu *dharma*. Like other similar organizations, the Samaj realized that the vernacular language was essential to preserving culture. It combined this with providing formal education through English schools. To achieve these goals, it tapped into the wealth of its own members. It recognized that Indian school-going population had increased phenomenally, and, in stepping forward to fill that need, the Samaj established its legitimacy in the wider Indian community. The Samaj used parameters defined by the state to achieve its goals. As an apolitical body, it established networks with financial institutions, and local, provincial and national decision-makers.

Scholars have written widely about the dynamics surrounding political, social and labour movements that went into the making of newer concept of what it meant to be Indian in the 1940s and 1950s (Bugwandeen 1995, Edwards 1989, Freund 1995, Ginwala 1974, Mesthrie 1984, Pahad 1973, Padayachee *et al.* 1985, Raman 2006, Vahed 1997). Few, however, have examined the apolitical orientation of voluntary bodies and their culturally defined notions of identity. Such groups, as Hilda Kuper (1960) argues, operated within the 'limits of policy and procedures set by local law and custom' and negotiated 'when necessary with the responsible authorities'.

This essay examines the circumstances around which the Samaj achieved its defined goals in its formative years from 1943 to 1960, and broadened its mission to include formal education through private and public funding. It operated beyond the needs of its narrowly defined regionalism by declaring its willingness to help others. It engaged in partnership with the state by utilizing a formula that succeeded with a white power structure eager to co-opt minority leaders in the highly charged political environment of the 1940s and 1950s. All the while, the Samaj continued to serve the narrower cultural and religious interests of its region-specific members.

We address more fundamentally the issue about Samaj members' ethnic and regional identification within South Africa's officially designated term 'Indian' for all who were ancestrally connected to the subcontinent. While Samaj members declared their intention to move away from caste-based distinctions in 1943, they nevertheless adopted an identity that separated them from their Gujarati and non-Gujarati compatriots. In part, the desire to identify with India in narrowly defined cultural and/or religious terms was a reflection of the South African state's failure to extend citizenship rights to Indians – it was only in 1961 that the state formally embraced them as part of the country. Furthermore, segregation and apartheid had alienated many and encouraged them to search for emotional connection outside of South Africa's borders; and India, newly independent, became a source of enormous pride. The reality, however, was that South Africa was their home. This created ambiguities. How did the Samaj negotiate these dualities? The Samaj adapted to newer developments. Once the state had taken over responsibility in formal education, it redirected its energies to other goals such as promoting Gujarati and liaising more closely with bodies like the Surat Hindu Association (SHA, f. 1907) to create greater cohesion among Durban's Gujarati–speaking Hindu communities. All of this culminated in 1993 in the creation of the Gujarati Sanskruti Kendra or Kendra for short. Leaders reached out to other South Africans. Apartheid ended in 1994, and a democratically elected Black majority government came into place. New uncertainties emerged. What did all of this mean for individuals who called themselves South Africans even as they retained Indianness?

Experience in all diasporas is marked by ambiguities as people with loyalties to their ancestral land endeavour to identify with their new homes; and simple binary oppositions do not adequately define the multiplicity of identities. South Asian communities settled outside of their original home acknowledged their loyalty and emotions to the 'old country'. They displayed a desire to 'retain, reconstitute, and revitalize the many aspects of their culture in an overseas setting', all 'lineaments' of cultural retention undergirded by religion, caste, traditions, emotions, and imaginings, as Cohen (1997) points out. Religion was an important facet of this experience. Bhikhu Parekh found, for example, that a 'distinctive diasporic consciousness' emerged around Hindus who adopted the *Ramayana* (Appadurai 2003, Cohen 1997,

Man in India 2008, Parekh *et al.* 2003, Vertovec 2003). In South Africa, exclusion, disfranchisement and racial discrimination created anxieties from the beginning. Marginalized sections of a population are always more likely to attach themselves to real or imagined 'homes'. From the beginning, Indians created voluntary and exclusive associations around defined needs. Even when they adopted political identities, they did not shed loyalties to their community organizations. In their study of colonial Natal, Bhana and Vahed discovered that 140 of the 167 organizations had narrow sectional orientations with strong links to India. Only 25 were secular. Some of these continued well into the twentieth-century; and new bodies emerged. Almost all of them maintained links with India through regular visits, funding of small village projects, or remittances to family members. They invested in promoting what they regarded as 'traditional' values; and in some cases they identified with political and social movements in India. They are an important part of the history of South Africa's Indians (Bhana and Vahed 2005, pp. 157–161, *Oriental Anthropologist* 2007).

Briefly, that history began when the first group of indentured Indians migrated to South Africa in 1860. State-sponsored indentured migration continued through 1911. Other Indians followed in search of trade opportunities. By 1910, there were 150,000 Indians in the country. White rule and domination had already become firmly entrenched by then. Small and large African polities experienced conquest and subjugation even as the Boers, the descendants of the original Dutch settlers, clashed with the British for hegemony. Everywhere, white South Africa moved to exclude Indians from its shores. Laws restricting trade, movement and immigration came into place. The Indians resisted. In 1894, they created the Natal Indian Congress (NIC). It became a vehicle for political expression around the notion of Indianness even though Indians remained primarily loyal to their caste, language and religious bodies. This dual identification continued well into the twentieth-century. In the late 1940s and 1950s, for example, the NIC created multi-racial alliances even though its membership was entirely Indian; and in the 1970s, its leaders embraced the term 'Black' for Indians to show solidarity with Africans. Indians never made up more than 3% of the total population (Bhana 1997). Their numbers increased to 200,000 in the 1930s and 700,000 in the 1970s. In 2000, they numbered 1.1 million out of a total population of 45 million, over 90% living in urban areas.

The 1940s and the formation of the Samaj

The early 1940s were a period of great changes. The Second World War sparked off momentous events in India and South Africa. In both countries, there was a strong movement to end religious sectionalism and racial discrimination. In India, the British government had hardened its position towards the Indian Nationalist Congress leaders and jailed many of its leaders, including Gandhi. The Muslim League led by Muhammad Ali Jinnah (1876–1948) grew stronger in its demand for a separate state. In South Africa, the country's participation in the war stimulated industrialization and greater numbers of African workers moved to manufacturing plants in cities. They engaged in trade union movements seeking an end to wage disparities. Politically, young Black activists sought bolder directions from their leaders. For example, youthful and talented individuals like Anton Lambede, Walter Sisulu, Nelson Mandela and A.P. Mda in the African National Congress Youth League (f. 1943–1944) challenged leadership in the liberation movement to take a more active role in their search for freedom. This kind of militancy was also evident among Indian activists such as Monty

Naicker, I.C. Meer and Yusuf M. Dadoo who argued for political equality. They challenged the state to address the needs of a rapidly growing Indian population, which included adequate educational facilities.

Running parallel with such developments was the Indian desire to promote vernacular traditions. This was a long-standing trend from the colonial days as we pointed out earlier. In 1928 K.P. Kichulu found 50 vernacular schools, most connected to mosques (Mesthrie 2002). The Arya Pratinidhi Sabha (f. 1925) supported the teaching of Hindi, promoted reform Hinduism through six Vedic conferences from 1925 to 1945, and built the Veda Mandir (Naidoo 1992, http://www.apssa.co.za/history_of_aps.htm). In 1956, some 35–40 Hindi schools enrolled 3000–3500 students. There were about as many Tamil schools that aimed to teach the vernacular language and 'right' behaviour (Kuper 1960). In 1948, the Mayville Sarasvati Tamil School spent £2000 to convert a furniture factory into a school for 300 children with the service of one teacher. It had been running a Tamil school in a garage of one of its members since 1943 (*Indian Opinion*, 8 October 1948). Advertisements appeared regularly in newspapers for vernacular teachers in Arabic, Urdu and Tamil (*Indian Opinion*, 9 May 1947, 11 April 1948). The Tamil Federation of KwaZulu Natal promoted the language and cultural heritage of people who came from southern parts of India (http://www.tamilsa.org/index.php). Numerous other organizations with similar cultural or language orientations were active across all religious groups in South Africa. Muslim bodies like their Hindus counterparts adapted to changing circumstances. To take one example, the Orient Islamic Educational Institute set out in 1938 to build community schools. In the next 20 years, it established primary and secondary schools in Durban. The schools were secular but incorporated 'a distinctive religious ethos' and were turned into private schools in 1998 (http://www.orientschool.co.za/resume.asp?pg=profile).

This is the context in which the Samaj was created. It traced its beginnings to 1894 when two of the earliest immigrants were Porbandar residents Vasanji and Sunderji settled in Tongaat. They returned four years later and encouraged others to migrate. Immigrants came from Kathiawad towns and villages like Ranvav, Gondal, Bhanvad, Jodiya and Morvi, representing Hindu castes such as *Brahmin*, *Vanik*, *Lohana*, *Khatri*, *Soni*, *Patani* and *Girnara*. These early migrants created caste and sub-caste organizations. Their basic objective was to maintain caste integrity locally, although like many such organizations, they promoted social and commercial welfare of members within the group. The 1956 brochure listed seven organizations before 1943 so as to place the Samaj's history as having evolved from narrower to broader concerns. These seven organizations had narrow caste orientation. Their members shared, however, much that was common. Membership was not exclusive and many members belonged to more than one organization[1] (*KHSS brochure* 1956, Gandhi 1928).

In the 1940s, the Kathiawadis saw value in moving away from narrowly-based parochialism so as to pool resources to promote broadly regional, cultural, religious and educational values. Besides having a common language, they shared the rich cultural and historical traditions of the region. Many acknowledged that the early forms of the caste system had prevented them in the past 'from taking part in wider opportunities' to serve a 'larger community'. They recognized that they could more effectively preserve their language and culture as a united group, and provide skills for their children to succeed in South Africa. The 1956 brochure stated that they had to respond to the 'ever present danger' that their young men and women would lose contact with the 'mainsprings of their mother tongue'. They made language a central concern because knowing Gujarati was essential to understanding their heritage (*KHSS brochure* 1956).

Yet it would be misleading to think that all caste-thinking was on the retreat. It was deeply embedded in their daily practices. Many still clung to narrow forms of sectionalism. Dhupelia-Mesthrie relates that since her grandmother, Sushila Gandhi was a Surti married to Manilal Gandhi who was a Kathiawadi, many in the Kathiawadi community were 'not very open in its acceptance of the family …' and some labelled their daughter Ela Gandhi, a 'half-caste' (Dhupelia-Mesthrie 2004, pp. 286–287).

At the forefront of the endeavour to unite Kathiawadi Gujaratis was Dr Nagindas P. Desai (1905–1992). Even if region became the strongest base around which to organize the Kathiawadis, it did not include Muslims. There was thus a strong religious divide in the creation of the Samaj. Desai was a charismatic individual who was the driving force in the creation of the organization, although others like N.V. Mehta, H.N. Naran, H.H. Dhupelia, P.H. Dhupelia, V.R. Parekh, V.P. Desai and N.S. Devshi also played leading roles. If we focus on Desai, it is because he best embodied the goals for the early period. As a professional of some standing, he commanded respect among community members willing to follow his lead. He was immersed in the Gujarati culture as a result of his experience in India. In India, he edited *Maha Gujarat* and the *Hindu*. Desai was educated in Tongaat before going to Mumbai to study at the Esplanade High School where he matriculated in 1923. There, he entered the National Medical College to become a physician in 1929. He practised medicine before joining government medical service in India. In 1936, he went to England for further studies. He spent four years at the medical schools in London, Glasgow and Dublin earning additional qualifications. He returned to Durban in 1940 to practise medicine. He would soon be drawn into community affairs. Desai was influenced by Gandhi early in his life. In 1912 when he was seven-years old, he stayed briefly at the Tolstoy Farm run by Gandhi. While in India, he became involved in the independence struggle, and spent three months in jail for promoting *khadi* by weaving and selling this home-grown fabric. In South Africa, Desai promoted cultural and religious values through his role as president of the Gujarati Cultural Society and the South African Hindu Maha Sabha (*KHSS brochure* 1956, 1993, *Indian Opinion*, 5 September 1952).[2]

Desai was aware of developments within the Kathiawadi communities as well as the broader South African society in the 1940s. He served as president almost continually from December 1943 to June 1958 except for two years, 1946 and 1950. Under his stewardship the Samaj established, briefly, the Kathiawad Hindu Govt-Aided Indian School in Lorne Street and a community hall with the help of £21,469 from 40 families, the largest donation of £1262 coming from Choonilal Bros. The total cost was £35,000. The Kathiawad Hall, later renamed Mahatma Gandhi Hall, offered everyone a 'sense of belonging' and became a nerve-centre of the community. The Kathiawad Hindu Govt-Aided Indian School opened its doors in April 1947 with R.P. Soni as principal. It ran as a school for girls until 1969. Two new schools, the Manilal Valjee State-Aided Indian Primary School and the Gandhi Desai State-Aided Secondary School, came into being, thanks to the largesse of V. Valjee and the Gandhi–Desai family which donated £10,005 and £10,000 respectively. The schools opened in January 1959. In 1960, the Manilal Valjee had 16 classrooms, 650 pupils and 18 teachers; and the Gandhi Desai had 14 classrooms, 500 pupils and 20 teachers. The Manilal Valjee became co-educational in 1969. A Gujarati school was started in April 1945 in Desai's home with his wife Bhadrakumari Desai serving as one of the teachers. In May 1947, the vernacular school shifted to the Kathiawad Hindu Govt-Aided

Indian School in Lorne Street by which time the number of teachers had grown to five with four aides. A Gujarati library was opened on 25 April 1948. In November 1949, the library moved to the basement of Gandhi Hall and ran until the late 1960s. The Kathiawad Hindu Youth Organization ran from 1956 to 1971 using the Hall as its venue in later years. In the early 1940s, women promoted cultural forms like *garba* (traditional dance) on a monthly basis. In April 1950, Gujarati Hindu *Stree* [Women's] Samaj was created whose name was changed to Kathiawad Hindu Mahila Mandal in May 1951. This essay explores these developments in greater detail below (*KHSS brochure* 1956, 1993, Nowbath *et al.* 1960, pp. 125–127).

Desai had great passion for Kathiawad as we can see from first paragraph of a one-page message he wrote on 7 October 1943 to fellow-Kathiawadis. Addressing them as 'dear Kathiawadi brothers', he called on them to unite as befitting the heroic individuals who came from their 'brave land':

> The auspicious moment has arrived. The brave land where Lord Shri Krishna arrived from the north, settled in Dwarika and ruled; the Sorath region where he breathed his last; the blessed town of Probandar, which is well known as Sudamapuri and where Mahatma Gandhi was born; the sacred land which gave birth to a great religious leader like Dayanand Saraswati, the land of the brave where even Sorathi bandits earned fame for their bravery; the Sorath region where the hill town of Junagadh inspired the devotee of Krishna, Narasinha Mehta, to sing *Prabhatia* [morning hymns]; and the land whose sons, through their courage, proved in the *satyagraha* of Rajkot that the flame of bravery has not been extinguished there; the natives of the same land who have ventured across the sea and made this continent their own land, o' Kathiawadi brothers, our auspicious moment has arrived. [Translated from Gujarati]

The statement does not acknowledge the Muslim heritage of the region, once again revealing the strong Hindu orientation of the movement. In another general communication dated 25 September 1944, the heading was *Jai Saurashtra*, *Jai Swadesh* (Hail Saurashtra, Hail Our Land), while the text referred to 'our history', meaning the history of the Saurashtra and India. Desai's passion for it comes through in a message he wrote on 15 October 1950, 'Saurashtra is a heroic land, [and you who come from there] can shape your lives accordingly so that others can benefit from its nectar'. In a section called 'Our Heritage' the history of Kathiawad is presented as the new Saurashtra with the liberal use of maps, pictures and illustrations of famous temples, buildings and historical figures from the distant past to the twentieth century. Music and folklore are highlighted as part of its illustrious legacy. Indeed, the brochure traced it to the time of Krishna. The writings of the legendary poet Nanalal Dalpatram singing the praises of Kathiawad are reproduced (*KHSS brochure* 1956).

Why did the Samaj not unite with Gujarati Hindus who had created the Surat Hindus Association (SHA) in 1907? Strong caste and regional forms of identification prevented a merger in the 1940s. Besides, SHA had developed deeply entrenched vested interest and was not ready then to share resources with another body. The association had created institutions around the cultural and religious needs of Gujarati Hindus who came from Surat and surrounding areas. It invested in properties, built a hall, and created schools. It imported Gujarati teachers from India for its vernacular school, ran a library, a cricket club and established the Surat Hindu Government-Aided School in 1951. It observed separately cultural and religious festivals. It did, however, combine occasionally with the Samaj in the 1940s and the 1950s to host cultural and religious events. The two organizations had much to gain by working closely, but it was only in the 1990s that they merged as we see later in this essay. A more pertinent question is why it took the Kathiawadis so long to create a unified body some 36 years after the Surat Hindus. Perhaps the answer may lie in why the Surat Hindus decided as early as they did to create a unified body. Only a detailed examination of their records can yield an answer (*SHA brochure* 1975, 1982, Nowbath *et al.* 1960).

Foundational years: 1943–1960

For the early period, we had access to general and committee minutes from December 1943 to July 1960 as well as the 1956 Samaj brochure. Samaj minutes placed great emphasis on correct procedure without revealing the process by which they handled potentially divisive issues. The minutes, all written in Gujarati, record the names of members who attended committee meetings, but do not always provide details that went into making decisions. The elegant handwriting free of errors would suggest pruning as considerable care went into what was included and excluded. The minutes refer to letters received, but rarely revealed their contents. The records for this 17-year period show that the Samaj had 16 general and special meetings and 78 committee meetings. The July 1960 minutes of the Annual General Meeting (AGM) were missing. The organization had its inaugural meeting on 26 December 1943. There were no AGM's for four years: 1944, 1948, 1952 and 1959. The Samaj had an average of four committee meetings per year, although in some years, as in 1947, it had as many as eight. All meetings began with the *Gayatri Mantra* (universal prayer) and ended with the *shantipath*, the peace prayer. In the first three years, the AGMs were held in the Arya Pratindhi Samaj Hall. After the Samaj built its own hall, the organization held its meetings in the Mahatma Gandhi Hall from 1947 forward. The business premises of Dhupelia & Sons was generally the venue of committee meetings until 16 April 1947. After that date, all meetings were held in the hall, usually in the office of the school principal. Almost all committee meetings occurred late in the afternoon or early evening around 5:30 or 7:30 p.m., although Sunday meetings began at 10:00 a.m.

Desai had the support of many other executive or committee members. Over 40 members played influential roles as Table 1 shows, although the years of service in some cases go beyond 1960. Some like Moolji Hirjee served in several capacities. He was vice president in 1945 and 1946, and secretary in 1947, but served on the management committee throughout. Nathalal S. Devshi served as president in 1950 and 1951 and as vice president in 1953. No woman served in any capacity. Their absence made the Samaj a heavily patriarchal body. Almost all were businessmen. Of the 46 names on the list, 25 were businessmen, 10 were jewellers, four were in real estate, and two were professionals. Some businessmen doubled as money-lenders.

At its inaugural meeting, the Samaj determined its goals to preserve and promote *matrubasha* (mother tongue), *dharmic* (religious) education and culture by building a temple as well as Gujarati and English schools. Members declared their support by pledging donations: Choonilal Bros £1001, Samjee Devshi £350, Nathalal Naran £250, Dhupelia & Son £251, Soni Kara Devraj £250, N.P. Desai £500, Jethalal Naran £101, Chimanlal Mehta £101, Goshalia & Son £201, M.K. Lodhia £101 and Lakhani & Son £251. These sums add up to huge contributions in today's values. A retail price index suggests that £100 in 1945 was equal to £3000 today while the average earning index increases that to £9000.[3]

In following a chronological order, we show how the Samaj reacted to challenges as they arose. Beyond the goal of acquiring sites for buildings and creating an infrastructure that would propel their goals, Desai and others in the organization acted

Table 1. Samaj officials, 1943–1993 (selective)

Name	Years	Name	Years
Chhagan, P.	14	†Mehta, N.V.	31
Desai, Kantilal P.	44	*†Naran, H.N.	37
Desai, Krishnadas P.	30	Naran, Ramdas	33
*†Desai, Dr N.P.	30	Nathoo, Damji	44
Desai, V.P.	33	†Parekh, M.	7
*†Devshi, Nathalal Samjee	15	Parekh, R.V.	16
Devshi, V.J. Thakker	40	†Premji, Soni Jeram	29
Dhupelia, H.H.	31	Samjee, Nathalal	15
*Dhupelia, P.H.	40	†Soni, M.H.	?
Garach, R.C	10	†Soni, O.M.	?
Harilal, Govind	18	Soni, T.K.	6
†Hirjee, Moolji	31	Tabha, N.	20
Jethalal, Dharmsee Naran	15	†Thaker, H.A.	15
Kara, D.J.	25	Thaker, Sr, S.J.	37
†Kara, Pragji	12	Thaker, V.J.	40
Kara, V.J	10	Thakker, H.	19
Lakhani, H.H.	23	Trikamjee, Ashwin	20
†Lakhani, N.N.	15	Trikamjee, Hirji	45
Lodhia, M.K.	36	Valjee, J.M.	20
Manji, M.	36	Valji, B.M.	39
Maghjee, Soni Kanji	7	Valji, Damji	7
Mehta, C.J.	17	Vallabhdas, N.	37
Metha, C.K.	25	Vasanji, Vallabhdas	23

Notes: *President; †Vice President.
Sources: *KHSS minutes*, 1943–1960, *KHSS brochure* 1993.

quickly when the need arose. A small coterie of well-heeled Samaj members usually came up with money at relatively short notice when it was needed.

During 1944, seven committee meetings made important decisions to set into motion the Samaj's main goals. The first of these related to the purchase of suitable land to build schools and a hall. The subcommittee members rejected a site on the corner of Stradford Street and Old Dutch Road valued at £11,000, but showed enthusiasm for a property in Lorne Street owned by a Samaj member. It cost £5650. The Samaj had over £5561 in cash by the end of October. It took out a bond of £5500 and paid £150 in cash. A separate subcommittee recommended the purchase of a property in Grey Street next to the Randeri building with a bond payment of £3500. Reference in the minutes to a bond of £2500 paid on the R.K. Khan Estate is not clear. The Samaj moved quickly to give termination notices to tenants living in the Lorne Street property and hired one architect to draw up a plan to build classrooms and a hall. A plan was ready by the end of November 1944. It calculated that £20,000 was needed to build a hall.[4]

The Samaj postponed decision about membership fees in its first year. Membership was open to all who came from Kathiawad. If there was a debate about this, the minutes are silent about it. Gandhi's son, Manilal M. Gandhi, resigned from the committee, but no reasons are given. It could be, as Dhupelia-Mesthrie has suggested, that Manilal Gandhi, like all members of his household, was open to 'people of any culture, religion, caste, race or class' and therefore did not feel comfortable associating with an organization that was narrowly caste- and region-based (Dhupelia-Mesthrie 2004, pp. 286–287). In its primary function of building schools, it decided early that it would provide education in Gujarati, and would solicit matching funds from the state to run English schools. A subcommittee was appointed towards the end of the year to determine conditions under which the Education Department would agree to a joint enterprise. Given the urgent need for education, Samaj members postponed the building of a temple. In the meanwhile, it affiliated with the South African Hindu Maha Sabha and sent seven delegates to its annual conference in Pietermaritzburg. In its endeavour to promote Gujarati, the Samaj decided to build a library. A library fund was created and members donated money, books and book shelves. Advertisements were placed in *Indian Opinion*, *Daily News* and *Natal Mercury* for a teacher and a priest.[5]

The Samaj sounded out the Education Department about running the Lorne Street premises entirely as an English school. Working with non-Samaj people like Sorabjee Rustomjee, H.R. Naidoo and P.R. Pather, Samaj members met the chief of Indian Education, Devlin (full name not available), and on Pather's advice met with the chief inspector. Pather was then head of a general education committee looking into ways of expanding resources and facilities for Indian schools. These non-Gujarati individuals had long been involved in promoting state-aided schools. We do not know the outcome of such deliberations. In any event, the Samaj hired the services of three architects in planning and designing the project in Lorne Street and launched a drive to collect funds. T. Manjee headed the collection drive in Natal, while a group headed by Desai went to the Transvaal for donations.[6]

As for Gujarati school teachers, the Samaj failed to get suitably qualified local teachers. It had greater success advertising in newspapers in India and many of the Kathiawad applicants seemed well qualified. Members visiting India were given permission to screen them further. Given immigration restrictions, the Samaj needed approval by the state to import teachers. The Gujarati library was making slow progress because war conditions had delayed shipment of books from India. Local members continued to donate shelves for the library. In the meanwhile, Hindu festivals were observed at the Surat Hindu Association (SHA) hall; and on 14 January 1945, the Samaj encouraged all to take part in a fun event, *makker-sankrati* (kite-flying). Throughout 1944, the Samaj engaged in activities to demonstrate its support for India's independence. It celebrated Gandhi's seventy-sixth birthday and organized prayers when he fasted from 6 to 13 May 1944, and there were the usual round of farewell receptions for Samaj members travelling to India.

There were three committee meetings in 1945. The Education Department spelled out conditions under which it would collaborate in running the English school. The Samaj decided to build five classrooms. For the time being, it delayed temple building to focus on getting the school started. Even as the Samaj was concentrating on its Lorne Street project, the Durban City Council offered it 1.75 acres of land in the Curries Fountain complex to build one or more schools. No details are given in the minutes, but members were surely excited by the possibility of adding another school under its control. Nathalal Samjee immediately offered £5000 in memory of his father, Samjee Devshi, towards the building of an English school on the new site. The Samaj considered this a great opportunity to shift state resources to the new project. Desai and others met with Education Department's Devlin to request a transfer of the government grant from the Lorne Street project to the new one at Curries Fountain, but Devlin thought it best to leave things as they were and suggested that the Samaj should seek another grant when the Curries Fountain project was completed. Should the Samaj return the Lorne Street school grant to the government? A special general meeting on 8 September 1946 voted against it, 47 to 5. Meanwhile, it took out a bond of £5000 to cover the cost of the Lorne Street project. Members came forward to extend interest-free loans. Parekh offered £1000 and H. Nathalal and P.H. Dhupelia each gave £500 for two years. A foundation stone was laid at the Lorne Street site. The hall was built, and the *vastu* (initiation) ceremony was performed on 25 October 1946 followed by a cultural show. As for the Curries Fountain project, the Samaj invited Indian High Commissioner Ram Rao Deshmukh to break ground at the site on 13 October 1946.[7]

Nineteen-forty-seven was a busy year. India's independence was celebrated in a grand style. Students at the Gujarati school received independence medals. There were eight committee meetings, two general meetings, and one special general meeting. The Samaj streamlined its regular work by creating subcommittees. The management committee was increased from 12 members to 17. The English-medium school began in January 1947 with 300 students. It was officially opened on 19 April 1947 in the presence of R.A. Banks, the Director of Indian Education and other dignitaries. Financial issues continued to dominate the year. Some £17,000–£18,000 had been spent on the Lorne Street complex when only £8000 had been projected. This generated heated discussion at the AGM on 4 May 1947. Raising funds became important. A special subcommittee was given the task of collecting money with permission to solicit donations from non-Kathiawadis. By the middle of 1947, unused building materials were sold for £1800. Hall rental at £15 to £20 per session brought some relief. By October, hall rental had earned over £73. The Gujarati school brought five shillings monthly in student fees as from July 1947, but the Samaj needed additional funds to pay off debts and to cover regular and incidental expenses. To cover these expenses, the Grey Street site was sold to M.R. Parekh for £4000. This lot had been earmarked for a temple, but members argued that the area was too small to accommodate a place of worship. The Grey Street property had been used as collateral for a £5000 bond provided by the Netherlands Bank and with its sale, one of the members stepped in to act as guarantor.[8]

With the hall built and the schools operating, the Samaj fulfilled its cherished goals. During 1948 and 1949, it concentrated on ensuring that things ran smoothly. Early in 1949, it had a cash reserve of £1500 which it placed in fixed deposit to earn extra revenues. The government increased its grant for the English school from 33% to 50% which translated into a subsidy of £8040. The Samaj extended a loan of £1500 to M.R. Parekh at 8% interest. It also took out bonds on properties in Riverside and Clairwood, about which there are no details in the minutes. Donors contributed regularly. Regular rental of the hall for weddings and other social events or special events brought much-needed revenues. After Gandhi's cremation in 1948, some ashes were brought to the hall for a special ceremony attended by hundreds of people, after which they were ritually released in the Umgeni River. From that point forward, the hall was renamed the Mahatma Gandhi Hall. It served as a popular venue for cultural and religious festivals like *Diwali*, *Krishna Jayanti*, *Ramnavmi* and *Gita Saptah*. Soon after Afro-Indian riots in January 1949, it was used to shelter some 1100 refugees. Individual organizations made use of the facility to hold meetings or to run special Indian language classes; or, as in the case of the Natal Indian Congress (NIC), to provide standard six classes for students who could not be accommodated at Sastri College, the only school in the area offering secondary education.[9]

The Gujarati school expanded rapidly. At the beginning of 1949, there were 160 pupils. Class 1 had 92 students, while upper levels (from standards 1 to 4) totalled 68. The emphasis was on *dharmic sanskaro* (religious principles) in which Hindu literature, prayers, *garba* (dance) and *bhajans* (devotional songs) took prominent place. There was a need to get qualified teachers from India as well as a priest knowledgeable about Hinduism. Many applied. Some of them dropped out because the Samaj could not get timely approval from the immigration authorities to import teachers. It improved pay scales and working conditions to attract teachers. Teachers were offered £25 per month and a six-year contract and had to give one-year notice to quit. Desai took over the management of the syllabus and examinations.[10] Later, a revised Gujarati syllabus focused on prayers, poetry, *bhajans* (devotional songs), Gujarati, arithmetic, *dharmic* studies and singing. On Fridays, pupils were instructed in prayer rituals like *sandhya* and *havans*. In addition, there was *Saptahik Satsang* (weekly devotional songs) every Sunday. There was greater success with the English school. The Samaj started pre-school classes, and in 1951 had an enrolment of 460 students. That year, they started standard five classes. In 1953, there were 454 students with 12 teachers. The school also introduced standard six and 25 of the 31 students who sat for this public examination passed.[11]

Long-postponed issues about membership and goals were taken up at a special general meeting on 10 July 1949. The Samaj defined its aims as promoting the interests of 'Kathiawadi Hindus' and reaching out 'to all sectors of the Indian community' in South Africa. Membership was open to 'all Hindus of Kathiawadi descent living in Natal', not less than 18 years old, but eligibility was left strictly in the hands of the management committee, which in terms of the new definition, consisted of 30 officials, the president, three vice presidents, two secretaries, two treasurers, five trustees and 17 members. We do not know if there was any dissension on membership issues. One issue hinted at in the minutes turned out to be incidental, but it showed how strongly the Samaj identified with issues related to India. An individual wrote anonymously to *Indian Opinion* on 8 October 1948 complaining about the way the Samaj changed words from the original Bengali version when the children sang India's national anthem, *Janaganaman*. Manilal M. Gandhi criticized the Samaj in an editorial column on 19 November 1948 for changing the words. The Samaj defended its action by saying that it had followed the version recorded and issued by Tagore's Viswabharati University at Shantiniketan. The minutes labelled Gandhi's position as 'sankuchit' (narrow-minded) (*Indian Opinion*, 8 October 1948, 19 November 1948).[12]

The Samaj continued its cultural connection with India. In 1949, India's independence was celebrated jointly with the Surat Hindu Association through a committee called 'Shri Bharat Prajasattaak Din Utsav'. The Samaj celebrated annually the birthday of Jawaharlal Nehru, India's Prime Minister, and memorialized the deaths of prominent individuals like Sarojini Naidu (1879–1949) and Sardar Vallabhbhai Patel (1875–1950). The Samaj's strong identification with India can be measured by its decision to sing at future meetings India's national anthem. It created the Gandhi–Tagore Lectureship Trust to host speakers regularly. There was no ambivalence about the pride Samaj members felt for India. If they felt any anxiety about the newly proclaimed apartheid policies of the Nationalist government, it did not show in the minutes. As in the past, they learned to play politics apolitically to advance their goals. So, the Samaj decided that there could be some advantage sending Christmas greetings to Nationalist party leader Dr D.F. Malan and other members of his cabinet as well to leading provincial officials. It saw itself as promoting the educational welfare of Indians while at the same time preserving Hindu cultural and religious values.[13]

The Samaj established its reputation as a successful organization in the first 10 years of its existence. Its members worked closely with city, provincial and national authorities in making a case for the need for additional government-aided schools. To this end, the Durban city council donated 1.75 acres of land in the Curries Fountain complex. The title deed was acquired only at the end of 1954. At a Special General Meeting called on 23 November 1954, the Samaj immediately went to work by appointing a subcommittee of 15 members.

Since 1946 when it first learned of the donation, the Samaj had envisaged building two schools and liked the Education Department's suggestion of a primary and a secondary school. It reassured the department that the schools would be strictly secular. Once again, the Samaj appointed a subcommittee to build the schools. An architect estimated the cost from £75,000 to £80,000. At the next two committee meetings, various individuals came forward with donations. Manilal Valjee and M.K. Lodhia promised to give £10,000 each.

At a special general meeting on 8 April 1956, the Samaj prepared the ground for contributions by adopting a resolution for a primary and a secondary school. The two largest donors, Valjee and Lodhia would be honoured by having the schools named the Manilal Valjee Government-Aided Indian School and the M.K. Lodhia Indian High School. The Gandhi–Desai family donated £5000 for the hall. Other donors would have their names dedicated to library or classrooms as requested. Committee members decided that 'Kathiawad' and 'Hindu' would not appear in the names. The Manilal Valjee School would be for boys, and the Lorne Street English School would be for girls. Donors promised a total of £52,000. A sum of £40,000 (later increased to £50,000) would come from the Education Department. A ceremony for ground-breaking took place on 20 July 1956 and Provincial Administrator D.G. Shepstone did the honour of laying the foundation stone on 25 August 1956. At a Special General Meeting on 21 August 1956, it was revealed that M.K. Lodhia was unhappy about the Samaj not meeting all his stipulated conditions. He lodged a complaint with the Education Department. A five-person delegation met him to resolve differences without success. It is not clear from the minutes why Lodhia was unhappy, but the Samaj resolved that the conditions he stipulated were not acceptable. Some three years elapsed before the Samaj finally rejected his terms, and accepted an offer by the Gandhi–Desai family to increase its contribution from £5000 to £10,000. The school would be named after the family.[14]

By the end of 1958, both schools were ready. The Samaj got clearance from the Group Areas Board about its legal ownership of the Curries Fountain complex. The date for the *vastu* (initiation) ceremony was set for 17 January 1959. B.D. Lala was appointed principal of the primary school with 11 teachers under his care, and S. Chotai was named the head of the high school. The *Leader* reported a rumour that Dr Desai as trustee may have had a hand in selecting Chotai, but this was discounted by 'knowledgeable persons'. The Manilal Valjee State-Aided Indian Primary School and the Gandhi–Desai State-Aided Secondary School opened their doors in 1960.[15]

As the projects got under way, membership of the Samaj shot up. It had established its credibility as a successful organization. Those who qualified for membership wanted to take full advantage of the Samaj's facilities. There were 129 new members in July 1958. A month later another 36 applied for membership. The Samaj at first amended the constitution to state that it was not obliged to give reasons for denying membership to anybody. Later it changed to say that rejection could be appealed. This led to fears of exclusion among non-Kathiawadis. Leading officials of the Natal Indian School Building Trust, A.D. Lazarus, Naidoo (full name not available) and Raidoo (full name not available), all teachers, sought reassurance from the Samaj that non-Gujaratis would be eligible for enrolment at the schools. Lazarus was a one-time president of the Natal Indian Teachers Society. An article in the *Leader* expressed similar concerns. The minutes do not show the Samaj's response, but members no doubt reassured the public that the schools would be open to all.[16]

By 1960, then, the Samaj had succeeded in its mission. Remarkably, some 40 individuals, all Kathiawadis, had come forward to underwrite the costs of its ventures in cultural and educational matters. Without their support, the Samaj's goals could never have been fulfilled. In 1944, for example, nearly all seven members on the management committee doubled their contribution from £1500 to nearly £3000. In 1946, three individuals offered to lend £2000 without interest. In 1947, a Samaj member acted as guarantor for a £5000 bond. In 1959–1960, two families (Manilal Valjee and Gandhi–Desai) donated over £20,000 to build schools in the Curries Fountain complex, and others supplemented this amount with an additional £3500 to help defray the cost of a library, woodwork laboratory, and class rooms.[17] They did not benefit directly from their largesse, but took great pride in their achievements as Kathiawadis, a gift to the community as a whole because the facilities they helped to build were open to all. It was an effective use of the Samaj's social capital. Having moved away from strictly 'ethnic social capital' for narrower objectives, the donors engaged in what is called 'cross-cultural social capital' to tap into the goodwill of the larger community. Such a gesture enhanced their stature, and directly and indirectly helped them in their standing as community members.

Desai's leadership is important, although the Samaj's success goes beyond the role of one individual. Strong leadership is usually the hallmark of a successful voluntary organization. He rallied Samaj members in the 1940s by referring to Kathiawad in heroic terms. Such language is somewhat muted in the 1950s, the decade during which the African National Congress and its allies built massive following among Black people. Samaj minutes make no reference to significant moments in the liberation movement such as the 1946–1948 Passive Resistance struggle or the 1952 Defiance Campaign or the 1955 Freedom Charter. Desai and his colleagues were fully aware of the political currents of their time and chose to follow conciliation rather than defiance. Other foreign-trained doctors like Dr Yusuf M. Dadoo (1909–1983), Dr G.M. Naicker (1910–1978), and Dr K. Goonam (1906–1999) threw themselves into the Congress movement in the 1940s and 1950s. They defined community broadly to include all Indians and insisted on rights rather than privileges, and Dadoo, a founding member of the 1938 Non-European United Front as well as a member of the South African Communist Party since 1939, embraced a wider political spectrum. Naicker was inspired by Gandhi much as Desai was, but engaged in passive resistance. He wrote in 1946 while in the Pietermaritzburg jail, his appreciation for the 'full power of the weapon of *satyagraha*'. Dadoo, Naicker and Goonam were in the forefront of those who re-defined their Indianness as part of their vision of an ideal modern citizenship (Digby 2005, Reddy 1991, Raman 2005b, Desai and Vahed 2010).

Desai like many other South African Indians followed India's anti-colonial movement with great interest, especially the role of fellow Kathiawadi Gandhi. He had taken part in protest against British rule in the 1920s when he was in India. The Samaj observed Gandhi's birthdays and named a hall after him. It also honoured other Indian revolutionary leaders. Desai and the others admired the liberation struggle in India. They welcomed India's help and were aware of Nehru's exhortation that Indians must identify with the country of their adoption. They likely opposed the racial system, but expressed no support for South Africa's liberation movement. As pragmatists they placed greater store in working through an organization over which they had greater control and negotiated for better opportunities. The Samaj's symbolic connection with India coloured the way it defined Indianness and this shaped its politics. It remained silent about the oppressive political system. Hence, while there is reference in the minutes to giving shelter for people displaced by the 1949 riots, the Samaj took no active steps to discuss racial animosities between Africans and Indians that underlay this catastrophic event. In this bitter racial conflict, 142 were killed, among them 87 Africans and 50 Indians. As an organization narrowly focussed on promoting Kathiawadi Gujarati Hindu values, it did little formally to reach out to Africans. However useful it was in creating unity within the group, its vision did not include creating understanding of its place within the broader South African ethnic and racial communities.

The Samaj argued that it was necessary to deal with people in power apolitically to achieve its goals. Samaj members were not seeking political power. They posed no threat to white rule. As influential businessmen, they cultivated relationships with people in power willing to help them. They presented themselves as representing an organization seeking to improve the community's educational standards. Even as a body representing 'Kathiawadi Hindus', it expanded its vision to include 'all sectors of the Indian community'. Its strategy was to extend its social capital across a network of support groups and in this it succeeded. The Samaj schools admitted all Indians and in this sense it played a vital role in promoting unity beyond ethnicity, caste, religion, class and region, even if inter-caste marriages were rare.

The state was happy to provide matching funds to build schools. It had no issue with the Samaj's goal to promote its cultural and religious heritage. White leaders at the national and local levels doled out favours and privileges if only to show up organizations that insisted on fundamental rights. The government spelled out its position in 1948 when Interior Minister T.E. Donges stated that it preferred to work through an 'acceptable channel' rather than one that flouted laws and sought the help of 'another country' (meaning India), although in this case he was showing preference for the compromise-leaning South African Indian Organisation instead of the politically defiant South African Indian Congress (Bhana 1997, p. 113).

Later in his career, Desai served on the South African Indian Council (SAIC) and likely saw himself as serving 'community interests' through this form of 'negotiated politics' much as he did with the Samaj. This consultative body simply bolstered white rule since it had no meaningful authority outside of parameters defined by the apartheid rulers. Many were critical of Indians who served on this body, and in the sometimes bitter politics of the period, labelled them as 'collaborators'. If Desai had hoped to serve 'community interests', they were much harder to define in this state-appointed body. The apartheid regime kept Blacks divided and disfranchised through rewards it alone had the power to define. This SAIC model would be extended to an all-Indian House of Delegates in Parliament in the 1980s, but failed as Black insurgency rejected all government-created forums. Some in the Samaj did not like the close association of individual members with state-created bodies since it gave it a bad name, as Ashwin Trikamjee recalls (Desai 1986, Trikamjee to Bhana (emails) 3, 5, 12, 17 May 2009).

Later years: 1960–1993

In the decades after 1960, the political dynamics would change radically and the Samaj adapted to them. The apartheid regime faced serious domestic and international challenges. The cracks became apparent after the mid 1970s. In some ways, the presidency of Ashwin Trikamjee was symptomatic of the changes that the Samaj experienced. His father, Hirji Trikamjee, who had run a cosmetic store, performed a priestly function and had served the Samaj for 45 years, persuaded his son to take part.

Ashwin Trikamjee was president in 1981 and 1982. His presidency indicates how the Samaj adjusted to changes. As a young man strongly opposed to apartheid, Trikamjee brought a different style of leadership. He had been president of the non-racial South African Soccer Federation Professional League and an active member in the 1970s Black Consciousness movement promoting self-help to free people of colour from dependency. It was therefore a challenge for him to lead an organization that was narrowly defined into one that was more strongly connected to South Africa. He tried to lead the Kathiawadi community away from its 'apartheid influenced mentality'. He set new parameters by extending membership to all Gujarati Hindus by birth or marriage. He freed Samaj of 'family political battles' by limiting the term of the president to two terms. As he explained, 'My major objective [was] to restore dignity and order to the conduct of meetings, making it very formal and businesslike. Meetings that took hours and hours of rhetoric and belaboured discussions without any solution suddenly became orderly and were completed within two hours'. Trikamjee continued, 'We … [turned] the New Year functions into a slick, brief, and orderly affair and swelled attendance to over a 100 persons. We also introduced a quarterly newsletter called the *Samachar* in both English and Gujarati'. It became a vehicle for open expression of ideas and promoted dialogue. 'We also forced an open dialogue with the Surat Hindu Association and organized many joint functions.' He re-defined what was culturally essential for the Samaj within a South African rather than an Indian context. The old guard was unhappy with some of these changes, but in their weakened state they were unable to mount a serious challenge to a person it regarded as an 'outsider'. He was not above using satire to keep the 'conservatives' at bay. He wrote, produced and acted in a satirical play called *Aapno Rangilo Samaj* (Our Colourful Samaj) to highlight some of their 'follies'. Others who succeeded him maintained the momentum (Trikamjee to Bhana (emails) 3, 5, 12, 17, 20 May 2009, conversation with Trikamjee, 24 September 2009, Durban).[18]

In the Samaj's stated objective of promoting Gujarati, it did not succeed mainly because of circumstances beyond its control. The Department of Indian Affairs decided in 1961 that it would not introduce mother-tongue education in Indian schools. It allowed the introduction of Indian languages at the secondary level in 1977, but few schools took the option. The Samaj no doubt welcomed the introduction of the Indian languages including Gujarati at the University of Durban–Westville in the 1970s. The number enrolled in Gujarati was 21 in 1979, but dropped to nine in 1991. This programme was discontinued when the university merged with the University of Natal in the 1990s to become the University of KwaZulu Natal (Pennycook 2002, Desai 1992, 1997, *NGP brochure* 1994, *KHSS minutes: AGM*, 30 April 1986). In KwaZulu-Natal, where 80% of Indians live, Gujarati-speakers make up only 7%. Tamil and Telugu are spoken by 51% and 6% respectively, while Hindi and Urdu are spoken by 30% and 5% respectively of Indians. Some may wish to see the basics of Gujarati introduced optionally at selected public schools since the emphasis on full-fledged

Gujarati education as in the 1940s and 1950s is no longer feasible (Heugh 2002, Mesthrie 2002).[19]

Indians proficient in vernacular languages including Gujarati have dwindled in the decades after 1960. Young men and women knew only too well that they would need proficiency in English to compete successfully in the job market and for most it has become the first language. In 1991, 95% of Indians declared English as their home language. In South Africa's changing environment, they feel less connected to India culturally and historically as the old generation of Gujarati speakers were. They learned about the history of South Africa in public schools and knew little about India. They see South Africa as home and India a place from which their ancestors came. Most were born after 1950, and had no first-hand knowledge about India's struggle for freedom in the way that their parents had. They feel little need to keep up with developments in India. Young professionalized Indians have assimilated to South Africa in ways that their parents could not. They were less likely to use religious beliefs and practices to define who they were or to see politics simply in ethnic terms even if recent trends seem to suggest a resurgence of narrow forms of identification.

Studies of other Indian communities have shown similar trends elsewhere. Second-generation Indian immigrants from the Caribbean to the USA or Canada do not consider ancestry significant because time and memory have dimmed their knowledge of places of origin. The Surinamese in the Netherlands, to take another example, are less interested in South Asian realities than they are in Bollywood movies (Oonk 2007). Diesel argues that the traditional divisions of caste and class are less relevant in present-day South Africa. Indians are taking interest in popular culture in films, music and fashion. The pride of young Indians for India should not be interpreted to mean that they wish to establish permanent links with the 'motherland'. It reflects rather the ambiguities of living in post-apartheid South Africa (Diesel 2003). The Samaj's 1993 brochure shows some awareness to the changing political terrain. It reproduced the country's two national anthems, but dropped India's national anthem. It retained *Bande Materam* (Hail to the Motherland) to remind Indians of the struggle for independence as well their ancestral connection. The Samaj saw a clear advantage in representing itself as part of a larger and more unified group of Indians.

The Samaj gradually adapted to changes after 1960 with regard to English schools under its control. After leasing the Manilal Valjee State-Aided Indian Primary School and the Gandhi-Desai State-Aided Secondary School to the House of Delegates in the 1980s, it closed them in 1992 when the leases expired. Since the state has taken over the responsibility for formal education, the Samaj took itself out of its direct role. It concentrated on promoting vernacular education and culture. Samaj minutes from 1979 to 1990 show that it adjusted to newer realities. It considered converting its school premises into a hospital complex, but decided against it. In the 1980s and early 1990s, members reached out more actively to a sister organization like SHA for closer cooperation. In its search for a suitable site to build a temple, it formed a committee in August 1988 to liaise with SHA. Old regional loyalties, caste- or language-based, have given way to a broader conceptualization of who they were. Such thinking contributed to the creation of the Gujarati Sanskruti Kendra or Kendra for short in 1993. The Kendra set out to serve all, but its cherished goal was to unite Gujarati Hindus in the region. The Samaj sold Gandhi Hall and transferred the proceeds to the Kendra and leased the land to it for an extended period.In a May 1993 minute, the Samaj congratulated itself for having taken a step that would 'go down in history' as being pivotally important for all Gujarati-speaking Hindus. The Samaj, SHA and the

Saptah Mandir run by the Arya Bhajan Mandal each contributed R75,000 (Rand) to meet the initial expenses. The Samaj donated R1.25 million and gave a loan of one-half million which has been repaid by the Kendra. The SHA contributed R500,000 in loans and an equal amount in donations.

The Kendra was completed in 2001. It consists of a community hall and a temple called Ekta [Unity] Mandir, which, as its president Prabhakant L. Patel claimed, united the Samaj, SHA and the Saptah Mandir. Patel estimated that there have been over 60 activities at the Kendra in the last two years with the *Navaratri* festival being the biggest and most important. The Ekta Mandir favours no individual sects or groups and is open to all, Patel pointed out. The Kendra has become a centre for cultural and religious events mainly for Gujarati Hindus. It offers Gujarati classes with emphasis on language and culture, very different from the syllabus that the Samaj followed in the 1940s and 1950s. It has also introduced special activities such as outdoor picnics, India tours, film shows and *bhajan* (devotional songs) sessions (conversation with Patel, 19 September 2009, Durban, *Ekta Mandir and Sanskruti Kendra: commemorative brochure* 2001, http://www.kendra.org.za/kendra_gardens.html).

Ashwin Trikamjee's assessment is that the Samaj has reverted to its earlier asset-protecting role and is less concerned with serving larger community interests. The Kendra, Trikamjee thinks, represents a 'noble idea … [to unite] the Gujarati community' but is faltering. The Kendra has built one of 'the finest venues for weddings', he concedes, but its efforts to promote culture and language have become mired in 'community politics' as in the old days. Even the temple 'has failed to attract the Gujarati community'. In his view, the Kendra has become primarily a 'business' organization tightly controlled by individuals with a 'commercial objective'. This was especially so with *garba* events with guest artists invited from India. Patel in his conversation with us countered this by insisting that the Kendra is not driven by the profit motive. To be sure, it earns revenues through hall rental and events like the bridal fair to meet its expenses and more recently to cover costs for a retirement home currently under construction. Both Patel and Jaisook Valjee admitted that not all SHA members were happy with the creation of the Kendra. Patel attributes the disunity to stubborn caste thinking prevalent among some segments of Gujarati Hindus, but he argues that the majority of Hindu Gujaratis support the Kendra. Even so, relations between the Kendra and SHA (more specifically its Saptah Mandir affiliates) soured to a breaking point in 1999, Trikamjee recalled, until he and Sudhir Pragjee smoothed things over in a series of meetings. There was 'genuine opposition to what was happening', he recalled. A series of cultural events early in 2000 at the Kendra healed the rift. Still, the Saptah group built its own temple in suburban Reservoir Hills (Trikamjee to Bhana (emails) 3, 5, 12, 17, 20 May, 5, 6, 14 October 2009, and conversation, 24 September 2009, Durban, conversation with Jaisook Valjee, 17 September 2009, Verulam, conversation with P.L. Patel, 19 September 2009, Durban, Patel to Bhana (emails), 25 September and 2 October 2009).

A thorough investigation of such groups focusing on language, religion, or caste will reveal much about how they have evolved in South Africa. Caste organizations like the *Rajput*, *Prajapati* and *Darjee* continue to flourish. In the last 25 years, uncertainties in South Africa have produced organizations based on narrow ethnic and religious forms of identification. Such developments should be examined against the backdrop of shifts in identity among Indians. Changes measured against the original sets of defined goals will reflect why and how they occurred. We will learn a great deal about the evolving multi-cultural setting in a democratic South Africa. As our study of the Samaj has shown, such groups start with narrow focus but often broaden their horizons to meet changing South African conditions even as they maintain some form of cultural and religious orientation. We learned how it negotiated with political authorities in the decades marked by resistance and non-collaboration. In the 1990s, the Samaj has assumed a passive role as it relegated its earlier function to the Kendra. Indeed, it will shortly be placed entirely in the care of seven trustees, as Jaisook Valjee explained. It has R2 million at its disposal for continuing to provide bursaries and loans to Gujarati students (conversation with Jaisook Valjee, 17 September 2009, Verulam).

While bodies like the Samaj have created greater cohesion for its members, they were surely aware of their insularity and isolation from other groups in the larger South African community. Younger Indians, politicized by developments in South Africa, are dealing with inherent cultural symbolism differently. Or to put it differently, their Indianness is more rooted in South Africa than India. Still, the ambiguities remain. Ronnie Govender testifies to this in his autobiography,

> Drugged by back-slapping self-assurances of how great one's culture is, we espouse a stubborn refusal to accept that there is no such thing as a pristine culture .... Yet, should tradition not have its place, and should there not be diversity of cultures within a single nation? Should young people not be taught their own language, their own culture? (Govender 2008, p. 23)

Even as he wrestled with this issue, Govender had no problem engaging in politics, sports, and the theatre that transcended his ethnic loyalties. This is true also of Ashwin Trikamjee. Early in the 1970s, he espoused non-racial causes in sports and politics. A lawyer by profession, he was president of the Natal Law Society in 1992–1994 and of the Law Society of South Africa in 1997. He is the president of the South African Hindu Maha Sabha. He has adopted a broad lens in defining community that includes his own as well as a wider South African set of interests across religious, cultural and political lines. Trikamjee sees no conflict taking part in community affairs and serving broader interests. Indeed, he doubles as the officiating priest during the annual nine-day *Navratri* festival at the Kendra devoted to Mother Goddess representing *shakti* (cosmic energy).

In their individual capacities, people like Govender and Trikamjee have moved effortlessly from within their cultural identities to reach out to the broader South African community across political and racial divides. Perhaps other cultural bodies (Indian as well as non-Indian) were making similar endeavours. What we might see then, is what Hilda Kuper calls 'overlapping ... sub-cultures' in South Africa and perhaps she is right asserting that each appears 'marginal to everything but itself' (Kuper 1960, p. 262). It is these overlapping experiences that have created a broad South African culture. If we have confined our discussion to Indians only, it is because this group – unlike Africans, so-called Coloured, or Whites – has always seen South Africa through a diasporic lens that connected them to India. The challenge is to discover layers of such experiences by examining closely hitherto understudied cultural organizations among Indians and non-Indians.

Acknowledgements

We are grateful to KHSS president Jaisook Valjee for giving us permission to examine Samaj minutes and to Kendra's Ramnik Juta for kindly providing us with post-1960 records. Past president Ashwin Trikamjee readily offered valuable comments and insights on the

Samaj. Dr Prabhakant Patel very graciously provided details on the Kendra and carefully read drafts of the paper. Professor Arvinkumar Bhana took great trouble to make electronic copies of KHSS minutes from 1943 to 1960. We are grateful to Anita Vallabh, Dr Hema Hargovan and Asha Bhana for their help.

Notes

1. The seven organizations were: Natal Lohana Niti Darshak Sabha (1905–1916), Kathiawad Arya Mandal (1907–1943), Kathiawad Pattani Soni Association (f. 1925), Saurashtra Hindu Association (f. 1927 or 1928), Girnaar Soni Hitvardhak Mandal (f. 1932), South African Vanik Association or Vanik Mahajan Association (f. 1934), and Pattani Social Club (f. 1941). See *Kathiawad Hindu Seva Samaj souvenir brochure*, Durban, 1956.
2. Desai's additional qualifications were: LRFP & S (Licentiate of the Royal Faculty of Physicians and Surgeons), LMSSA (Licentiate in Medicine and Surgery of the Society of Apothecaries), and LM (Licentiate in Medicine) (Dublin). Among some of the other positions he held were: Indian Goodwill Club (president), Natal Indian Congress (vice president), Gandhi-Tagore Lectureship Trust (trustee), Candella Hindu Sungatan Government-Aided Indian Girls School, M.L. Sultan College (council member), M.C. Varman Trust (trustee), and the Hindi Shiksa Sang (trustee). In 1952, he served as Durban Centre's Commissioner for Hindi Examinations. The Hindi examinations were conducted by the Rashtra Bhasa Samiti of Wardha in India.
3. Minutes: KHSS General Meeting, 26 December 1943. These figures are for the UK, but are relevant since South Africa used sterling as a monetary unit. See http://www.west-egg.com/inflation/
4. Members often increased their donations when the need arose. Donors who contributed £100 and more were promised that their donations would be prominently displayed on a plaque after the building was completed. *Minutes: KHSS Committee* [*Samiti*] *Meetings*, 3 January 1944, 19 March 1944, 6 August 1944, 13 August 1944, 28 October 1944, 1 November 1944, 21 November 1944 and 22 November 1944. Members who increased their donations were: Natha Naran Pty Ltd, from £251 to £501, Dhupelia & Son from £251 to £501, Samjee Devshi & Son from £301 to £501, Soni Kara Devraj from £251 to £501, C.J. Mehta from £101 to £151, M.K. Lodhia from £101 to £301 and M. Lakhani & Co. from £251 to £501. Some new donors were: Victoria Produce Co., £501, Jeram Premjee, £251, Mooljee Hirjee, £101, Odhavjee Mavjee, £101, Mistry Bros, £25 and Ratanjee Pragjee, £25.
5. *Minutes: KHSS Committee* [*Samiti*] *Meetings*, 3 January 1944, 19 March 1944, 6 August 1944, 13 August 1944, 28 October 1944, 1 November 1944 and 21 November 1944, contd. 22 November 1944.
6. *Minutes: KHSS Committee* [*Samiti*] *Meetings*, 25 March 1945.
7. *Minutes: KHSS Committee* [*Samiti*] *Meetings*, 25 April 1945, 9 August 1945 and 16 October 1945; *Minutes: KHSS Committee* [*Samiti*] *Meetings*, 28 February 1946, 19 July 1946, 14 August 1946, 4 September 1946, and *Special Meeting Minutes*, 8 September 1946.
8. Special committees or boards were created for handling things like drawing up hall rental rules, managing the Gujarati school and raising funds. The monthly salaries for a Gujarati teacher and the priest were £10 and £15 respectively. *Minutes: KHSS Committee* [*Samiti*] *Meetings*, 14 January 1947, 22 January 1947, 16 April 1947, 21 June 1947, 28 August 1947, 19 October 1947, 26 October 1947, 21 December 1947; *KHSS Special General Meeting*, April 1947; *AGM*, 4 May 1947, 10 August 1947.
9. The Samaj secured a license to use the hall for entertainment and was required to implement safety measures. It spent £900 to purchase chairs for the hall. Extra classrooms were created by building partitions and windows. It built three stoves to provide meals for students. The Samaj also took advantage of the state subsidy to run a feeding scheme at the rate of six pence per student. *Minutes: KHSS Committee* [*Samiti*] *Meetings*, 3 July 1948, 21 November 1948, 13 February 1949, 19 March 1949, 8 June 1949, 13 November 1949; *AGM*, 20 March 1949, *Special General Meeting*, 10 July 1949.
10. In 1948, the shortage of teachers forced the school to close for eight months. A library (Gujarati Hindu Pustakalay) was opened on 25 April 1948. In the beginning, there were some 2000 books and 30–35 magazines and newspapers. A reading room was created in

the basement of the hall. *Minutes: KHSS Committee* [*Samiti*] *Meetings*, 3 July 1948, 21 November 1948, 13 February 1949, 19 March 1949, 8 June 1949, 13 November 1949; *AGM*, 20 March 1949, *Special General Meeting*, 10 July 1949.

11. In addition to observing major festivals in 1950 and 1951, the Samaj organized a *mahayagna* (fire ceremony) on 18 June 1950 in which six other Hindu bodies took part. The Gujarati school had 140 pupils in 1950 with only three teachers, but the number dropped to 88 by May 1953 and increased somewhat two years later, but the AGM report still described the situation as 'dollum-doll' (precarious). In 1953, Samaj assets stood at £23,253 with a cash balance of £2372. The hall as an asset was acknowledged in following idiom, 'Lagna kahe ke mane aadri juwo, and makaan kahe ke mane ukheri juwo' ('Marriage says, try building me; and a house says, try uprooting me.' *KHSS Minutes: Committee* [*Samiti*], 8 January 1950, 1 February 1950, 19 March 1950, 24 September 1950, 10 January 1951, 19 February 1951, 4 March 1951, 21 March 1951, 24 May 1951, 1 August 1951; *AGM*, 5 February 1950, 5 February 1951; *KHSS Minutes: Committee* [*Samiti*], 5 February 1952, 14 September 1952, 18 September 1952, 16 January 1953, 5 February 1953, 11 February 1953, 14 April 1953, 12 May 1953, 28 July 1953, 6 October 1953; *AGM*, 14 May 1953; *KHSS Minutes: AGM*, 11 June 1955.
12. *KHSS Minutes: Committee* [*Samiti*], 21 November 1948; *Special General Meeting*, 10 July 1949.
13. Some others who contributed were: £1001 from Dharamsi Jethalal for library, £440 from V.S. Lakhani for the principal's office, £1000 from P.H. and H.H. Dhupelia for woodwork room, £1100 from H.N. Naran for two classrooms and £5000 from an anonymous donor for the school hall; V.V. Devshi £1500, N.S. Devshi £1500, H. Naran £375 for vice principal's office, N. Vallabh £251 for secretary's office, the Mathurdas Vassanjee Estate £525 for a classroom, and Visram Mooljee £375. Non-Kathiawadis were free to donate money, but we have no figures for them. *KHSS Minutes: Committee* [*Samiti*], 11 May 1954, 18 July 1954, *Special General Meeting*, 23 November 1954; *KHSS Minutes: Committee* [*Samiti*], 23 March 1955, 7 July 1955, 23 June 1955, 13 October 1955; *AGM*, 11 June 1955; *KHSS Minutes: Committee* [*Samiti*], 9 February 1956, 1 March 1956, 5 March 1956; *KHSS Minutes: Special General Meeting*, 8 April 1956; *Committee* [*Samiti*] Meeting, 8 July 1956. *KHSS Minutes: Committee* [*Samiti*] *Meeting*, 4 March 1957; *KHSS Minutes: Special G. Meeting*, 21 August 1956; *KHSS Minutes: Committee* [*Samiti*] *Meeting*, 16 August 1956; *KHSS Minutes: Committee* [*Samiti*] *Meeting*, 16 January 1959, 21 April 1959, 8 November 1959, 15 March 1960, 24 July 1960.
14. The building got under way on 3 August 1957 with Owen Dick as the builder. The minutes provide details about rising building costs leading the Samaj to take out bank overdraft to keep up with the increases. Once again, generous members came forward to stand guarantors or lend money without interest to make up for shortfalls. *KHSS Minutes: Committee* [*Samiti*] *Meeting*, 8 January 1959, 16 January 1959, 21 April 1959, 8 November 1959, 15 March 1960, 24 July 1960; *Leader*, 23 January 1959.
15. *KHSS Minutes: Committee* [*Samiti*] *Meeting*, 18 June 1958, 22 July 1958, 19 August 1958; *AGM*, 24 August 1958.
16. *Minutes: KHSS Committee* [*Samiti*] *Meetings*, 3 January 1944, 19 March 1944, 6 August 1944, 13 August 1944, 28 October 1944, 1 November 1944, 21 November 1944 and 22 November 1944; *KHSS Committee* [*Samiti*] *Meetings*, 28 February 1946, 19 July 1946, 14 August 1946, 4 September 1946, and *Special Meeting Minutes*, 8 September 1946; *Minutes: KHSS Committee* [*Samiti*] *Meetings*, 14 January 1947, 22 January 1947, 16 April 1947, 21 June 1947, 28 August 1947, 19 October 1947, 26 October 1947, 21 December 1947; *KHSS Special General Meeting,* April 1947; *AGM,* 4 May 1947, 10 August 1947.
17. Trikamjee was treasurer of the radical South African Student Organization (SASO), chairman of NIC's Durban central branch and founding member of the Black People's Convention. Together with other Black Consciousness (BC) activists, Trikamjee organized the Theatre Council of Natal which produced plays along BC lines. As a student on Salisbury Island, he was part of an informal group, the Cafe Clan that opposed Republic Day celebrations on the campus. In the play 'Black on White', Trikamjee collaborated with drama student Subhas Maharaj and others like Strini Moodley, Kogs Reddy, Dennis Pather, Sam Moodley, Asha Rambully and Kriba Pillay. This play enjoyed 38 performances throughout South Africa in 1967 and 1968 after its initial showing in Durban. The

play satirized the SAIC and other conservative bodies that collaborated with the apartheid regime.

18. The 1996 South African constitution recognizes 11 official languages: Afrikaans, English, *isiNdebele*, *Sesotho sa Leboa*, *Sesotho*, *siSwati*, *Xitsonga*, *Setswana*, *Tshivenda*, *isiXhosa* and *isiZulu*. The constitution promotes respect for minor languages such as German, Greek, Gujarati, Hindi, Portuguese, Tamil, Telugu and Urdu; and recognizes that Arabic, Hebrew and Sanskrit are used for religious purposes.
19. *KHSS Minutes: AGM*, 25 May 1933 and 1936; *KHSS Minutes: Management Committee Meeting*, 25 August 1988, 17 November 1988, 23 February 1993, 4 June 1992.

Notes on contributors

Surendra Bhana taught at the University of Durban–Westville (now University of KwaZulu Natal) from 1972 to 1987. He joined the History Department at the University of Kansas in 1988 and taught there until his retirement in May 2006, and is now Professor Emeritus. He is the author, co-author, editor and co-editor of numerous books including: *The Making of a Political Reformer: Gandhi in South Africa, 1893–1914* (2005); *Gandhi's Legacy: The Natal Indian Congress, 1894–1994* (1997); *Indentured Indian Emigrants to Natal, 1860–1902: A Study Based on Ships' Lists* (1991), *Essays on Indentured Indians in Natal* (1990) and *Setting Down Roots: Indian Migrants in South Africa, 1860–1911* (1990).

Kusum K. Bhoola is an independent researcher based in Durban, South Africa. She graduated with an Honours degree in Oriental Studies at the University of Durban–Westville (now the University of KwaZulu Natal). She has translated Gujarati texts into English in Nardev Vedalankar's *Essential Teachings of Hinduism* (1979) and *A Concise Study of Hindu Scriptures* (1981). Most recently, she and Surendra Bhana translated a serialized Gujarati novel that appeared in South Africa in 1911 entitled *Introducing South Africa OR Dialogue of Two Friends (Dakshin Afrika Darshan yane be Mitreno Samvaad), By Ek Hindi* (An Indian), 1911 (2004).

References

Appadurai, A., 2003. Disjuncture and difference in the global cultural economy. *In:* J.E. Braziel and A. Mannur, eds. *Theorizing diaspora: a reader.* Malden: Blackwell Publishing, 25–48.

Bhana, S., 1997. *Gandhi's legacy: the Natal Indian Congress, 1894–1994.* Pietermaritzburg: University of Natal Press.

Bhana, S. and Vahed, G., 2005. *The making of a political reformer: Gandhi in South Africa, 1893–1914.* New Delhi: Manohar.

Brettell, C.B., 2005. Voluntary organizations, social capital, and the social incorporation of Asian Indian immigrants in the Dallas-Fort Worth Metroplex. *Anthropological Quarterly,* 78 (4), 853–883.

Bugwandeen, D.L., 1995. *A people on trial for breaking racism: the struggle for land and housing of the Indian People.* Durban: Institute of Black Research.

Cohen, R., 1997. *Global diasporas: an introduction.* Seattle: University of Washington Press.

Desai, A. and Vahed, G., 2010. *Monty Naicker: between reason and treason.* Durban: Shuter.

Desai, U.K., 1992. The Gujarati language among Gujarati-speaking Hindus in Natal. Unpublished thesis (MA), University of Durban–Westville.

Desai, U.K., 1997. An investigation of factors influencing maintenance and shift of Gujarati language in South Africa. Unpublished thesis (PhD), University of Durban–Westville.

Dhupelia-Mesthrie, U. 2004: *Gandhi's prisoner? the life of Gandhi's Son Manilal.* Cape Town: Kwela Books.

Diesel, A., 2003. Hinduism in KwaZulu Natal, South Africa. *In:* B. Parekh, G. Singh and S. Vertovec, eds. *Culture and economy in the Indian diaspora.* London: Routledge, 33–50.

Digby, A., 2005. Early black doctors in South Africa. *Journal of African History,* 46 (3), 427–454.

Edwards, I.L. 1989. Mkhumbane our home: the African shantytown society in Cato Manor Farm, 1946–1960. Unpublished thesis (PhD), University of Natal.

Ekta Mandir and Sanskruti Kendra: commemorative brochure, 2001. Durban.

Freund, B., 1995. *Insiders and outsiders: the Indian working class of Durban, 1910–1990.* Portsmouth: Heinemann.

Gandhi, M.K., 1928. *Satyagraha in South Africa.* Ahmedabad: Navajivan Publishing House.

Ginwala, F.N., 1974. Class, consciousness and control: Indian South Africans, 1860–1946. Unpublished thesis (PhD), Oxford University.

Govender, R., 2008. *In the manure: memories and reflections.* Cape Town: David Philip.

Heugh, K., 2002. Recovering multilingualism: recent language-policy developments. *In*: R. Mesthrie, ed. *Languages in South Africa.* Cambridge: Cambridge University Press, 449–475.

KHSS, 1956. *Kathiawad Hindu Seva Samaj souvenir brochure.* Durban: KHSS.

KHSS, 1993. *Kathiawad Hindu Seva Samaj fiftieth anniversary brochure, 1943–1993.* Durban: KHSS.

Kuper, H., 1960. *Indian people in Natal.* Pietermaritzburg: University of Natal Press.

Man in India: An International Journal of Anthropology, 2008. Special issue on Indian diaspora in the Caribbean, 88 (1).

Mesthrie, R., 2002. Language change, survival, decline: Indian Languages in South Africa. *In*: R. Mesthrie, ed. *Language in South Africa.* Cambridge: Cambridge University Press, 161–177.

Mesthrie, U.S., 1984. From Sastri to Deshmukh: a study of the role of the government of India's representatives in South Africa, 1927–1946. Unpublished thesis (PhD), University of Natal.

Naidoo, T., 1992. *The Arya Samaj movement in South Africa.* New Delhi: Motilal Banaridass.

NGP, 1994. *Natal Gujarati Parishad: silver jubilee brochure.* Durban: NGP.

Nowbath, R.S., Chotai Sookraj and Lalla B.D., eds., 1960. *Hindu heritage in South Africa.* Durban: South African Hindu Maha Sabha.

Oonk, G., ed., 2007. *Global Indian diaspora: exploring trajectories of migration and theory.* Amsterdam: Amsterdam University Press.

Oriental Anthropologist, 2007. Special issue on Indian diaspora in South Africa, 7 (1).

Padayachee, V., Vawda, S., and Tichmann, P., 1985. *Indian workers and trade unions in Durban, 1930–1950.* Durban: Institute for Social and Economic Research.

Pahad, E., 1972. The development of Indian political movements in South Africa, 1924–1946. Unpublished thesis (PhD), University of Sussex.

Parekh, B., Singh, G., and Vertovec, S., eds., 2003. *Culture and economy in the Indian diaspora.* London: Routledge.

Pennycook, A., 2002. Mother tongues, governmentality, and protectionism. *International Journal of Sociology of Language,* 154, 11–28.

Raman, P., 2005. Yusuf Dadoo: a son of South Africa. *In*: S. Dubow and A. Jeeves, eds. *South Africa's 1940s: worlds of possibilities.* Cape Town: Double Storey, 227–245.

Raman, P. 2006. Being Indian in a South African way: the development of Indian identity in the 1940s. *In*: A.E. Coombes, ed. *Rethinking settler colonialism: history and memory in Australia, Canada, Aotearoa New Zealand and South Africa.* Manchester: Manchester University Press, 193–208.

Reddy, E.S., ed., 1991. *Monty speaks: speeches of Dr. G.M. (Monty) Naicker, 1945–1963.* Durban: Madiba Publishers, 54–56.

SHA, 1975. *Surat Hindu Association diamond jubilee brochure, 1907–1975.* Durban: SHA.

SHA, 1982. *Surat Hindu Association platinum jubilee brochure, 1907–1982.* Durban: SHA.

Vahed, G., 1997. The making of Indianness: Indian politics in South Africa during the 1930s and 1940s. *Journal of Natal and Zulu History,* 17 (1), 1–36.

Vertovec, S., 2003. *The Hindu diaspora: comparative patterns.* London: Routledge.

Religion and gender: the Hindu diaspora in Portugal

Inês Lourenço

CRIA – Centre for Research in Anthropology, Lisbon, Portugal

As perpetuators of what is considered traditional knowledge, Hindu women in Portugal are assigned a new status through religion, thus replacing the male *pujari*. This article focuses on the Hindu diaspora in Portugal, and specifically on the role played by women in the construction of gender and religious identities, who, entrusted with new social and ritual responsibilities, contribute towards the cultural replication of their traditional community. As anthropological studies on gender in diaspora show us, the assignment of religious roles are used to recreate women's social status in the 'host' country.

Introduction

The Hindu community of Santo António dos Cavaleiros (in the Greater Lisbon area, Portugal) possesses a cohesive group structure, in part owing to the diversified aspects of cultural reproduction, carried out almost exclusively by women, whose activity is essential for the consolidation of the group's collective identity. These women, considered the 'guardians' of the group's traditional identity, assume the responsibility of transmitting traditional references involving the negotiation of social status and manipulation of the religious structure, and taking upon themselves the task (in the sense of fulfilling their *dharma*[1]) of maintaining, and thus inevitably transforming what they consider to be the group's cultural identity in the diaspora.

This anthropological perspective of the Hindu diaspora in Portugal, combines notions of religion and gender to facilitate privileged insight into the dynamics of perpetuation and transformation of ideological and gender practices in the process of this group's adaptation to Portuguese society. Studying a diaspora should not imply isolating the primary analytic categories. Elements that are intrinsically connected to the process of cultural reproduction, for example, caste, social mobility, family and language, have not been excluded from the ethnographic study on which this essay is based. Likewise, the multi-local dimension that characterizes studies of the diaspora has been taken into account, combining the study of this group with the surrounding social space, as well as transnational elements that impact upon the group.

As the expression 'Hindu community' itself indicates, religion is one of the key defining features of the diasporic community that is the object of this study, distinguishing this group from others who may share the same country of provenance. Cohen (1997), who maintains that it is not possible to claim the existence of strictly religious diasporas, does accede to the notion that the consolidation of a diasporic consciousness is comprised of a few essential elements, among which religion may be particularly salient. The author's position is particularly bound with the fact that he considers religions to concentrate on a variety of cultural contexts while at the same time finding that most universal religions, except the Jew and the Sikh, do not mythologize and idealize their origin. We must also point out that even though Cohen does not acknowledge the existence of religious diasporas, he states that 'religions can provide additional cement to bind a diasporic consciousness' (1997, p. 189).

Vertovec (2000), however, adds Hinduism to the two religions that Cohen has identified as possible exceptions. Unlike Christianity or Islam, Hinduism assumes a strong association with a national territory, in the sense that virtually all Hindus are Indians. The feeling of a bond with India in the form of spiritual reverence, of the great sacredness attributed to religious locations and the geography itself, is enough to demonstrate the significance of India's civilizational heritage in the consolidation of this diaspora. In *Desh Pardesh*, Roger Ballard (1994) considers religion an essential element in the consolidation of South Asian diasporas in the UK. Martin Baumann speaks of the establishment of 'Little Indias' beyond the subcontinent, where Hinduism is not simply maintained but transformed through reinterpretations of this religion and its reification (cf. Baumann 1998).

Therefore it makes sense to speak of an extensive Hindu diaspora, composed of groups with specific characteristics deriving either from their cultural and regional backgrounds within India itself (Gujarati, Punjabi, Bengali, for example), or from the specificities of the countries in which they settle, whereby it is not the same to speak of the Hindu diaspora in the USA, in the UK or in Portugal. Even still, the unifying elements are strong enough to overcome the internal differences of the global Hindu diaspora.

Religion acts as a preferential device in the consolidation of the Hindu diasporic identity and simultaneously as a means of transformation and re-creation. Likewise, gender is also a key element in any approach to diasporic terrains, which constitute a privileged context for the observation of changes in gender roles, particularly of the increasing responsibility placed on women in their community's cultural reproduction. Clear shifts in the feminine status in terms of the formal structure and public sphere, as well as in areas of artistic practice, political involvement and religious domain have been observed within the Hindu diaspora (cf. Rayaprol 1997). The diasporic logic of mobility in itself influences the reconfiguration of gender roles. Resettling in a new social and cultural environment that has different perceptions of the role of women and combined with the media's influence, impacts on their position and mobility inside their group, however discretely these appear to occur. Processes of mobility can also promote feminine and masculine labelling, given the need to preserve gender statuses (cf. Glick Shiller 2007) and become a means to ensure the logic of family institutions. The Hindu communities initially established in Trinidad provides an example where the shortage of women disrupted traditional patterns of family life and the group's social norms. When the arrival of women corrected this imbalance, a reestablishment of family life that acted as a source of social cohesion was observed (cf. Cohen 1997). Alongside this development, the freedom and autonomy of the few women who were previously a minority in Trinidad diminished as a consequence of male efforts to reinstall the patriarchal family system.

The internal complexity and specificities of Hindu diasporas is a fertile domain for the consideration of the changing position of women even if these continue to be conditioned by conservative and patriarchal logic. In the diaspora, women assume religious tasks that were previously male dominated, altering traditional gender roles albeit within a patriarchal social structure. Furthermore, the acquirement of these new tasks fosters freedom from male dominance and greater openness to socialization. Speaking about Hindu women in diaspora therefore implies analysing their relation with the religious sphere, in which images of female autonomy and conservatism that are influenced by Indian nationalist ideologies and are subtly integrated in these women's daily activities are simultaneously present. While religion can potentially lead to gender equality, in most cases, religion is used to perpetuate patriarchy.

Reconfiguring Hinduism

The development by women of empowerment strategies through attempting to equal men in the performance of ritual tasks is not exclusive to the diaspora. Neither is transforming ritual practices connected to gender status. Nevertheless, the diasporic setting is propitious in effecting the emergence of new ritual tasks bestowed upon women who thus gain privileges over religious activity and ritual practice (cf. Knott 1986, 2000, Rayaprol 1997).

Throughout the last two centuries, in India and beyond, numerous changes have been evident in Hindu religious practices. The emphasis on rationalizing creeds and practices and the progressive decrease of the so called 'lower tradition'[2], substituted by the 'higher tradition', and the resulting importance paced on the *bhakti*[3], are the most noticeable characteristics of diasporic Hinduism. Due to its adaptation to new social settings, diasporic Hinduism has been described as a shifting religion, included in a transformation process that has been labelled as 'new Hinduism' (Eck 2000), 'American Hinduism' (Eck 2000, Kurien 1998), 'British Hinduism' (Knott 1986, p. 58) or 'Ecumenical Hinduism' (Williams 1996, p. 238). Some contexts provide a more clear setting for the manifestation of these changes in sect and ritual, as in the Canadian case where the role of the *guru*[4] has become preponderant and substituted Hinduism's ritual and devotional diversity, by concentrating on the spiritual doctrines of the guru figure (cf. Coward 2000, Williams 1996).

In the UK, Hindu rituals are characterized by changes in the rhythms of *performance* and in the specialists' roles (cf. Knott 1986, 1987). The demand for new responses to external pressure has led to the framing of new ritual forms in order to preserve religious tradition and adapt it to aspects of the new surrounding cultural context (Venkatachari 1996, p. 198). Similarly, the inclusion of new holydays in the religious calendar, the adaptations made to the lunar calendar – so that celebrations are adjusted to the western calendar and schedules – and the transformation of festivities to suit each community constitute the experience of religious life in Hindu communities scattered around the world.

Most authors agree on the weight of religion in the constitution of Hindu communities in diaspora, emphasizing the centrality of women's roles regarding their group's religious replication. In this respect, I will rely on Kim Knott's perspective to establish a clear articulation between the notions of gender and religion: 'In order to understand fully the nature and development of Hinduism in Britain it is essential to hear separately from women' (Knott 2000, p. 98). For Knott, the new form of British Hinduism, more open to the participation of young people and women, gives women new public responsibilities and opportunities for leadership, thus becoming essential to listen to dissenting voices – mostly young and female – to understand and interpret the transformation processes evident in British Hinduism (Knott 2000, pp. 97–98).[5]

Interpretations of Hinduism in diaspora arose from the growing need to solve the doubts raised by second and third generations regarding their own religion, and led to the development of religious and cultural organizations. Kurien (1998) shows how the emergence of devotional and educational groups – *satsang* and *bala vihars* respectively – was meant to face an absence of proper cultural channels of transmission of Indian values to the young who had no direct contact with India.

The process of institutionalizing a reinvented form of Hinduism, to which the negotiation between personal and cultural identities, of values and practices acquired in and outside the home, was aimed to build new, more structured forms of interaction (Kurien 1998, p. 44). Narayan also mentions the difficulty in reproducing tradition without investment in the community's formal education: 'it is always difficult to perceive oneself clearly and to articulate one's faith and tradition to oneself, the community and to one's children especially if one has had no formal training or education in the field' (1996, p. 172).

The transformation of traditions always results from processes of adjustment to the circumstances found in the new places of settlement. In view of this, individuals find the need to remember physically and geographically distant traditions so that they can later adapt them to the new place of residence, thus creating new traditions for themselves and their descendants. This theme is thoroughly analysed by Raymond Williams, who illustrates it through the metaphor of the sacred thread, according to which this thread symbolizes the process of religious transmission down the generations (Williams 1996). Therefore, according to Williams, the Hindu tradition would resemble a bundle of threads – similar to the sacred thread used by Brahmans – representing the various historical configurations it has undergone throughout time. According to this perspective, the process of religious transmission is considered an essential task in diaspora. The youngest are the target of these transmission processes, usually befalling on the second and third generations the investment on education.

The production of dialects of power and resistance originated from globalization, fostering negotiations that mobility legitimizes, reveals new and old oppressions but also opportunities to defy them through a claim to citizenship. These dialects produce new men and women who redefine territories of regional, national and individual identity, thus producing new histories with multiple agendas (cf. Sarker and Niyogy De 2002, p. 2).

Diasporic heterogeneity must not be ignored in favor of dominant patterns. Neither must member's identities, particularly women's, who are traditionally cast in stereotypical images that are built on reified models of femininity. The diaspora should be conceived of as a space for the creation of new identities that surpass usual patterns. Women are key elements in those processes:

> It is no wonder that there is no homogeneous South Asian minority or community, even though the media sometimes portrays migrants and their children in this way. Nor is there one South Asian woman's experience, though again the media may portray the South Asia woman in the Diaspora as oppressed by patriarchy, secluded and ill-educated. For every women from a conservative family who fits this description there are South Asian women who go out to work, who increasingly control their own incomes, who are themselves educated and see that their daughters are educated, who are rising high on major issues, such as working conditions, treatment of women and human rights. This mirrors, of course, the changes also occurring on the subcontinent, where women are now a force to be reckoned with in public and political life, as they have always been in the domain of the family. (Brown 2006, p. 174)

The object of analysis: the Hindu community of Santo António dos Cavaleiros

The settlement of Hindus in Portugal dates back to the end of the 1970s and the beginning of the 1980s. Resulting from processes of de-colonization in the former Portuguese territories in Africa – particularly in Mozambique, where significant communities from India were settled – the mass movement of Indians towards Portugal can be characterized as follows: Hindus, Muslims, Ismailis and Christians (cf. Malheiros 1996), from Goa, Daman and Diu and from the state of Gujarat, in which the latter two colonies of former Portuguese India – Daman and Diu – are geographically situated. Their settlement took place with recourse to strategies of re-communitarization and spatial congregation (Bastos 1990), with the majority concentrated in the Greater Lisbon Area, initially in the rundown neighbourhoods of Areeiro and Portela de Sacavém – and subsequently re-housed in other residential areas of the capital – in Santo António dos Cavaleiros, and also in smaller communities located in the cities of Oporto and Coimbra. The pioneering work on the presence of Hindus in Portugal undertaken by Bastos (1990, 1992) and by Bastos and Bastos (2001) dates from the end of the 1980s and the beginning of the 1990s, and is centred on the processes of identity construction developed by these groups, as well as their cultural reconstruction in the migratory context (cf. Bastos and Bastos 2001, pp. 14–15).

In relation to the Hindu community living in the district of Santo António dos Cavaleiros – a district in the Lisbon suburban area, part of the Loures municipality – this was an area which, at the time of the arrival of the Hindus in Portugal, was undergoing great residential expansion. The increase in the population of this area was due to a large extent to the arrival of groups from the former Portuguese colonies, among them Hindus. Here, similarly to what happened in other neighbourhoods with a concentration of Hindus, there was a process of spatial congregation, following on from the processes that had already been carried out in Africa – particularly in Mozambique (cf. Bastos 1990, Bastos and Bastos 2001) – albeit with the necessary readjustments. Unlike in the other areas of Hindu spatial congregation, there was a greater heterogeneity in Santo António dos Cavaleiros in relation to the origins of the individuals. Whereas in the neighbourhoods of Areeiro and Portela de Sacavém, for example, there was a congregation of a majority of Hindus from Diu, belonging to service castes, Santo António dos Cavaleiros presents a greater variety in relation to origin. Service castes and merchant castes from other areas in the state of Gujarat (cities like Rajkot, Porbandar or Junagadh) share the same residential space, as well as a common place of worship, the Shiva Temple. The differences between castes – belonging to different *varna*[6] – also correspond to cultural divergences and diversities of worship, particularly manifested in the distinction between Vaishnavism and Shaivism. Nevertheless, despite its internal differences, this community has a cohesive identity, reinforced by a religious basis, Hinduism. The internal differences are superseded by a common unity that overcomes the internal distinction, permitting it to be situated in Portuguese society and, at the same time, to preserve harmony within the group.

The present article is based on ethnographic research carried out among this community since 2000 and more concretely, on the female section of this group. Empirical data was collected on the basis of informal interviews with women belonging to various social backgrounds and different ages. The so-called *satsang* group was the priority focus of this research, and emphasis was also placed on a heterogeneous group of young women. Participation in female devotional moments, as well as in public ritual performance, together with my presence during day-to-day domestic activities, were the main sources of information. The fieldwork undertaken in Portugal was complemented by research periods in India and in the UK.

What distinguishes the two age groups referred to above is that the 'group of older women' or the '*satsang* group', comprising around 25 women[7] aged over 50, brings together women belonging to different castes, with different geographical origins – and respective cultural backgrounds – whereby what they have in common is the fact that they do not work and they take on the task of organizing the religious activities of the community. In relation to the 'group of younger women', composed of women between 24 and 37 years old, this group is more dispersed in relation to their insertion into the labour market and the family patterns of these women. Unlike the *satsang* group, in which the older women show traditional family patterns, the family composition of the group of young women is more variable, diverging between an extended family and a nuclear family.

In relation to insertion into the labour market, while the older women do not work, and when they do, they do it in the context of the family business, the group of younger women is, also at this level, more varied, presenting a dispersion between the women who do not work, those who work in the family business and those who – a minority – have accessed the independent labour market.

Religion and gender: negotiating identities in diaspora

Women's role in Hindu cultural transmission is a constant element throughout different diasporas (cf. Knott 1986, 1987, 1996, 2000, Rayaprol 1995, 1997, 2001, Pearson 2001, Hole 2001). The ethnographic case presented here aims to show how women accepted that task, throughout a process in which new forms of Hinduism were developed through the combination of traditional values with new elements introduced by the influence of the countries of settlement. In the Hindu case, religion is one of the key features of cultural identity reproduction, whose transmission relies on the preservation of certain values and the elimination of others. The principles of female conduct are considered essential within this process and are often the cause of tension between generations, thus requiring negotiation. This negotiation involves some compromise on the part of parents regarding their daughters' behaviour, giving them some freedom in terms of dress codes or socializing with friends. Among the more conservative families this negotiation is virtually inexistent, often resulting in acts of disobedience that can have serious consequences. Parents' expectations do not always match their daughters', marriage being a frequent source of disagreement.

Marriage within the caste or at least within the religious community is one of the principles of female conduct, just as are the tasks most obviously connected with the domestic family space. Young women's adoption of western values goes against these rules of behaviour and could in theory seem to threaten the moral structure of families, and consequently the survival of the group's identity. Family structures try to control the actions of their young girls, a control the latter feel in their everyday lives within a context where there is a strong spatial concentration of Hindus and where older women are permanently watching over the activities of young women. In cases like this, working outside the family environment of their residential area acts as an escape to community pressure. The growing arrival of Hindu women to the work market derives from the negotiation of gender roles, which involves combining family life and what is considered their main role as women with the new emerging roles – managing and ensuring the family's well being – results in their more active involvement with the surrounding society.

Older women in turn are responsible for maintaining order within the family group while negotiating new responsibilities in the sphere of religious activity. Their performance, considered vital for the preservation of religious practice has led to the transformation of their gender status, as the acquisition of new ritual roles demonstrates. These women's knowledge of the religious texts and their prestige as bearers of such knowledge has concrete consequences, namely taking charge of organizing rituals and religious celebrations of the Hindu calendar; acting as priestesses and presiding over rituals such as the *hawan*[8] and katha,[9] thus defying both male exclusiveness regarding ritual performance and their own widower status, which Hinduism traditionally considers extremely unfavourable and implies the exclusion of widows from the ritual sphere;[10] and finally, acting as the vehicles through which goddesses manifest themselves, receiving and embodying these divinities, which communicate with the followers through these women's words and body language in very specific ritual events through the enactment of performances of possession.

In many ways, women assume the *dharmic* task of religious transmission while simultaneously firmly consolidating their power through religion. On one hand, the code of female conduct, the *stridharma* (*stri* = woman; *dharma* = duty), seeks to regulate female behaviour based on the idea that the unstable, weak and impure nature of women must be kept disciplined. Accordingly, a woman must marry and become an exemplary spouse, never letting herself be controlled by her own nature, as dictated by the *Laws of Manu*, the most ancient Hindu law code. On the other hand, religious teachings are open to negotiation and change, and may lead to new forms of resistance and opportunities of power for women.

Nevertheless, Brahmanical views on the duties of women are conveyed through the more expedient channels of diffusion such as television or the internet.[11] Even in a context where the impact of Hindu nationalist movements is not directly felt by the communities in question such as the Portuguese case, other means of ideological transmission contribute towards the construction of feminine stereotypes, according to which the woman is held responsible for preserving family. Where lies the proof of female power? In married women's fertility as the warranty of the group's continuity, and therein possibly lies the origin of women's subordination. In her research on a caste of untouchables from Gujarat, Rosa Maria Perez not only demonstrates that women are responsible for social perpetuation, but also that this fact is the reason for the apparent disqualification of the feminine status:

> This apparent constancy in the disqualification of the female sex is undoubtely misleading. A married woman's segregation, her excessive submissiveness, in fact seems to be a smoke-screen for the admission of a power totally concealed by society: the woman is the guarantor of social survival by her procreation. Even if the bloodline is ascribed to the son (an attitude suited to the apparent disparagement of the daughter), it is in fact the son's wife who is responsible for the continuity of the line. (Perez 2004, p. 100)

Women's power is actually camouflaged under this disqualification:

> Therefore we will have to search for the reason why the woman is subjected to this peculiar treatment, by the society to which she belongs in her fecundity, and the reason for the power she retains through it. In other words, the outer signs of segregation, frequently interpreted as a sign of submissiveness, in reality cover up the great power which a woman has as a result of her capacity to perpetuate the family and society in

> general – a power camouflaged by the apparent disparagement of the woman and the great inequality in the functions ascribed to each sex. (Perez 2004, p. 100)

Besides their reproductive role, women must also summon divine protection for their home and family, taking vows (*vratas*) to ensure family stability. Single women wish to find a good husband, while married women pray to the gods for their husband's health and longevity, or for the birth of a son. In exchange for these requests, they take vows, make offerings and fast. Placing responsibility for the family's survival on women encourages them to control the fate of their family, as well as their own, through negotiation with the gods (Knott 1996, p. 23).

According to Kim Knott, Hindu women in the UK perpetuate vows as a way to accomplish their wishes and at the same time protect their honour, thus fulfilling their duty as women and wives. However, younger women offer resistance to the models their families expect them to follow. Their lives are filed with anxiety over marriage, and sometimes they oppose their parent's attempts to arrange their marriage (Knott 1996, p. 24). Resistance to *dharma* may be punished by the family that in extreme cases expel or break contact with them. Secretly eloping with their boyfriends is usually the result of the family's inflexibility and refusal to accept any other fate for their women other than marriage inside the caste or religious community.

The duties of Hindu women in Santo António dos Cavaleiros far exceed, as we have seen, the family and domestic circles. Their *stridharma* has extended to religious performance and transmission and to the responsibility over the survival not just of the family but of the whole group. When asked the reason for having this task as their mission, the women of the *satsang*[12] group explain: 'it is our *seva* (service). *Seva* is our *dharma* as well. We must ensure continuity.' One of them, a 62-year-old woman, continues:

> There is a temple. It is built. If there wasn't one, we would pray at home, it is already our tradition. We have two *agyiaras*[13] a month. Then we also have to read the Bhagavata Purana or Shiva Purana for instance … we have to give continuity. So that our children will follow this path; So they know God, the meaning of the Bhagavata Purana, the Ramayana. We have to teach them.

The education of their descendants is their chief concern, while both the youngest and the oldest consider the transmission of Hindu principles to their children and grandchildren a crucial task, which ensures their group's perpetuation. Contact with the surrounding society is seen as a bad influence, and despite considering it important to prevent children from being discriminated against, they believe that it must be complemented with an education that will teach them their ancestor's religion and cultural references.

Ignorance of the mother tongue is the most obvious sign that children and young people are losing contact with their traditional references. Thus, young and old female groups face the task of filling the gaps in the education of the young Hindus. The Gujarati school, which gathers the younger women around the goal of teaching, not just the language but the mythological references and moral principles of Hinduism as well, acts directly on this problem. The *satsang* group, in a more indirect and broad manner, ensures religious and ideological transmission to descendents and promotes the group's religious dynamic.

The task of ensuring the group's cultural and religious continuity faces difficulties in the confrontation between traditional values and those of their host countries. As Hole observes: 'Removed from the familiar, cultural surroundings, women have to balance the demands and impacts of the ancestral culture as well as the impact, questions and cultural demands for acceptance that the receiving culture puts on them' (2001, pp. 457–458). In fact, the search for equilibrium between the surrounding society's influence and the preservation of traditional Hindu religious beliefs and practices is, as we have seen, the resource found by Hindu diasporas in order to face younger generation's demands.

At the same time, the increasing responsibility of women in the religious sphere confers them autonomy of action in the process of cultural transmission, altering the meaning of the *stridharma*, extending it from the domestic to the public and communitarian spheres. By embracing the task of religious transmission and divine service (*seva*) as two of their primary duties, women gain new social and gender statuses. Older women are allowed to cross the boundaries of the traditional female sphere due to the freedom derived from their age status. Besides the freedom from behaviour constraints imposed on younger women, the former are most of the time out of the reach of male control. Therefore, in the course of the years, women have developed strategies of ideological transmission, ritual practice and management that have become gradually stronger. Segregating men from this process, women have occupied their spaces, having nevertheless left the community's official direction, as well as its visibility in Portuguese society, to the male universe.

The existence of a single ritualist (*pujari*) resulted in women's acquirement of the male ritual roles, initially performed by the Brahman widows and later in their absence, by women from other castes. Asked about its relevance in the process of cultural reproduction within their group, women asserted their importance and claimed that without them the group's identity references would disappear within the next generations. They are therefore conscious of their role's significance and the promotion of their status that resulted from strategies of adjustment of Hinduism to a diaspora context.

We should nevertheless emphasize that the attainment of autonomy and prestigious roles within the community occurs within a patriarchal logic. Even so, women who move within a sphere of patriarchal dominance should not be looked at through the perspective of subordination implied by this hegemony. It is also necessary to frame this phenomenon within Indian society on the whole. As Kakar and Kakar mention:

> To view Indian women solely through the lens of patriarchy, therefore, is to see the resemblance – in fact only superficial – to women in other patriarchal societies. But the image in such a case is always fuzzy and indistinct. Once we use the zoom lens of Indic culture (and its contemporary ferment), however, the picture becomes more focused and nuanced as unexpected details emerge. (Kakar and Kakar 2007, p. 41)

Unexpected details mark their difference from other types of patriarchal dominance:

> Thus, for example, in India, caste almost always trumps gender in the sense that a Brahmin woman will have higher status than a low-caste man. Or, to take another example, the powerful role played by mother-goddess in the Indian cultural imagination – and by mothers in the inner worlds of their sons – imbues male dominance with the emotional colours of fear, awe, longing, surrender, and so on. (Kakar and Kakar 2007, p. 41)

When asked about the possibility of a priest remaining in the Shiva Temple, women stated that their public ritual duties would cease to exist. Each gender's traditional duties must only be altered when there is need of adjustment and this fact becomes clear in the statement given by one of the *satsang* group's main supporters, at the age of 59:

> If in the future there is a fixed priest in the Shiva Temple, it is he who will carry out the work we are doing now; because it is his work, not ours. We won't stop participating, but we will no longer recite the texts. Meanwhile we will not give up this tradition: Chaitra mahino,[14] Bhadarvo *mahino*, Janmashtami, Divali, Navratri, Purshotam *mahino*: so far we have never failed because it is our tradition. If a priest ever comes everything goes back to him.

The potential return of this female performance to a future male priest therefore implies a recoiling of women's leadership and its 'restoration' to male dominance. Male supremacy is nonetheless recognized by the women themselves and transmitted within a conservative and patriarchal context where mythological references serve to corroborate gender roles. Feminine stereotypes are conveyed through Hindu nationalist ideology, which albeit indirectly, influences the reproduction of female models based on the idea of connection between womanhood and tradition. Sangeeta Ray ironizes the essentialist attitude she discovers in the fact that women defend traditional forms of Indian dressing outside of India as a form of identity perpetuation:

> Generally, tradition is a hard thing to let go of, and more significant, even if man had to adapt because they were part of the ephemeral public life, women could always be counted on to affirm the continuity of tradition. Thus, if Indian women continue to wear Indian clothes while living in the United States, then the fear of 'tradition' and 'culture' being contaminated in India is minimal. (Ray 2000, pp. 1–2)

The effect of Hindu nationalist movements in the diaspora enables the sustention of traditional Hindu standards, whose perpetuation women are responsible. At the same time, the *hindutva*[15] provides a universal form of Hinduism, fostering a spirit of national communion in communities of the diaspora through which conservative values are conveyed. The mechanisms of globalization lend a strong support to the dissemination of the nationalist ideological message (cf. Burlet 2001, p. 15).

The community in which this study focuses does not possess a sufficiently solid economic basis to proceed with the building of a permanent temple nor to accommodate a resident priest for the next few years, pointing to the likelihood that women's activity in this sphere will remain a constant in the near future. We must however, take new elements that may lead to future changes into consideration, namely the effect of the ideological dissemination of nationalistic nature, the involvement of youth groups and a more intense contact with the remaining diasporas; phenomena that began in the first decade of the 21st century and that may change Hinduism, as well as its main actors, in Portugal.

Regardless of the changes that are forthcoming, the relevant idea to retain is that these women's autonomy is restricted by a set of notions that, curiously enough, they themselves specifically convey. The vows and acts of abstinence performed on behalf of the family's well-being, as well as the transmission of mythological references in the domestic and public spheres, transform the gender roles in a context where male dominance is accepted by women themselves and where their subordinate role is inherent to their own *dharma*. The involvement of the Portuguese Hindu diaspora with its counterparts may bring a strengthening of nationalist ideology that has so far been virtually absent from individuals' discourse, despite being present in the endorsement of certain values such as the gender roles.

As we have seen, all these transformations have been taking place since 2008, like for example the regular visits of religious specialists that were practically nonexistent when this research was started, in 2000, and which have been significantly intensified.

In an age of swift social change, gender roles remain subjected to the rule of patriarchal control; however, social changes in women's role are inevitable, and the reconfiguring of Hinduism, inside which women build new gender statuses, gives a significant contribution.

Final remarks: age status and religion

The involvement of Hindu women in the religious sphere is a constant fact in their everyday lives, especially considering that most women in Santo António dos Cavaleiros do not work away from home. Nevertheless, we find two distinct positions regarding religion: those who repeat what they learnt from their family's elder without questioning its grounds, and those who do question themselves and seek answers for their theological doubts. Female religious tradition is passed down from older to younger women in a family environment, from mother to daughter and from mother-in-law to daughter-in-law.

Older women master the religious texts and some even control the traditionally male ritual practice, a knowhow they acquired when their age released them from the family duties. In their wake, younger women perpetuate this knowledge, particularly in the domestic religious practice. While until the first decade of the 21st century younger women received this information and accepted it unquestioningly, today a section of young women is not content with repeating the ritual acts and sacred formulas, questioning and searching for answers that the older women cannot give them.

Some younger women resent the fact that many others still lack a critical attitude towards their religion. According to them, without criticism, they cannot deepen their knowledge of the religion they profess. Many young women, not just the older ones, ignore the reasons behind the practice of certain ritual acts and the meaning of the sacred formulas they recite. The fulfilment of the female duty does indeed imply carrying out certain religious acts, often ignoring the reason for them besides having been dictated to do so by the mother or mother-in law, just as the women before them had done. However, not all women accept this mimicry and among younger women who furthered their formal education, whether in Portugal or in India, the need for an understanding of their religious principles is higher. Furthermore, this position widens the existing breach between those who had the chance to continue their studies and establish a professional career and those who remained confined within their domestic nucleus, deprived of direct contact with the surrounding environment.

The distinction between younger and older women reflects itself in the different spheres and activities associated with each of them. Older women occupy the space of the *satsang*, while the youngest are concentrated in the Gujarati school. Likewise, the spaces and leisure moments are separate: it is common for the Gujarati school to organize parties that are related both to the Hindu and the Portuguese calendar, the latter case including for instance organizing Christmas and Easter brunches and dinners, or Carnival parties. These celebrations for children and teachers do not count on the participation of older women, who consider that it is important for the younger relatives to socialize away from their controlling presence. As a 62-year-old woman referred: 'That is strictly for the young. If we go they cannot enjoy themselves freely'. Female leisure activities are age-related and connected with women's body language, so that the youngest must control their self-expression while the elder are free from the behavioural constraints in their public actions that derive from the transformations of their gender identity.

Between the beginning of the reproductive cycle until the end of their procreative powers, women are subjected to strict behavioural rules that restrict their sexuality. Freed from the constraints associated with their reproductive phase, a new period in their life begins in which control over their sexuality has ceased to be a concern and a transformation of their gender identity and corresponding public and private behaviour takes place. The effect of ageing on gender definition is linked to the transformations the body goes through in the course of a lifetime. According to Lamb, exploring gender issues necessarily implies understanding how women interpret, resist and criticize dominant gender ideologies in their society, while at the same time analyzing conceptions regarding physical transformations, identities and forms of power and subordination throughout life (Lamb 2000, p. 198).

Looking at gender relations from the perspective of women's experience of their roles in the different stages of life allows us to conclude, according to Perez's thesis (2004), that female segregation serves to camouflage and control their power. The power of ensuring the group's continuity – which according to the author resides in the exclusively female ability to guarantee social survival – assumes new forms in diaspora. In this context, it surpasses the merely reproductive task, and women have also made it their goal to ensure the perpetuation of the group's cultural references through their descent.

The foreseeable estrangement of the community's younger members from traditional reference values once again places the task of ensuring the group's perpetuation – not just physical, but cultural and religious[16] as well – in the hands of the mothers and grandmothers. The concern with their descent and the survival of Hinduism's traditional values are the driving force behind their actions, in the absence of which this community's survival would be impossible: such is the female power. It has become public besides private and it is proof of women's centrality for Hinduism's perpetuation and dynamics of adjustment. The terms perpetuation and adjustment point to the confluence between strategies designed to preserve conservative ideologies – in which gender identities are included – and the transformation of gender roles in the public sphere. In this sense, women's acquirement of autonomy emerges in a context where they themselves uphold conservative discourses on womanhood.

Notes

1. Socio-cosmic order or moral duty the individual must comply to in order to respect his/her individual and social condition.
2. The terms 'high tradition' and 'low tradition' were made popular by the Chicago school, particularly by Robert Redfield and Milton Singer (1954) to designate in the first case a set of canonical texts, religious practices and ritual representatives associated with the historical past of a particular group, and in the second case, a group of 'low' local religious traditions expressed by local dialects, which differ from the unified body of the 'high traditions' of Hindu Sanskrit. Cristopher Fuller emphasizes the need to not separate these two levels of Hinduism, calling our attention to their complementary nature: 'It is now generally accepted that the religion is not split into two (or more) separate strata, each with its own body of distinctive beliefs and practices. In fairness to Srinivas, Redfield and Singer, it must be said that they always insisted that the higher and lower strata are interconnected' (Fuller 2004, p. 26).
3. *Bhakti* means devotion and expresses the relationship between the devotee and a particular deity. This current was revealed in the Bhagavad Gita, where Krishna, the central character of this odyssey, expresses each individual's need to fulfill their *dharma*, while at the same time he teaches the secret of the encounter with the divine by assuming a universal form. This message encourages harmony between the *bhakti* and the *dharma*. The utmost example of devotion towards the deity is fulfilling the *dharma*, however difficult or painful it turns out to be.

4. The Sanskrit term to designate the spiritual master, whose task is to guide the disciple through his teachings and religious knowledge.
5. In the process of interpreting Hinduism, Kurien, regarding the reading and discussion of the Hindu religious texts, highlights women's interpretation of the female characters through a feminist perspective which heightens their power (Kurien 1998, p. 54).
6. Sanskrit term (meaning colour) used to describe the four classifying units that comprise the Hindu social hierarchy: Brahmins (priests), Kshatryia, (aristocracy), Vaishya (merchants and farmers) and Shudra (services castes).
7. It is not possible to cite a fixed number given the frequent mobility of these women between Portugal, India and other countries where contacts with the Hindu diaspora in Portugal are deeper, as is the case with the UK.
8. The cult of fire through a Vedic ritual.
9. A history with a moral lesson usually implying a ritual that includes making offerings to the deities.
10. The female role in India that finds an approximate Portuguese counterpart is that of 'temple attendants' or 'pujarini' (cf. Marglin 1985, p. 54) in certain tasks where we register the participation of post-menopausal widows aiding in the temples religious duties, which they are allowed to do because, despite their widowhood, their advanced age confers them a status of purity. Such tasks are usually minor duties and never imply – similarly to what we observe in Portugal – presiding over rituals that require the presence of a male priest.
11. Television shows such as the serial on the Ramayana epic convey a conservative image of women of which Sita is the perfect model.
12. Group of women aged over 50 who meet to carry out devotional gatherings (*satsang*), and the main focus of my research.
13. Also called *ekadashi*, the eleventh day of each lunar phase.
14. Means month in Gujarati.
15. This term expresses the Hindu essence, the link between Hindu religious heritage and India's national identity. This notion finds its foremost expression in the context of Indian political and religious nationalism connected with the ideological structure of the BJP (Bharatiya Janata Party). The movement known as *hindutva* intervenes through campaigns that trigger feelings of Hindu revivalism, proclaiming this religious source as the foundation of Indian nationalism. Besides their action in Indian Territory, this movement is active in most transnational Hindu communities.
16. Being young in diaspora in many cases implies searching for stable points of reference, in a context where religion emerges as a national language (Shukla 2005, p. 233). As Shukla points out, some young people reject the flexibility of cosmopolitan identity and try to organize themselves around the identification with the cultural values of the subcontinent, although not those necessarily associated with nationalist movements. However, Shukla points out that: 'In all these cases, movements in the subcontinent reach out to their wayward sons, even if they are in a new generation and have a relatively abstracted relationship to the nation' (Shukla 2005, p. 233).

Notes on contributor

Inês Lourenço is a researcher at CRIA (Centre for Research in Anthropology – ISCTE/Lisbon University Institute) and post-doctoral fellow at the Science and Technology Foundation. She has published 'Diu: a Meeting Place' (2005), 'Gender and Diaspora in Portugal: the Hindu Community of Santo António dos Cavaleiros' (2007) and 'A partir de Diu: diáspora hindu e género em Portugal [From Diu: Hindu diaspora and gender in Portugal]' (2010). Her research is centred on the Hindu diaspora in Portugal and her main interests relate to the social uses of culture and the consumption of goods of Indian origin, particularly cultural products such as Bollywood films in Portuguese society.

References

Ballard, R., ed., 1994. *Desh Pardesh: the South Asian Presence in Britain.* London: Hurst.

Bastos, S.P., 1990. *A Comunidade Hindu da Quinta da Holandesa: um estudo antropológico sobre a organização sócio-espacial da casa.* Lisbon: LNEC.

Bastos, S.P., 1992. *A frigideira sagrada e o fio de algodão – A prática vrata cathâ numa comunidade hindu gujarati do Sul do Saurasthra (Diu).* Thesis (M.A.). FCSH/UNL, Lisbon.

Bastos, J.G. and Bastos, S.P., 2001. *De Moçambique a Portugal. Reinterpretações Identitárias do hinduísmo em Viagem.* Lisbon: Fundação Oriente.

Baumann, M., 1998. Sustaining little 'Indias': Hindu diasporas in Europe. *In*: G.T. Haar, ed. *Strangers and sojourners: religious communities in the diaspora.* Leuven: Peeters Publishers, 95–132.

Burlet, S., 2001. Re-awakening? Hindu nationalism goes global. *In*: R. Starrs, ed. *Asian nationalism in an age of globalization.* Richmond: Curzon Press, 1–18.

Brown, J., 2006. *Global South Asians: introducting the modern diaspora.* Cambridge: Cambridge University Press.

Cohen, R., 1997. *Global diasporas: an introduction.* London: UCL Press.

Coward, H., 2000. Hinduism in Canada. *In*: H. Coward, J. Hinnels and R. Williams, eds. *The South Asian religious diaspora in Britain, Canada, and the United States.* Albany, NY: State University of New York Press, 151–172.

Eck, D., 2000. Negotiating Hindu identities in America. *In*: H. Coward, J. Hinnels and R. Williams, eds. *The South Asian diaspora in Britain, Canada and the United States.* Albany, NY: State University of New York Press, 219–238.

Fuller, C., J., 2004 [1992]. *The camphor flame: popular Hinduism and society in India.* Princeton, NJ: Princeton University Press.

Glick Schiller, N., 2007. The centrality of ethnography in the study of transnational migration. *In*: A.K. Sahoo and B. Maharaj, eds. *Sociology of diaspora: a reader.* New Delhi: Rawat Publications, 118–155.

Hole, E., 2001. Ethnicity and symbolism among Hindu women in a small diaspora community. *In*: T.S. Rukmani, ed. *Hindu diaspora: global perspectives.* New Delhi: Munshiram Manoharlal, 443–469.

Kakar, S. and Kakar, K., 2007. *The Indians: portrait of a people.* New Delhi: Penguin India.

Knott, K., 1986. *Hinduism in Leeds. a study of religious practice in the Indian Hindu community and Hindu-related groups.* Leeds: Monograph Series, Community Religious Project, University of Leeds.

Knott, K., 1987. Hindu temple rituals in Britain: reinterpretation of tradition. *In*: R. Burghart, ed. *Hinduism in Great Britain: the perpetuation of religion in an alien cultural milieu.* London: Tavistock, 157–179.

Knott, K., 1996. Hindu women, destiny and *Streedharma*. *Religion,* 26, 15–35.

Knott, K., 2000. Hinduism in Britain. *In*: H. Coward, J. Hinnels and R. Williams, eds. *The South Asian diaspora in Britain, Canada and the United States.* Albany, NY: State University of New York Press, 89–108.

Kurien, P., 1998. Becoming American by becoming Hindu: Indian Americans take their place at the multicultural table. *In*: R. Warner and J. Wittner, eds. *Gatherings in diaspora: religious communities and the new immigration.* Philadelphia, PA: Temple University Press, 37–70.

Lamb, S., 2000. *White saris and sweet mangoes: aging, gender, and body in north India.* Berkeley: University of California Press.

Malheiros, J.M., 1996. *Imigrantes na Região de Lisboa: Os Anos da Mudança: Imigração e Processo de Integração das Comunidades de Origem Indiana.* Lisbon: Edições Colibri.

Marglin, F.A. 1985. *Wives of the god king: the ritual of the Devadasis of Puri.* New Delhi: Oxford University Press.

Narayan, V., 1996 [1992]. Creating South Indian Hindu experience in the United States. *In*: R. Williams, ed. *A sacred thread: modern transmission of Hindu traditions in India and abroad.* New York: Columbia University Press, 147–176.

Pearson, M., 2001. *The Indian Ocean.* London: Routledge.

Perez, R.M., 2004. *Kings and untouchables: a study of the caste system in western Gujarat.* New Delhi: Chronicle Books.

Ray, S., 2000. *En-gendering India: woman and nation in colonial and postcolonial narratives.* Durham, NC: Duke University Press.

Rayaprol, A., 1995. Gender ideologies and practices among South Indian immigrants in Pittsburgh. *Sagar: South Asian Graduate Research Journal,* 2 (1), 268–270.

Rayaprol, A., 1997. *Negotiating identities: women in the Indian diaspora.* New Delhi: Oxford University Press.

Rayaprol, A., 2001. Can you talk Indian? Shifting notions of community and identity in the Indian diaspora. *In*: S. Jodhka, ed. *Community and identities: contemporary discourses on culture and politics in India.* New Delhi: Sage, 163–190.

Redfield, R. and Singer, M., 1954. The cultural role of cities. *Economic Development and Cultural Change,* 3, 53–73.

Sarker, S. and Niyogi De, E., 2002. Introduction: marking times and territories. *In*: S. Sarker and E. Niyogi De, eds. *Trans-status subjects: gender in the globalization of South and Southeast Asia.* Durham, NC: Duke University Press, 1–27.

Shukla, S., 2005 [2003]. *India abroad: diasporic cultures of postwar America and England.* New Delhi: Orient Longman.

Venkatachari, K.K.A., 1996 [1992]. Transmission and transformation of ritual. *In*: R. Williams, ed. *A sacred thread: modern transmission of Hindu traditions in India and abroad.* Columbia, NY: Columbia University Press, 177–190.

Vertovec, S., 2000. *The Hindu diaspora: comparative patterns.* London: Routledge.

Williams, R., 1996 [1992]. Sacred threads of several textures: strategies of adaptation in the United States. *In*: R. Williams, ed. *A sacred thread: modern transmission of Hindu traditions in India and abroad.* Columbia, NY: Columbia University Press, 228–257.

Young, K., 2002. Women in Hinduism. *In*: A. Sharma, ed. *Women in Indian religions.* New Delhi: Oxford University Press.

Talking 'gender superiority' in virtual spaces: web-based discourses of Hindu student groups in the US and UK

Anjana Narayan[a] and Bandana Purkayastha[b]

[a]*Sociology, California State Polytechnic University, Pomona, USA;* [b]*Sociology and Asian American Studies, University of Connecticut, Storrs, USA*

This study focuses on the public assertion of gendered ethno-religious identities on the websites of Hindu student groups (HSGs) in the South Asian Diaspora in the USA and UK. HSGs are a part of a larger phenomenon of individuals and organizations engaged in creating and promoting ethnicities in virtual spaces. In this paper we focus particularly on the HSGs deployment of 'strong woman' imagery to assert their 'superior cultures'. We find that while the HSGs appear to challenge the gendered/racialized construction of minorities in Western societies as traditional, and non-modern, their construction of 'strong Hindu women' is replete with gendered inequalities. In addition, such constructions also implicate 'their women' into the process of drawing racialized boundaries against other groups. This paper explores how the processes involving the construction, representation and reproduction of Hinduism and Hindu identity on the web, from locations in the USA and the UK create contemporary gender hierarchies.

Introduction

The rapid growth of the web continues to raise interesting questions about contemporary social identities of marginalized groups that have been negatively affected in tangible (i.e. non web-based) social spaces by hierarchies imposed by the dominant groups through a combination of ideologies, interactions and institutionalization (e.g. Diamandaki 2003, Ignacio 2005, Macfayden 2006). Some scholars have documented that individuals try on less-essentialist, choice-driven, multiple, fragmented and hybrid identities on the web and thus dilute the consequences of gendering, racialization, class and other social hierarchies to which they are subjected in their tangible lives (e.g. Mitra and Gajjala 2008). Other scholars have documented that organizations are active in the web-world in trying to expand their reach to potential members by emphasizing selected aspects of identities that individuals might share with others but in affirming ways that help them to deal with the negative aspects of these social identities in tangible spaces. (e.g. Earl 2006, Howard 2006, Narayan and Purkayastha forthcoming, Pudrovska and Ferree 2004). While much of this research has focussed on ethnic, racialized and gendered identities at the individual level, and political organizing at the group level, this paper focuses on South Asian groups in the UK and USA and their constructions of ethno-religious identities.

As the religions of 'new' immigrants and the supposed backwardness of norms about treatment of women in Islam and Hinduism have entered into the UK's and USA's mainstream political discourse, many ethnic groups have been active in attempting to counter these characterizations by deploying affirming ethno-religious identities (see Narayan and Purkayastha forthcoming, Purkayastha and Narayan 2009, also Kurien 2004, 2005). Yet there is no large-scale research, as far as we are aware, that systematically examines these group identities on the web. This paper fills that gap by examining discourses deployed on the websites of ethno-religious Hindu student groups in the UK and USA. Since the processes of gendering – the ideologies, interactions and institutionalization that create and maintain hierarchies between men and women – is an ongoing central feature of contemporary life, we focus particularly on the discourse relating to women to examine whether these are constructed in ways that challenge gender hierarchies. We argue that such 'affirming' identities about 'gender superiority' of Hindu women simultaneously inscribe gendered/ethno-religious hierarchical boundaries so that Hindu men remain more powerful than Hindu women, and Hindus appear to be better than Muslims and Christians.

Gender and ethnic women

In recent years, gendered ideologies and practices in religions has become enmeshed in discussions about the assimilation of new immigrants in many Western countries (Ebaugh and Chafetz 2000). Since religions such as Hinduism and Islam are seen as 'new' religions in the West, much of the scholarly discussions about these practitioners have been framed within larger discussions about modernity and traditionalism. Assuming gender equality is a hallmark of modernity, much of these discussions' focus is often on ethnic women and their experiences of these religions. Western theorists continue to assume that increasing modernity and consequently decreasing gender inequalities, is crucial to improving women's position in society (e.g. Chafetz and Dworkin 1986, Okin 1999). In terms of immigrant communities, scholars argue that women from more traditional cultures tend to replicate their cultural values within ethnic communities, and gender hierarchies only change when they – particularly second-generation daughters – adopt more modern cultural values of the West (e.g. Ebaugh and Chafetz 1999, Yang and Ebaugh 2001).

Yet another source of sustaining this modernity/tradition dichotomoy has been the mainstream feminist literature. Ideologies about subordinated women in 'other' cultures continues to survive in the twenty-first century; such ideologies are most starkly evident in framing discussions about women in 'other' religions, even though a significant body of literature has begun to question the construction of this overgeneralized, ahistorical construction of 'the oppressed woman', without reference to her multiple social locations (e.g. Narayan and Purkayastha 2009, Zia 2009). Part of the problem is that discussions of religion in the feminist literature are based on an assumption that the ideologies, organizations and histories of women within Christianity in the West is the template through which all other women and their experiences with their religions should be studied. For instance, in a summary of feminism and religion, Andersen (2005) lists feminist scholarship on the historical relationship of women, religion, feminism; women's religious beliefs and status within churches; the role of churches in minority communities; and new perspectives inspired by feminist spirituality and theology, as key arenas of feminist scholarly contribution to our understanding of women and religion. Discussions about the ideologies, organizations and histories of non-church based religions and long established ideas of women's spirituality (e.g. Ahmed 2002, Saxena 2004), appear to have little effect in expanding and deepening such discussions of 'feminism'. The other part of the problem is that feminist scholarship has mostly focused on what happens in tangible religious spaces shaped by social and political institutional imperatives within nation-states, while mostly ignoring the virtual social spaces where 'the woman question'[1] has been discussed and framed for nearly two decades.

In contrast to the two sets of literature that emphasize gender inequalities alone, some of the diasporic literature which focus on ethnic women have pointed out that as ethnic groups recreate 'culture' in their host countries, women become the symbols of 'tradition' and their behaviours are strictly controlled to maintain the boundaries of ethnic groups (e.g. Kabeer 2002, Das Gupta 1997, Dasgupta and Dasgupta 1996, Yuval-Davis 1997). They do not assume that female migrants from the 'third world' are subordinate because of the 'gender backwardness' prevalent in non-Euro-American parts of the world; instead they describe how ethnic women in minority groups become subject to new controls that are specifically reflective of their positions as racially marginalized groups in the West. Their racialized/gendered marginalization in countries such as the USA and UK is further complicated because their lives are constrained within ethnic communities where they are expected to be the keepers of 'traditions' within ethnic groups, with conservative men often assuming the role of defining what 'tradition' is, and setting up a series of mechanisms to control their behaviour (Anthias and Yuval-Davis 1989, Kabeer 2002).

In this paper we focus on Hindu student groups (HSGs) in the USA and UK and their assertions about 'Hindu women' on their websites. We use the example of HSGs to show that contemporary gendered/raced ideologies are produced, while using a strong woman frame. Such websites have a significant reach,[2] bridging geographical dispersion, and breaching boundaries between the real and virtual worlds to manage the way people perceive the world (Howard 2006).

Using this example of HSG discourse, we show that over-generalized assumptions about subordination of women through religious ideologies – which continues to shape much of the mainstream discussions on religion – need to be replaced by discussions that recognize the existence of strong women ideologies in 'traditional cultures' and that these 'strong women' ideologies can be used to promote contemporary ideologies of subordination. While many scholars have discussed how women find ways of empowering themselves despite the existence of ideologies of subordination (e.g. Katzenstein 1995), we illustrate that the opposite is also true; new ideologies of domination and subordination can be constructed out of ideologies of strong, powerful women. We show that HSGs' discourses profess the distinctiveness of Hindu female identities as a way to construct a positive identity to challenge the negative racial categorization of Hindus among many sections of the mainstream; but they also use erasures and silences to construct gendered family oriented roles for women, while drawing ethnocentric boundaries between themselves and Muslims.

The case

This paper is part of a larger study that draws on the experiences of Indian-origin groups in the USA and UK to examine transnational ethnicity, focusing on ethno-religious organizations engaged in constructing transnational ethnic identities by using religion as a means for constructing new, virtually linked communities. We focus on Hinduism because it is a religion with no uniform sets of practices – religious texts, practices and beliefs are culturally-, regionally- and family-dependent – providing a good basis for examining whether the identities constructed by these groups are transnational. This paper specifically examines whether these identities are gendered, and in what way, by focusing on HSGs in the South Asian diaspora in the USA and UK, countries with very diverse migration histories. There are now hundreds of student organizations in these two countries that are asserting 'a' Hindu identity (Kurien 2005, Rajagopal 2000). Scholars have begun to document how pan-Indian umbrella organizations (both secular and religious) that present the face of Indians abroad have had the task of codifying Indian ethnicity and communicating what Indian culture and Indian religion stands for (e.g. Kurien 1999, 2004). The HSG websites serve to virtually assert an ethno-religious identity. Overall, they emphasize certain aspects of identities, present certain histories and selected 'traditions' (in the case of ethnic groups) to make and claim new believers to their version. Since they have a potentially worldwide audience, they are able to attract a much wider viewership with their versions of ethno-religious identity. Scholars who have begun to study such virtual constructions of ethnic identities emphasize the growing importance of such forms among geographically dispersed ethnic groups, especially those that transcend the day-to-day interactions within enclaves (e.g. Purkayastha 2005).

Methodology

This study focuses on the US HSG and the UK HSG, selected because they are the most prominent and the largest in both countries. Established in the early 1990s, both have similar organizational structures: a national association with an overarching website, and local university chapter websites across geographical zones.

The sample size numbered 18 websites: two main websites, seven UK chapter websites, and nine US chapter websites. We used computer-assisted text analysis software and a statistical data analysis tool to locate recurrent themes across the total sample, as indicated by common or identical terminology. Phrases that recurred most frequently were then classified in terms of taxonomy. In other words, phrases that meant the exact same thing or were closely related were first grouped together in categories called dictionaries. A KWIC (Keyword in-context) tool was used to analyse the phrase in the context of the site content and inconsistent terminology was deleted.

The larger study identified seven themes: gender superiority, world religion, history and scriptures, modern and relevant, universal applicability, beliefs and rituals, and gods and gurus. We used the emergent categories based on the quantitative data to qualitatively analyse the textual evidence from the websites. In other words we used a summative approach, wherein the preconceived code categories or dictionaries were used to analyse the qualitative data. It allowed for the understanding of the context connected with the application of the word or phrase as well as to demonstrate that the quantitative data is consistent with the textual evidence.[3]

In this paper we focus on the gender superiority theme that was consistently prominent on UK and USA websites. We present the discourse on the dimensions of gender superiority by focusing on the three most frequently occurring sub-themes: goddesses and epic women, role of strong Hindu women and segregated spheres.

Web-based discourse on gender superiority

The data indicates that the combined categories *goddesses and epic heroines* and *role of strong Hindu women* together form 72% of the total frequency distribution of the overall category of gender superiority, with segregated spheres occupying only 28% of the total frequency distribution for the USA and UK combined. An analysis of the distribution of gender categories across websites for the USA and UK separately indicate that *goddesses and epic heroines* and *role of strong Hindu women* together occur in 12 websites in the USA and 11 websites in the UKA, with only eight and seven websites showing segregated spheres for the USA and UK respectively.

Thus, a simple descriptive examination of the frequency counts and category distribution across websites gives the overall impression that the discourse professes an ideology of strong women as central to the construction of a Hindu ethnic identity. However, a substantive reading of the gender-related themes presented in the next section clearly establishes that an emphasis on strong Hindu women is a reaction to racist views and embedded gender distinctions.

To understand these themes, it is important to note that Hinduism is 'brimming with imageries of goddesses who are warriors, destroyers, creators, guardians of wealth, education, and ultimate liberators' (Narayan and Purkayastha 2009, p. 16). Such goddesses could be important in their own rights or in their symbolic roles as mothers, wives, daughters. In Hinduism, 'god' is neither man nor women; s/he is *ardhanariswara* (half woman, half man) and beyond such male/female dichotomies based on physical bodies or essential natures. The worship of these female forms of goddesses varies significantly across India based on social and historical forces that shape particular regions. Kumar (1993) for instance, discusses how goddesses – Durga and Kali – became important in the Bengal region of India as part of the growing socio-cultural resistance against the British colonial and missionary practices in the region. Others document that these practices continue in contemporary times (Saxena 2004, Saha 2008, Purkayastha 2008). Thus there is no single set of religious ideologies, or actual practice that is 'the' Hindu form; rather, diversity and variety mark the ways in which goddesses are imagined in different regions.

Goddesses and epic women

The websites affirm the feminine by positioning women at the centre of the worldview. While women from Hindu history, literature and mythology are eulogized as role models for all Hindu women, the websites deploy two specific configurations to drive home the message: powerful Hindu goddesses and dutiful epic women.

While there are innumerable Hindu goddesses, the autonomous figure of Durga or Kali is 'the goddess' personifying Shakti.[4] They highlight the feminine principle (Shakti) inherent in Hinduism as the fundamental reason for the high status accorded to the Hindu womanhood. In an article titled 'Shakti and Hinduism' on a US HSG website, the author states:

> Shakti can be translated as meaning 'power', 'force', or 'energy' … feminine principle. Shakti is synonymous with the great Devi, or the great goddess of Sanatana Dharma (Hinduism) … . As a natural consequence of this view, Sanatana Dharma encourages all people to have respect and reverence for women … Hindu women have not only historically enjoyed the respected status of being repository of Shakti, but have very often had the opportunity to wield quite a bit of actual power and authority in the everyday world.

The other goddesses mentioned in the websites include Lakshmi and Saraswati, the consorts of the great gods Vishnu and Brahma respectively.[5] Once again the discourse underlines that according to Hindu belief the principle of energy consists of the feminine and that every male deity is activated by his consort's Shakti. Her role is not merely supportive, but enabling. The numerous consort goddesses ultimately manifest the pre-eminent goddess herself as the primary embodiment of Shakti. On the US HSG national website an article titled 'Hinduism as a Liberating Force for Women' the author states:

> Almost every god (deva) of the Hindu pantheon has a feminine companion, a consort, a goddess. This is an idea which is an indispensable element of every major sect of Hinduism. ... These goddess-consorts are said to personify nothing less than the essential energy of the god .... Thus it is the feminine principle, which is the animating force of life itself.

The websites also highlight that the worship of God in the form of Mother is a unique feature of Hinduism. Tracing the lineage of mother-worship to the Indus Valley civilization, they argue that, through the ages, the doctrine of the Motherhood of God has established a firm root in Hinduism and that Hindus worship the Divine Mother in many popular forms such as Durga, Kali, Lakshmi and Saraswati. In this sense, we are all children of the 'Divine Mother'. An article titled 'The Worship of God as Mother' on a UK HSG chapter website states:

> The position of women in the Hindu religion is dignified because each woman is considered a manifestation of the Divine Mother .... Through the worship of God in the form of Mother, Hinduism offers a unique reverence to womanhood.

The mother goddess is also portrayed as 'Mother Earth' permeating all living things through the energies of the soil. The mother's fecundity and affection is represented in the fertility and bounty of the soil, and conceptualized as the blessed motherland. 'Mother India' (Bharatmata) is a favourite theme of Indian nationalism and she is represented as a woman whose body defines the frontiers of the subcontinent.

Mainstream feminist discussions rarely recognize the prevalence (indeed tradition) of strong women motifs in religions such as Hinduism. It is clear from these websites, however, that 'traditional' religious motifs are being used to construct the notion of 'gender superiority'. At this level the modern-traditional dichotomy that frames so much of mainstream work fails to explain the persistent occurrence of these goddesses. Part of the explanation can be traced to racialization, while part is simply that strong women motifs are widely available in Hinduism; these groups use them much as feminist groups have added women to their scholarly and activist projects.

The motif of strong women on these websites includes other figures, bringing us to the second symbolic configuration: epic women who are behaviour models for women. Mother Earth is sometimes associated with Sita, the devoted wife of Rama in the epic *Ramayana*.[6] Rama's unfair treatment of Sita when he doubts her virtue has aroused much condemnation over centuries. Some websites emphasize Sita's heroism, as is evident from the quote by on the US HSG national website:

> In the Ramayana, we meet Sita, the wife—and Shakti—of Rama, an incarnation of God. Though arranged marriages are the norm in Hindu society, we find that Sita chooses her own husband in a svayamvara ceremony. Also of her own free will, she chooses to accompany Rama to the forest when he is sent into exile, thus exhibiting her strength and commitment to loyalty. While living in the forest, she continues to display her independent

> nature, as when she convinces Rama to chase the gold-spotted dear. Hindu literature is full of such examples of strong, heroic women …

Thus the discourse elides two different aspects of Hinduism. The symbolic importance of mother goddesses (emphasized only in parts of India) is presented as the 'natural' cause of the high status of women. At the same time, mythological characters such as Sita that embody absolute devotion to their husbands are equated with the independent goddesses such as Durga and Kali, and depicted as strong-willed, liberated women.

Overall, these images of goddesses and epic heroines are portrayed as allowing Hindu women a wide array of role choices. The implicit message is that Hinduism encourages women to assume powerful roles in the public domain provided they remain dutiful and devoted in the familial sphere. The question that remains unanswered is in which arenas do these 'strong' women exert their power? The answer is suggested in the discussions on the next theme.

The role of 'strong' Hindu woman – construction of rigid boundaries

A persistent theme in these websites is the reprocessing of the universal image of the 'Indian woman' who is seen as a metaphor for the purity, chastity, and sanctity of the ancient spirit that is India. Indian women embody aspects of 'the ideal woman' based on romanticized myth of womanhood in the Vedic age. The timeless essence of India, derived from its distant past and unfettered by the struggles and miseries of the present, is constantly constructed and reconstructed, eternalized, celebrated and eulogized like an ancient artefact in the discourse.

A fundamental aspect of the discourse is the belief that ancient India embodied the ideal society whose essence was sullied by the invasions of Muslims, the British, and the postcolonial domination of 'pseudo-secular' Indians. The 'Hindu groups' that create these websites consider themselves part of a movement that aims to restore the ancient glory of Hinduism. The centrality of gender is very clear in this version of history and of Hindu revivalism. In a posting titled 'Hindu heritage and women' the US HSG National website quotes Swami Ranganathanda:

> When we study our Hindu history of the last 5000 years, we come across many changing phases of women's status in our society. In the beginning, in the Vedic period, it is perfect equality. Then the feudal period came, foreign invasions came, women's freedom became abridged. But now all that is over, that is all yesterday. When we enter the modern period, a new situation had arisen … .

Thus, there is a gendered construction of India's glorious heritage and a significant aspect of Hindu revivalism is the celebration and the vision of the 'New Hindu Woman' as an essential category that could preserve society from destruction. She is the staunch upholder of the cultural essence of Hinduism. Most important, the 'new strong Hindu woman' presents the ideal middle ground between 'Islamic culture' (criticized for repression of women) and 'Western culture' (criticized for promiscuity and materialistic lifestyle).

(a) Separation from Muslim culture

The websites use a discourse of 'superior culture' and 'model minority' to correlate (as causation) the achievement of Hindus with the gender ideologies presented by these groups. A central issue is demarcation of social boundaries different between 'our women' and 'their women'. Boundaries between Hindus and Muslims is a clear and ongoing theme. For instance, an article on the US HSG national website states:

> The Islamic rulers basically imposed the rules from their scriptures (Quoran and Hadith) in this newly conquered society in India … Purdah was enforced on both Muslim and non-Muslim population, since it is a basic idea of Islam … Child marriage became rampant to prevent forceful abduction by the aggressors … Dowry became a tradition because parents had to get their daughters married by hook and crook or … otherwise would face abduction or forced marriage by powerful Muslim men … .

The next posting states:

> … let me make my final statement that the Hindu Scriptures do not support practice of dowry and bride burning. People who indulge in this abominable practice are either ignorant of Hindu Dharma or have lost contact with their own conscience … .

Thus, the rhetoric is often couched within a discourse on gender equality, with the emphasis on the woman-empowering factor that distinguishes Hindus from other South Asians, especially Muslims. Hindu women allegedly enjoy a parity power status with their male counterparts, a phenomenon unique to Hinduism and absent in all other South Asian religions – particularly Islam. As a case in point, when the US HSG launched the 'Hindu Women Project', they promoted it as a 'forum for Hindu women to discuss and address their concerns in order to foster unity, strength and understanding and to promote full social, political, spiritual, and educational opportunity for them'. An article on this Project claims:

> Hindu women have historically easily risen to heights of power within various monastic and religious hierarchical structures, parallels of which would have been unheard of in other religions … . Considering that Indian culture has always been a culture in which religion has always been the most important social institution in society, it is no small accomplishment for women to have risen so high in the echelons of Hindu leadership.

Similarly, in an article titled 'Ten questions people ask about Hinduism … and ten terrific answers' the authors try to answer the question why women wear a dot in the middle of their forehead:

> Do not be ashamed to wear the bindi on your forehead in the United States, Canada, Europe or any country of the world. Wear it proudly … . The sacred forehead dot is an easy way of distinguishing Hindus from Muslims.

Another boundary the groups try to establish is between 'Hindus' and pan-ethnic groups. HSGs in the US mirror the UK group's denial of an Asian/South Asian entity by objecting to the British usage of the term 'Asian' when referring to the race riots of 2001 in Northern England. In the words of the author of an article on the Hindus in the UK on the US HSG website:

> For example, in 2001 there were major riots in parts of North England between Pakistani/Bangladeshi and white communities. This incident was described by the media as 'Asian' vs. white, although there were no Hindus involved. Many Hindus have now rejected the term 'Asian', but that leaves a question as to what our identity is. Are we Indian? But most of us were born in the UK and our parents in East Africa or Fiji,

> Guyana, Trinidad etc. The links to India seem to be distant in this respect. To resolve this there has been an assertion of a new term – British Hindu, which National Hindu Students Forum (NHSF) is actively promoting – the theme of the 2002 Annual Conference being 'Be British, Be Hindu'.

The UK websites constantly highlight a sense of pride in their identity as 'Hindu' vs 'Asian' or 'African.' Interestingly, a vital factor in the construction of this Hindu culture was the construction of the 'modern' Hindu woman who was as successful as men at every level, in terms of class and accomplishment. In the words of one of the leaders of the UK HSG, 'Hindu women do not hide behind the purdah and are no longer subject to forced marriages. Hindu women have been successful in every field'.

Notably, the references to purdah – an ongoing theme in the writings of many Western feminists (e.g. Daly 1978, Okin 1999) and non-feminists – is used without any discussion of or challenge to the processes of racialization. Instead, the attempt is to separate 'Hindus' from the groups that are considered to be the actual political pariahs. The events that followed 9/11 and the 7/7 London bombings have also provided HSGs in the USA and the UK with abundant reasons to further disparage the 'Asian/ South Asian' label. The websites highlight that in the wake of the terrorist events the majority of Americans and British perceive all Asians as a single ethnic entity and cannot always distinguish between Muslims and non-Muslims.

HSGs in the USA and the UK are rallying their (considerable) forces to underline the distinction between Hinduism and Islam. A conference entitled 'British Hindus and the War on Terror' by the UK HSG was intended to 'discuss values of justice, tolerance and respect for all regardless of race, religion or creed just as passionately as some groups believe in fanatical hatred'. On 26 September 2001, only weeks after 9/11, the US HSG launched the Dharma Life Project 'to bring the powerful messages of the sages of Sanatana Dharma (Hinduism) to students and youth'. The website states, 'these universal messages find extreme relevance and importance during a time when peace, harmony and protection are the things that the world is aspiring most'. Notably this rhetoric once again focuses on the feminine principle innate in the Hindu religion to demonstrate that tolerance is one of the central tenets of Hinduism. The feminine principle is used to methodically define the Hindu entity as non-violent, tolerant, progressive in its thinking. This strategy is encapsulated in an article on the website of the US HSG's Hindu Women's Universe project:

> If the feminine qualities of the divine were recognized some of the evils which have occurred in the name of God would not have happened.

(b) Separation from Western culture

The websites highlight the continual denigration of Hindus and Hindu women by the academia, Christian evangelists and the Western media. They argue that it is Western thinking (often anti-Hindu) that speaks for women from non-Western cultures/ ideologies, resulting in Hindu-bashing at human rights seminars, feminist events, religious and social studies conferences. Presenting such misconceptions on the US HSG national website, the author argues, '"Caste, Cows and Curry" or "Women oppressed in Hinduism"' theme is predominant'. The discourse is also very critical of the Western exploitation of Hindu imagery and symbolism for commercial purposes, vociferously protesting against Western designers derogating their deities by using them as a motif on 'demeaning' articles like lingerie or bottled beer.

Thus, the websites call for the need to establish a forum where *Hindus* can find a voice of their own – a forum where Hindu women can interact, discuss issues important to them and project their own unique perspectives, rather than accept ideologies that have been forced upon them. The Hindu Women Project, launched by the US HSG had modest beginnings as a discussion forum, the 'Hindu Women Talk Net', which was popular enough to be housed in its own website.

The discourse emphasizes that Hindu women must safeguard against negative Western influences. The 'new Hindu woman' is one who has successfully done so and who has thereby intrepidly protected the sanctum sanctorum of the Hinduism she symbolizes. Thus, the 'strong, modern, Hindu woman' rhetoric within the 'model minority' rhetoric is astutely positioned alongside the more traditional discourse, which argues that feminine power is only acceptable if chastity and virtue remain important norms. The US HSG national website quotes the views of ISCKON on women:

> What have 'equal rights' and 'high profiles' brought woman anyway? Exploitation, broken marriages, an animalistic chain of uncaring sexual partners, abortion, children bereft of parental love, and above all, no time for Krsna [God] consciousness. (*Back to Godhead Magazine*, March/April 1991, p. 53)

Thus, this strong new Hindu woman is the antithesis of the Westernized feminist woman who does not fit the prototype and is consequently morally inferior, sexually promiscuous and seduced by a career to the detriment of her family and home. Interestingly, there are no objections to the new Hindu woman working outside the home, as long as her priority lies in fulfilling her familial obligations, without allowing 'polluting' Westernized influences – such as career-mindedness, feminism and sexuality – to encroach on the sanctity of the Hindu family.

Segregated spheres

The focus of the 2004 UK HSG national conference in London was to examine the shifting role of British Hindu women, focusing on women's traditional role in Vedic society. According to the speaker:

> Throughout the many years of the Vedic culture, women were given the highest level of respect and freedom, but they were also protected by the men. Women need protection, not because they are weak, but because they are so precious and so delicate, they should be protected like children … .

The issue of 'protection' became progressively more evident (and complex) toward the latter part of the conference, when an interesting event took place. The entire female body of the audience was requested to move to the back of the conference hall, as a member of the Swaminarayan sect was going to address the audience.[7] When later asked about his views on this incident, one of the leader's remarked:

> I have a lot of Swaminarayan friends. I am not a Swaminarayan myself, but … I know all the swamis at the Swaminarayan temple, including the one who spoke. If you ask him 'Why do you have to divert your eyes from women?' I like his argument … . In Islam, women have been asked to cover themselves; however, in Hinduism, and the Swaminarayan philosophy in particular, they say that we are not going to ask women to cover themselves, we will divert our eyes. Thus, we will not inconvenience women by asking

> them to dress a certain way, but we will inconvenience ourselves by not looking at them … it is extremely difficult for them to avoid looking at women, you know. So it is more challenging for them, because they have to follow the Swaminarayan philosophy.

Thus, while the separation of sexes is intended to safeguard both genders from sexual temptation, the leader explains that it does not imply female inferiority in any form.

Similarly, other websites argue that there is much criticism surrounding a verse in the Manusmriti[8] in which it is said that a woman requires lifelong protection. They highlight that it is common knowledge that women are vulnerable to attacks by 'males with evil propensities', which is why Manusmriti imposed the obligation of protecting young girls and women on their fathers, husbands and sons respectively. In response to the criticism surrounding Manusmriti, the US National HSG quotes British author Kerry Brown:

> In Hinduism a woman is looked after not because she is inferior or incapable but, on the contrary, because she is treasured. She is the pride and power of the society…No extra burden of earning a living should be placed on women who already bear huge responsibilities in society: childbirth, childcare, domestic well-being and spiritual growth. She is the transmitter of culture to her children.

This adds a new dimension to gender 'equality'. Equality means an affirmation of the differences between men and women and of their corresponding roles that are aligned to these differences.

This view is echoed by the authors of a handout that was distributed at the 2004 UK HSG national conference, titled 'Changing Role of Hindu Women: Struggles, Responsibilities and the Future'. The authors validate their view by quoting Swami Vivekananda:

> Any attempt to modernize our women, if it tries to take [them] away from [the] ideal of Sita, is immediately a failure … .

In Hinduism, the legendary figure of Sita is believed to embody the virtues of the 'ideal' woman, where 'virtue' primarily amounts being a 'good' Hindu wife. The rhetoric reiterates that men and women are indeed different, but these are positive differences that must be honoured, protected and reinforced. A US HSG quotes Swami Harshananda:

> Thus, in this respect she enjoys equal freedom with man … . However, the fact that she differs from man both biologically and psychologically, has not been overlooked … . The perfect housewife is the ideal presented before the Hindu woman. She is the personification of the ideal wife, friend and mother, all rolled into one. Thus, she complements man. But, at home, she plays the major role.

Finally, the ideals of female virtue and chastity are embedded within the discourse of the harmonious Hindu family through the concept of Vasudhaiva Kutumbhkam (one world family).[9] What is less obvious is that this is also the central tenet in the social structure, where gender roles are the core focus. Therefore, while it is the chaste, uncorrupted family that universal Hinduism seeks to preserve, the onus of preserving this sanctity lies with the women. In an article published on the US HSG, the author states:

> Women should take work outside as an extension of their family, to project their care, goodwill and organizing ability to a larger family. Does not our age-old Indian saying

describe 'Vasudhaiva Kutumbhkam' – the whole world as our family? It is easier for woman to feel this as she is the creator.

The contents of the 2004 UK HSG annual conference kit included a speech delivered in 1980 by a renowned Hindu sage. It asserted that in contemporary society of nuclear families women are only truly liberated when they return to the natural scheme of things dictated by their dharma instead of being seduced by careers and worldly ambitions: 'A mother's place is within the home and not out in the world working. This is the great power held by the mother and by no one else'.

The web page of the US HSG's Dharma Life Project quotes the same swami, echoing the same message: the mother alone holds the power to preserve and strengthen family bonds.

> It is … a proven fact that nearly all parents who mistreat their children were themselves mistreated by their parents. Unless mothers care and love their children, society will inherit an entire generation of frustrated adults who were once frustrated children.

The authors of the webpage elaborate on this message:

> … an in-depth study of the family system in India is sure to show that it is the women who by playing their role in the capacity of wife, mother, sister, sister-in-law, grandmother, etc. was able to protect and preserve our cultural values despite the many invasions and acts of destruction that went [on] through India.

Thus, the global dharma has ordained a woman to be a devoted sister, a committed bride, a devoted wife, a selfless mother and a dutiful daughter-in-law, among similar roles. The more dutiful a woman, the stronger her power to keep the family unit intact, creating harmony and prosperity in the household, which contributes to the welfare of the community, leading to the prosperity of the nation. If, however, she falls short of these duties, she loses her power, thereby dooming herself, her family and her community.

Reflections on the construction of 'strong' Hindu women

Overall, these websites show that the 'strong woman' discourse is consistently deployed to emphasize the superiority of Hindus, while it is infused with patriarchal notions that subject women to various forms of control in the name of tradition and culture. It is difficult to grasp this apparent contradiction if we only consider women *qua* women without any reference to the ways in which structures of racism intersect with structures of gender (Purkayastha and Narayan 2009). The HSGs are using the concept of 'ethnic pride' and the notion of the group's distinctiveness through their discourse on gender equality. Set against the structural racism they encounter and the ideologies about their inferior cultures and religions in their daily lives (Narayan and Purkayastha 2009), these groups challenge stigmatized aspects of their culture by drawing attention to selected facets of their group. Since the supposedly inferior position of women, especially through religious ideologies and practice, is the key symbol of their denigration, this emphasis on strong women challenges such racialization. This strategy attracts members who are looking for ways to collectively construct a positive cultural identity that is directly opposed to the negative racial categorization of their cultures (Purkayastha 2005, Kurien 2004, Rajagopal 2000).

Along with the assertion of religio-cultural nationalism and ethnic pride, as predicted by scholars such as Kabeer (2002) and Yuval Davis (1997), the data indicates that gender inequalities in ethnic communities do not reflect prior gender ideologies and norms alone. In fact the deployment of feminine symbols of power by these organizations is actually grounded in accurate reflection of Hinduism, establishing the need to move beyond assumptions used in the recent literature that traditions – participation in rooted ways of life that mitigate individual empowerment – are deeply ingrained in immigrants who reproduce traditions in modern host countries (Ebaugh and Chafetz 1999, Okin 1999).

However, what is being violated in these web-based discussions of 'strong women' and 'equality' is evident through the depiction of where the strong women are supposed to be confined. The web-discourses talk about Durga/Kali, but erase their independent status by their repeated emphasis on a clear separation of male and female roles and the ideal 'traditional' family. There is an insistence on roles of women as good mothers and wives and women are perceived as guardians of the good old ways reclaiming the former glories of ancient Hinduism.[10] The strong overtones of sexuality encapsulated in Kali (and the tantric traditions through which Kali became codified as a goddess), and the veneration of power of Durga without any reference to her husband Shiva, are also totally erased in these discussions.

These reconstructed discourses emphasize a version of Hinduism as 'the' version of Hinduism. By erasing the diversity within Hinduism, such ideologies attempt to centralize power to define the religion, in the hands of a few, in a centralized way.[11] Even though scholars such as Ebaugh and Chafetz (1999) concluded from their study of temples in Atlanta that the presence of a few females on temple executive boards was a sign of new gender emancipation (resulting from assimilation into American ways), paying attention to the websites indicate that the opposite is true. New gender hierarchies are being re-inscribed in the USA and UK, as the makers of these websites seek to become the voices that define Hinduism and women's position within this religion.

Reflections on feminist theories on religion

Our research leads us to two main conclusions about theorizing on religion. First, most scholars tend to build theories about ethnic religions without interrogating the assimilationist, Christianity-centred bases of their theories. Instead, we argue that theories of religions need to seriously integrate an intersectional approach that looks at religions as dynamic entities whose ideologies and practices emerge in response to socio-historical conditions. Equally important, such theories have to move away from the assumptions about ideologies of inferiority of women/females in other religions. Instead, more nuanced theories should be able to document and acknowledge the co-presence of strong/empowered women ideologies and subordinated women ideologies in religions and focus on the conditions under which such ideologies are translated into practice and the reasons for doing so. Such an approach would bring discussions of racism (and other axes of subordination) centrally into discussions of gendered ideologies of religions. The case described here shows that mainstream feminism is complicit in the construction of controlling (racialized) ideologies about Hindu groups with the constant emphasis on subordinated women (and by implication predatory men). A serious intersectional approach, which includes self-reflection on the effect of mainstream Western feminism, would help to develop more valid theories about religions; it is important to examine who has the power to define the social situation (Katzenstein 1998).

Equally important, contemporary scholarship needs to seriously consider the porous nature of the 'real' and 'virtual' social spaces in which religious ideologies are being created. Thus there is a need to break away from the idea that religions are practiced in 'churches', and ideas about religions are mostly kept alive through congregation-members. Websites indicate a wider sphere of religious endeavour and indicate the need to conceptualize a wider diffuse audience (instead of membership) of such religious ideologies. We argue that there is a need for breaking out of Semitic religion framework to unlock the puzzle of how diverse, diffuse, dispersed religious groups with very significant variations of gender regimes are transformed into homogenized and centralized forms of religious communities. Homogenization, centralization of power, within socio-historical contexts that demand sharply demarcated identities, are key factors for understanding the gendering/racialization of religions.

Overall, this study indicates the need to reflect the diversity of religious practices instead of assuming that the all religions are organized by the same principles. Second, it needs to consider the nature of modern host societies and structures of racialization, to understand the construction of power relations in ethnic communities in ways that create new gender distinctions, instead of assuming traditional ethnic women become modernized in the West. Women become subjects of extra scrutiny precisely because the groups that are able to rise to power in the new structural circumstances are more patriarchal. Third, religious ideologies are now being created through web-based social spaces, with the ability to reach geographically dispersed, transnational audiences. The processes on the web only partially resemble what happens in churches and other politically demarcated religious spaces; tracking these 'new' processes are important to deepening feminist theorizations of religions and religious ideologies.

Notes

1. Popularized by Partha Chatterjee (1993) in his discussion about the question of women's status within the nationalist movement in India, this term, continues to be an important indicator of the discussion and framing of women within movements.
2. When we focus primarily on what happens in tangible spaces we often assume that small numbers translate to smaller effect unless a group has significant amounts of money and power to bend others to their will. When we study the web, the relative size of the group is less relevant, nor is the issue about money per se, since technical expertise to develop websites that rise in search engine rankings is the source of the power to reach significant numbers of people.
3. We also conducted six semi-structured interviews with the leaders of the national organizations and leaders from a small sub-set of chapter organizations. Additional data was collected by participating in the annual conferences of both organizations. A methodological challenge of studying websites is that the discourse changes with time and therefore we consider this as data at a specific point time. A detailed description of the methodology is available in Narayan (2006).
4. As Purkayastha has described elsewhere (2009), in Hindu mythology, Durga is the embodiment of strength and power. According to a legend when one particular *asur* (demon) got too strong for the male gods they collectively appealed to Durga to vanquish the demon. They showered her with their most potent weapons and she left to confront the evil force that was overpowering the gods. The form of Durga that is worshipped in Bengal represents this tableaux: Durga, standing on her attendant lion, her ten hands carrying different weapons, with the virile Asur, who has partly emerged from the body of a buffalo, pinned down by the force of her trident, semi-prone at her feet. This tableaux also shows Durga's children: Lakshmi the goddess of wealth, Saraswati the goddess of learning, Kartik the god of war,

and Ganesh, the god of benevolence. In other regions Durga could be seated on a tiger, with or without the demon, with or without her children. Kali is the dark naked goddess, who is worshipped with a garland of skulls around her neck, standing on a male god, Shiva associated with the Tantra tradition. Kali has become 'the' patron goddess of Bengal. Her temple in Kolkata is one of the significant points of pilgrimage for Hindus. Kali also represents strength, power of a more fierce, unrestricted variety than Durga's power. She is depicted as a female without 'family connections' that are associated with Durga.

5. Lakshmi is the Hindu goddess of wealth and prosperity and Saraswati is the Hindu goddess of knowledge, music, and art. They exercise their own independent mandate as goddesses with specific functional domains.
6. As a foundling discovered in a ploughed field, Sita is regarded as the daughter of the Earth. She willingly follows Ram into exile, where she is abducted by Ravana. After her rescue, when Ram has misgivings about her virtue, she readily undergoes an agni pariksha (trial by fire) that attests her purity. While the Ramayana is essentially about the cosmic struggle between good and evil (symbolized by the hero Ram and the demon Ravana), Sita reinforces her husband's morality with her devotion, intelligence, and strength and symbolizes wifely duty and devotion.
7. The Swaminarayan sect is committed to a stringent ethical code that demands institutional segregation of the genders. Women and men worship separately at the temple and women are barred from contact with religious specialists and gurus.
8. The Manusmriti (Laws of Manu) is a discourse on the 'law of social classes' by the sage Manu, believed to be composed between 200 BCE and 200 CE when the caste system was prevalent in India. While it is a valuable source for sociological, historical and political studies, it has drawn heavy criticism from Hindu reformists, and feminists for casteism and gender discrimination and for justifying oppression of the weak. Its position on women has especially been debated. While some sections treat women with scorn and suspicion, reducing them to little more than domestic menial workers, others glorify women and urge their protection.
9. The concept of Vasudhaiva Kutumbhkam uses the family metaphor at a micro and macro level, visualizing the community, society and the universe as a close-knit familial unit.
10. In our larger study we found that themes of gender superiority co-occurs the most with the category history and scriptures, gods and gurus (the websites list several gurus and their organizations, presenting these masters as guardians of Hindu spiritual and social values), world religion (Hinduism is not merely as a religion practiced by people in India, but as a world religion) and universal applicability (Hinduism as Sanatana Dharma (Eternal Tradition), not confined to the tenets of any particular group, class of people, or form of worship).
11. Our larger research also shows that the websites link to each other and repeat, most often, the discourse of right-wing Hindu groups that built a significant web presence.

Notes on contributors

Anjana Narayan is an Assistant Professor at California State Polytechnic University Pomona. Her areas of interest are ethnicity, migration, and gender. She is the co-author of *Living our Religions: Hindu and Muslim South Asian-American Women Narrate Their Experiences* (Kumarian Press 2009). She is a recipient of the American Sociological Association Section on Asia and Asian America 2010 'Early Career Award'. She also has a postgraduate degree in Social Work from the Tata Institute of Social Sciences (TISS), Mumbai (India). She was associated with a range of innovative initiatives in the field of women and development in India.

Bandana Purkayastha is an Associate Professor of Sociology and Asian American Studies at the University of Connecticut. Her current research and publications focus on the intersection of racialized ethnicity, gender and class. She has published several book chapters and articles on multiple marginalities that affect Asian American women. She is the author of *Negotiating Ethnicity – Second Generation South Asian Americans Traverse a Transnational World* (2005), and the co-author of *Living our Religions: Hindu and Muslim South Asian-American Women Narrate Their Experiences* (2009). She has won several awards including University of Connecticut Women of Color Award for Excellence in Leadership, Achievement, and Service.

References

Ahmed, D., 2002. *Gendering the spirit: women, religion and the postcolonial response.* London: Zed Books.

Andersen, M., 2005. *Thinking about women: sociological perspectives on sex and gender.* 7th ed. Boston, MA: Allyn and Bacon.

Anthias, F. and Yuval-Davis, N., 1989. *Woman, nation, state.* Basingstoke, UK: Macmillan.

Chafetz, J. and Dworkin, G., 1986. *Female revolt.* Totowa, NJ: Rowman and Allenheld.

Chatterjee, P., 1993. *The Nation and its fragments: colonial and post colonial histories.* Princeton, NJ: Princeton University Press.

Daly, M., 1978. *Gyn/ecology: the metaethics of radical feminism.* Boston, MA: Beacon Press.

Das Gupta, M., 1997. What is Indian about you? A gendered transnational approach to ethnicity. *Gender and Society,* 11 (5), 572–596.

Dasgupta, S.D. and Dasgupta, S., 1996. Women in exile: gender relations in the Asian Indian community in the U.S. *In:* S. Maira and R. Srikanth, eds. *Contours of the heart.* New York: Rutgers University Press, 324–337.

Diamandaki, K., 2003. Virtual ethnicity and digital diasporas: identity construction in cyberspace. *Global Media Journal* [online]. Available from http://lass.calumet.purdue.edu/cca/gmj/sp03/graduatesp03/gmj-sp03grad-diamandaki.htm [Accessed 15 June 2010].

Earl, J., 2006. Pursuing social change online: the use of four protest tactics on the Internet. *Social Science Computer Review,* 24 (3), 362–377.

Ebaugh, R. and Chafetz, J., 1999. Agents for cultural reproduction and structural change: the ironic role of women in immigrant religious institutions. *Social Forces,* 78(2), 585–613.

Ebaugh, R. and Chafetz, J., 2000. *Religion and the new immigrants: continuities and adaptations in immigrant congregations.* Walnut Creek, CA: Altamira Press.

Howard, P., 2006. *New media campaigns and the managed citizen.* New York: Cambridge University Press.

Ignacio, E., 2005. *Building diaspora: Filipino community formation on the Internet.* New Brunswick, NJ: Rutgers University Press.

Kabeer, N., 2002. *The power to choose: Bangladeshi women and labor market decisions in London and Dhaka.* London: Verso.

Katzenstein, M., 1995. Discursive politics and feminist activism in the Catholic church. *In*: M. Ferree and P. Martin, eds. *Feminist organizations: harvest of the new women's movements.* Philadelphia, PA: Temple University Press, 28–35.

Katzenstein, M., 1998 *Faithful and fearless: moving feminist protest inside church and military.* Princeton, NJ: Princeton University Press.

Kumar, R., 1993. *A history of doing.* London: Verso.

Kurien, P., 1999. Gendered ethnicity: creating a Hindu Indian identity in the United States. *American Behavioral Scientist,* 42 (4), 648–670.

Kurien, P., 2004. Multiculturalism, immigrant religion, and diasporic nationalism: the development of an American Hinduism. *Social Problems,* 51 (3), 362–385.

Kurien, P., 2005. Being young, brown, and Hindu: the identity struggles of second-generation Indian Americans. *Journal of Contemporary Ethnography,* 34 (4) 434–469.

MacFayden, L., 2006. Virtual ethnicity: the new digitization of place, body, language, and memory. *Electronic Magazine of Multicultural Eductation* [online]. Available from http://www.eastern.edu/publications/emme/2006Spring/macfadyen.pdf [Accessed 15 June 2010].

Mitra, R. and Gajjala, R., 2008. Queer blogging in Indian digital diasporas: a dialogic. *Journal of Communication Inquiry,* 32, 400–423.

Narayan, A. (2006) *Ethnic organizations and ethnic identities: the use of websites for creating transnational gendered identities.* Dissertation (PhD), University of Connecticut.

Narayan, A. and Purkayastha, B., 2009. *Living our religions: Hindu and Muslim South Asian-American women narrate their experiences.* Stirling, NC: Kumarian Books.

Narayan, A., Purkayastha, B., and Banerjee, S., forthcoming. Constructing transnational identities: a study of the discourse and networks of ethnic student organisations in the US and UK. *Journal of Intercultural Studies.*

Okin, S.M., 1999. Is multiculturalism bad for women? *In:* J. Cohen, M. Howard and M. Nussbaum, eds. *Is multiculturalism bad for women?* Princeton, NJ: Princeton University Press, 7–24.

Pudrovska, T. and Ferree, M.M., 2004. Global activism in 'virtual space': the European women's lobby in the network of transnational women's NGOs on the web. *Social Politics: International Studies in Gender, State and Society,* 11 (1), 117–143

Purkayastha, B., 2005. *Negotiating ethnicity: second-generation South Asian Americans traverse a transitional world.* New Brunswick, NJ: Rutgers University Press.

Purkayastha, B., 2008. Beyond the private-public, sacred-secular divide. *In:* A. Narayan and B. Purkayastha, eds. *Living our religions: Hindu and Muslim South Asian American women narrate their experiences.* Stirling, NC: Kumarian Books, 23–46.

Purkayastha, B., 2009. Transgressing the sacred–secular, private–public divide. *In:* A. Narayan and B. Purkayastha, *Living our religions: Hindu and Muslim South Asian working women narrate their experiences.* Stirling, NC: Kumarian Books.

Purkayastha, B. and Narayan, A., 2009. Bridges and chasms: orientalism and the making of Indian Americans in New England. *In:* M. Chiu, ed. *Asian Americans in New England.* Durham, NH: New England University Press, 124–149.

Rajagopal, A., 2000. Hindu nationalism in the US: changing configurations of political practice. *Ethnic and Racial Studies,* 23 (3), 467–496.

Saha, M., 2008. Red, bulls, and tea: cultural hashing of a 1.5er (a.k.a. second-generation reflections). *In:* A. Narayan and B. Purkayastha, eds. *Living our religions: Hindu and Muslim South Asian American women narrate their experiences.* Stirling, NC: Kumarian Books, 129–145.

Saxena, N., 2004. *In the beginning is desire: tracing Kali's footprints in Indian literature.* Delhi: Indialog Books.

Yang, F. and Ebaugh, R., 2001. Transformations in new immigrant religions and their global implications. *American Sociological Review,* 66, 269–288.

Yuval-Davis, N., 1997. *Women and nation.* London: Sage.

Zia, A., 2009. The reinvention of feminism in Pakistan. *Feminist review,* 91 (1), 29–46.

From the fringes of the diasporic garment: creative pageants of Indian Christian identity from Malaysia and Singapore

Shanthini Pillai and Sharenee Philomena Paramasivam

School of Language Studies & Linguistics, National University of Malaysia, Malaysia

There is no denying the great power invested in the inventiveness of the diasporic imaginary to reterritorialize Indian culture-scapes into local contexts. Malaysian and Singaporean Indian diasporic writers are no exception. For a long while, the tendency of most discussions of writings from these countries has been to focus on the syncretism of identity politics of a mainly Hindu experience. Yet, the Indian diaspora in Malaysia and Singapore consists also of those who are Christians. Would there be different modulations to the tones, inflections of the diasporic experience when the creative imaginary intersects and negotiates with the Christian, the Indian as well as the Malaysian and Singaporean experience? Would the attendant myths and metaphors also take on different characteristics as a result? These are issues that this paper aims to investigate through a study of selected writings from Malaysia and Singapore that reflect nuances of an Indian Christian heritage. The ultimate aim of the paper is to highlight the reterritorialization of the Indian self from a community that has remained on the fringes of the garment of discussions about writings from the Malaysian and Singaporean diasporic Indian community.

Introduction

Steven Vertovec has recently commented that while theoretical formulations of the subject of diaspora have engaged with many new dimensions, the aspect of religion has remained largely at the margins (2009, p. 132). This is indeed true as ethnicity, cultural conflicts and the road to nationhood and multiculturalism have often remained the centre of most discussions of the diaspora, and the Indian diaspora is no exception. In the moments when religious aspects do appear at the heart of a discussion of this community, the tendency is to focus on the identity politics of a mainly Hindu experience (p. 1). However, this denies the heterogeneity of the Indian diaspora as there are also communities of other religious beliefs, such as the Jains, the Muslims and the Christians who occupy this common diasporic space. If we were to extrapolate the lived experiences of such communities, we might in all probability witness common cultural echoes in aspects such as clothing, food and language. However, if one were to pay closer attention, different tones and rhythms will become apparent as there will be different trajectories to this diasporic experience when it emerges from different religious ensembles. The Indian-Christian diaspora is no exception. As Jacobsen and Raj (2008) point out:

> Christian immigrants from diverse ethnic, linguistic and cultural backgrounds have largely been overlooked by academics. Consequently, this important constituency has largely been a silent and invisible community, underrepresented in scholarly literature and public academic discourses … diaspora studies and scholarship on South Asia ought to truly represent and mirror the true complexion and the rich internal plurality and diversity of the South Asian religious landscape. (p. 1)

Most discussions of Indian diasporic fiction too are more often than not pivoted on the Hindu or Vedic myths and metaphors. What about the Indian-Christian experience? Would there be different modulations to the tones, inflections of the diasporic experience when the creative imaginary intersects and negotiates with the Christian? Would the attendant myths and metaphors also take on different characteristics as a result? This paper chooses to investigate this issue by focusing on the Malaysian and Singaporean Indian-Christian experience that has remained largely on the fringes of the garment of discussions about diasporic Indian writings from the region.

Christianity in the Indian historical context

The spread of Christianity in India is generally believed to be linked to Western missionary proselytization during the age of imperialism through the Portuguese, the Dutch and the British. Because of this link to the conquistador races, those among the Indian community have been conceived as aligning themselves to and abetting with the imperial force and thus betraying their own. According to De Mendonca (2002), 'The missionaries believed that to increase the number of converts it was urgent and absolutely necessary to help the Christians and disfavour the Hindus' (p. 161). He also notes that this method, while proving to be beneficial for the Christian converts, also had adverse effects. For instance, he cites accounts of governmental jobs and tax evasion that privileged the Christian community. It is also worthy to note that the methods of conversion that were instigated by imperial forces might have played a role in intensifying conflict between Christians and Hindus in India. Ludden (1985) remarks that communities that underwent conversion would deface and in some cases destroy temple idols and places of worship. Churches were then built upon the rubble of shattered Hindu worship sites by these new converts:

> Village after village of Shanars converted to Christianity, and many converts celebrated their rejection of the rituals that constituted their subordination by tearing down temple idols, making churches where Hindu gods has reigned. (p. 192)

Ludden further adds that missionaries supported the actions of these converts and saw this method of conversion as a means to rid the country of its pagan practices and instil a brand new, civilized religion. This disrespectful action, one can speculate, could have ignited strong animosity and discontent toward the new converts, because of the partiality that they received from the imperial race. All these various acts would have been the catalyst for the label 'traitor' that came to be associated with all Christian converts regardless of whether they participated in such acts or not. Conversion thus became a marker of betrayal towards the nation. This placed the new converts within an unfavourable position by other religious groups. With the rise in nationalistic fervour Indian Christians became caught within situations that were rather violent. There are many records of episodes where converts were forcefully humiliated and embarrassed by those of Hindu faith if they did not rescind and return to Hinduism

(Oddie 2001, p. 162). Frykenberg (2010) writes that 'A local *zamindar* arrived in his palanquin accompanied by troops of *lathi-wallahs* to whom he gave orders to demolish Christian buildings, appropriate belongings, and drive converts into the jungle to be "hunted like wild beast"', Frykenberg goes on to cite George Pettitt of 'The Vibuthi Sangam or "Sacred Ashes Society" …' which forced converts 'to swear, by the sacred ashes, that they will be true to the old religion and customs of the country and stand firm in their opposition to Christianity. The chief object is to insist upon every native continuing to smear his forehead with ashes, well knowing that compliance with this heathenist customs is in fact a ruination of the Gospel' (p. 277).

However, one should note that Indian Christians were also subjected to racial discrimination from the very people that urged them to convert. The Portuguese and the British, regardless of the propaganda put forth of their support for the converts, still treated the local Christian community as foreign and alien even though they practised the same religion. Imperial forces observed racial disparity within both the colonial administrative space and the Christian churches and missions. Oddie (2001) provides accounts of Indian ministers and missionaries that were denied the opportunity to serve a congregation and upon graduation were offered lowly jobs that were in many cases unrelated to the church and its services. These principle positions remained more often than not occupied by Western missionaries. In many instances, Indian-Christian priests who rebelled and demanded for more responsibility were sent away from the diocese. For instance, there was, 'the case of Lal Behari Day who started a movement against the exclusive missionary control of the church and who was sent upcountry after advocating that Indian-ordained ministers should be put on an equal footing with the missionaries and have full membership of the Scottish Church Council' (Oddie 2001, p. 5). Lal Behari Day is one among many priests who fought for equality within the church ministry. From these personal accounts, it is apparent that within the gaze of the imperial forces local priests were perceived as incapable and untrustworthy to maintain a diocese. It became obvious that although these individuals were practising and evangelizing the same theological discourse, their race and place of origin still placed them on a lower strata within the church.

It then becomes apparent that these multiple historical accounts of the space inhabited by the Indian Christians was a space of conflict and uncertainty. They were associated with labels such as 'traitor', by fellow countrymen for taking up the 'enemy's' religion and betraying the country, and also for embracing Western ideals, all of which placed these individual in an unfavourable light within the native space. However, not all Indian Christians were the quintessential mimic men/women; there is record of many instances where Christianity was nativized by the local Indian community.

Interweaving India within the Christian apostolic garment

As Western discourse was being disseminated by most imperial evangelizing methods there were also other threads that were interwoven within the Indian-Christian apostolic garment, that reflected nativized shades as Christian doctrine met with and was interpellated with Indian culture and custom. For instance, in the early stages of Western colonial history in India, the Portuguese noted that because of what they term guidance, or the proper method of adhering to Christianity and its teaching, the Indian Christians had amalgamated Hindu systems into their own understanding of the Christian religion.

The Portuguese missionaries saw the importance of Indianization of Christian ideology not merely as a means to preach to the Indian Christians but to attain new converts within the country. If one were to read narratives on missionary work in India, there are multiple accounts of missionaries expressing the need for intermixing native Indian belief and customs with their evangelizing practices. One such example is the arrival of Jesuit priests who saw the need for cross cultural engagement and took the initiative to familiarize themselves with 'local languages, customs and ceremonial rites' (Daniel 1992, p. 25). For instance, the Jesuit priest Robert De Nobili saw the need for converting the Brahmin population as he believed that if this community embraced the faith they would be a crucial factor in influencing others from different social stratus or caste to follow suit.

Geoffrey Oddie speaks of the setting up of Christian *ashrams* throughout India, a practise that was commonly associated with the Hindu community. The *ashram*, as M.M Thomas and P.T Thomas define it, is 'A Hindu pattern of community living under a *guru*' (Oddie 2001, p. 354). Similarly, this method of existing and preaching within a community was taken up by Indian Christians, with the first Christian *ashram* being Christukula (Family of Christ) that was set up in Tiruppattur, Tamilnadu in 1921. The basis of this Christian *ashram* was built on the guru being Jesus Christ. Oddie goes on to report that:

> The specific nature and purpose of Christian *ashrams* which were founded in increasing numbers during the period from 1921 to independence varied considerably. Many were founded by European priests or missionaries and Indian Christians working in collaboration, with the idea that the *ashram* would demonstrate the social equality implicit in Christian teaching, including equality between races so conspicuously absent in Indo-European relations elsewhere. (2001, p. 354)

The importance of the *ashram*, denotes the cultivation of a space that routinely promoted the blending between Indian cultural values and practices within Christian doctrine. The *ashram* created a living community whose basis or foundation is rooted in Indian tradition, yet it is re-spatialized to include Christian theology.

The British became aware of the importance of this hybrid space after the famed (mutiny). For instance Sir Sayyid Ahmad Khan (Dirks 2001) remarked that the rebellion was instigated through a lack of understanding and respect that the church and its missionaries practised on its Indian subjects. He commented that the 'Government has not succeeded in acquainting itself with the daily habits, the modes of thought and of life, and likes, and dislikes, and prejudices of the people … passing of such laws and regulations forms of procedure as jarred with the established custom and practice of Hindustan' (Dirks 2001, p. 6). Sayyid makes reference to the importance of merging Indian customs and beliefs into Christian religious doctrine. He further asserted that British missionaries should practice such interlinking and assimilation within their evangelizing because it would first reach a wider demographic within India and also placate the masses that were discontent with the manner that religious freedom was treated within India.

Such nativizing practices began to gather full force when the spirit of nationalism came upon most Indians. Geoffrey Oddie writes that as the sun began to set on the British Empire in India, many converts felt the need to reassess and reclaim the cultural aspects of India. For instance, Oddie makes reference to 'attempts to further indigenize forms of worship, especially through the introduction of Indian styles of song and dance and by modifying European forms of religious architecture' (2001,

p. 354). All of this points to a strong sense of nationhood in the Indian-Christian community. The Indian-Christian congregation thus re-territorialized and made familiar sacred spaces thereby carving a nativized or Indianized Christian identity to which they could belong too.

With the advent of the British forces into India, it led to the creation of diasporic Indian communities throughout the globe as many were sent to work on the infrastructure and also to open plantations in various colonies governed by Britain. Similar aspects of nativization of Christianity can also be seen in these diasporic Indian communities throughout the globe and among these are the Indian-Christian communities in Malaysia and Singapore, which will be discussed in the next section.

Indian Christians in Malaysia and Singapore

The history of the Indian-Christian community in Malaysia and Singapore can be traced to the early 1800s. The significant denominations are Roman Catholic, Anglican and Protestant, with the majority being from the Roman Catholic Church. According to Thomas, Catholic missionary work developed soon after the arrival of the British in Penang, and culminated in the establishment of the East Asia Seminary, the first college for the training of Asian priests. Subsequently, the Cathedral of the Assumption in Penang was built. This coincided with the arrival of immigrants from South India recruited specifically to aid in the building of key infrastructure as well as in the agricultural sectors in the coffee and rubber plantations. Early missionary work concentrated mainly on the downtrodden labouring population, especially those who were victimized in the plantations and labour camps they were sent to. The East Asia Seminary was largely responsible for the spread of Christianity among this disenfranchised population as there were a number of student priests from the Tamil community who were able to reach out and 'to practice their evangelistic and missionary zeal by converting Tamil non-Christians to Catholicism' (Thomas 1978, pp. 94–96).

In contrast to the Catholic community, the Anglican Indian community in Malaya consisted of those who already belonged to the Anglican Church in India prior to their arrival in the country. In the early years, missionary work by the Anglican pastoral community was stronger in Singapore but in 1871, the European chaplain in Penang arranged for Royappan Balavendrum, a Cathechist from Tanjore to help build an Anglican parish among the Indian community in Penang. Because of ideological and racist practises of the age, Indian labourers were not permitted to worship together with the Europeans though it was Indian convict labour that was largely responsible for the construction of the first Anglican Church, St George's. This led to the setting up of a separate place of worship for non-Europeans behind the main church and the growth of the Anglican Indian-Christian community. Amid this racial strife, churches of various dominations began to be built progressively within the peninsular. In the early years, service was mainly conducted in Tamil or any one of the languages of the dominant group in a particular parish.

The practise of conducting sermons and the entire liturgy in these various languages, would have ultimately lead to the malleability of the sacramental discourse. This is because the language of the liturgy would have been appropriated by and interpellated with the various nuances of Indian linguistic and cultural practices thus nativizing Christian forms of worship. As the majority of the Indian

Christian community was from the South of India this would have made the Tamil language most predominant. This 'Indianization' of Christianity can best be described as a form of religious syncretism. However the perception of religious syncretism is often open to debate, when bound by the regulations of keeping to the fundamental grounds of Christian theology. Victor J. Vethamani speaks of the 'dangers of religious syncretism', arguing that the Indian Christian community needed to be able to 'distinguish between what is cultural and what is religious in their Indian/Tamil heritage', be aware of the dangers of 'participating in Hindu festivals, ceremonies and practises' and last that the church should 'take necessary action against those who persist in syncretism' (1987, p. 66). In direct contrast, we argue that religious syncretism is an integral part of the Indian-Christian consciousness and that this pervades in all areas of daily cultural practise, often reflecting a blend of values that are simultaneously Christian and Indian. We choose to see this as creative strategies through which the Indian Christian community is able to reterritorialize Christian experience into Indian culture-scapes. Daniel (1992) has written extensively about this aspect in a discussion of the cultural life of Indian Christians in Malaysia. Most significant is his exposition of ritual items, kinship terms, life cycle rites and family genealogy and socialization. With regards to the first, he speaks of the significance that is accorded to the *thali* either in the form of 'the golden necklate that is attached to the middle of a string with turmeric' or 'a gold chain' (p. 148). An even more significant strategy of syncretism can be seen though the amalgamation of Christian spiritual symbols embedded within the *thali*, such as the image of the crucifix, the Holy Mother and the Holy Spirit. Daniel (1992) also refers to the Indian cultural aspects retained in matrimonial talks amid Indian Christians, such as the exchange of the 'tambulam' a tray in which significantly symbolic cultural items such as the betel leaf and betel nut are placed. He also speaks of the retention of Tamil kinship terms by the community, such as the honorific's *appa* for father, *amma* for mother, *annan* for elder brother, *periappa* (father's elder brother), *chitappa* (father's younger brother), *anni* (sister-in-law) and *thanggai* (younger sister), among others (p. 156). Also significant is the fusion of Christian and Tamil names. Daniel (1992) speaks of the tendency for many Methodist and Anglican Indians to 'give three types of names which represent their genealogy, linguistic affiliation and a Biblical name' (p. 157), the examples cited are Kalavathy Hilda Daniel and Gnanadas Chandran Peter. We could also add the names Jeyamari Anthoniamal Ratnam and Chinnaiah Subrailu John Pillai as other examples. Also, common among the Indian Christian community is the nativizing of Biblical names, such as *Soosay* for Joseph, *Davidoo* for David and *Lourdesamy*, a Tamil variation of Lourdes, as well as the example cited above, Jeyamari and Anthoniamal, Indianized versions of Mary and Anthony. With regards to life cycle rites, Indian death ceremonial rites are often observed such as ensuring that a lamp or candle is kept aflame, the pouring of milk over the grave and the burning of incense (Daniel 1992, p. 154). Many Indian Christian families also ensure that parents or elders of the family play a central role in initiating and arranging marriage proposals, organize social gatherings for suitors and prospective brides as well as their families to meet and if successful, arrange an engagement ceremony. All these are conducted in similar manner as Hindu marriage related ceremonies, with the appropriation of Christian customs. For instance, the bride to be is often dressed in an engagement saree that is purchased by the family of the groom to be, that is subsequently blessed by either a local pastor or a priest. The groom's family would normally arrive at the residence of the bride to be complete with *tambulams* filled with gifts and other Indian cultural items such as bananas, coconuts and sweet *pannir* or rose water (Daniel 1992, p. 152).

While the above introduction has mainly concentrated on the peninsular of Malaysia, parallels can also be drawn with the founding of the community of Indian Christians in Singapore. It is common knowledge that Tamil convicts were mainly responsible for the building of the island's first church, St Andrews, completed in 1837. In 1856, William Humphrey, Chaplain of the East India Company raised his concern about the need for evangelism among the native Chinese and Tamil population and subsequently created a committee to engage a Chinese-Christian and Tamil-Christian Catechist for the respective local communities (Poon 2005a, p. 2). Humphrey's mode of evangelism rested on the following decree that he set down in a letter to the C.M.S Madras committee:

> From the little experience I have had of natives (Hindus), I judge, that, in order successfully to combat the vast influence which their vast and spacious sacred courts … their secret recesses, hallowed by many a tradition – if we would successfully compete with these, it must be, not to destroy but to transfer; not by despising or ridiculing the things which they hold so sacred, but by showing them a *more excellent way*; by providing hallowed fanes, with hallowing Services; and *putting such garb on our Religion, that they may at least not spurn it for its nakedness.* (Poon 2005a, p. 3)

The crux of the view presented above lies in the acknowledgement of the centrality of the Indian culture in the consciousness of the Tamil population and the strategy of subtle amalgamation of Christian theological discourse with the tenets of traditional customs. Some of the strategies that he outlined were, as in Malaya, the conducting of sermons in Tamil and also the incorporation of 'an organ with chanting; which is much more agreeable to Tamul [*sic*] rhythm than is the singing of Tamul hymns to English Psalm-tunes, by which sound and sense is often sacrificed to the metre' (p. 4). The last is extremely important on a number of levels, pointing as it does to the recognition and acceptance of difference within the church, the centring of local perception and identity and most significantly the commingling of biblical sacrament and Indian culture, influences that were to reach far into the future, among the Indian Christians in contemporary Malaysia and Singapore. This fusion of East and West can be read in the edifice of St Andrews in Singapore, which though built to model most nineteenth century English churches, contained fortified interior walls which were coated with building material procured from India mainly 'Madras *chunam* made from shell lime without sand; … whites of eggs and coarse sugar, or "jaggery" beaten together to form a sort of paste, and mixed with water in which the husks of coconuts had been steeped' (Poon 2005b). This combination of materials in the formation of the church could be read as a metaphor of the Indian-Christian consciousness, whereby the bedrock of Christianity is interpellated and cemented with significant Indian cultural items. Added to this is also the fact that the jaggery and the coconut are also central ingredients in Indian cuisine and this is another significant aspect in the lives of Indian Christians. As Ganguly puts it, 'the connection, we might even say conflation, of territorial and dietary matters underlines the intimacy among what we eat, how we belong and who we are. However, the connection is not merely metaphorical and synecdochical (as in the saying we are what we eat) it is substantive in so far as the materiality of social identities are given their most solid value in food' (2001,

p. 137). This, she contextualizes against Norbert Elias's concept of *habitus* which is the 'second nature or the forms of embodied social learning underwriting all attempts at subjective self-consciousness' (p. 117). This is especially significant to the Indian Christian context, where the intimacies of the Indian dietary fundamentals are integrated to the daily living practices and celebratory festivals such as Easter and Christmas. Christmas for instance is traditionally associated with the Western yuletide culinary fare of dishes such as the traditional roast and Christmas pudding. However, if one were to visit the homes of any number of Indian-Christian families in Malaysia and Singapore, one would most probably find dining tables laden with the traditional Indian palate of curry and rice, reflecting the habitus of the social identity of being Indian and simultaneously Christian. This latter aspect can be divined through glimpses of an altar within which would reside the picture of the Sacred Heart of Jesus, a Crucifix and figurines of Mother Mary, set aglow in the light of a burning candle.

Such reterritorializations of religion and culture are manifested in Indian Christian families to this very day and creative works by authors from this community can be a pathway to witnessing the minutiae of the pageant of Indian Christian identity politics. The following discussion will focus on a selection of such writings from Malaysia and Singapore, namely two novels, *Abraham's Promise* by Philip Jeyaretnam (Singapore), *Love's Treacherous Terrain* by Shobha Mano (Malaysia) and one short story, *The Kiss* by Malachi Edwin Vethaman (Malaysia).

Creative pageants of Indian Christian identity politics

Philip Jeyaretnam's (1995) *Abraham's Promise* revolves around Abraham and the interweaving of memories of relationships with his father Isaac, his sister Mercy, his wife Rani and his son Victor. Interspersed into this familial network is the complex attachment to Rose Chinappa, a friend of the family. All of these characters are Singaporean Indians grounded in the Christian faith. In each of the separate encounters between Abraham and the aforementioned characters, we witness the pageantry of the interpellation of Indian Christian identity politics as discussed in the section before.

In the first act of Jeyaretnam's testament of Abraham's story, it appears as if his existence is based on a Eurocentric Christian existence, grounded as he is in the scholarship and discourse of Latin, of what he asserts is the 'vehicle for the spread of the gospel' (p. 13). However, a mere two pages later, we witness the intertwining of Indian cultural tenets, through Abraham's recollection of his childhood and particularly the scene of him and his sister at dinner 'refusing to eat the rice and curry that mother had prepared' (p. 15). Immediately we are made aware of the cultural habitus of the Indian Christian family through their daily consumption of a predominantly ethnic palate. Though our first impression of Abraham and Mercy is this refusal to partake in the ethnic meal, it is interesting that years later, in the present, as an older Abraham partakes in yet another ethnic meal, this time in Singapore's Little India, as he bites into a *vadai*, his favourite Indian teatime snack, it immediately becomes a locust of personal memory as he is transported into a scene from his past, of 'another teatime … many years before, when *vadai* too was served' (p. 77) by his sister Mercy. As he tries to resist the pull of the memory, the very texture of the morsel transports him into the very arms of that which he is keen to shrug off, the tumultuous family past. This portal of memory presents an intricate array of socio-cultural details of the Tamil Christian community, reflecting many of the elements discussed in the previous section. This is especially significant in the recollections of encounters between Abraham's family, the Isaacs with the Chinappas, another Tamil Anglican family. At the centre of this is the close bond that he shares with Rose, the younger daughter of the Chinappas, which dates back to the time when both were choir members in the Anglican Church.

The interspersing of the Chinappas into the fabric of memory is sparked off by a letter from Rose that Abraham finds among his personal belongings. This letter is the first of many that are interpolated into the textual space and each plays a significant role in presenting the intermingling of a deep seated awareness and foundation in Tamil cultural identity and Christian ecumenism. Rose always concludes her letters on a note of their Christian fellowship, with variations ranging from 'May God bless your endeavours' (p. 25) 'May the Lord bless you Abraham' and 'May the Almighty bless you and guide you' (p. 59). However, within each space, we hear articulations of the cultural dialectics of Tamil identity, in Rose's fears on not being accepted as a Tamil daughter in law by her white British in-laws and her reference to mutual friends whose ethnicity is made evident from their Tamil names: 'It was wonderful to see Sushila again … . I also met George, her husband. He is dark, with thick eyebrows and bushy sideburns. … George's sister, Shantini, has married Sushi's brother, Joshua' (p. 26). This dialogical synthesis appears to be a characteristic of the novel, as we witness smooth transitions between Tamil and Christian identity markers. When Abraham's parents discuss serious issues, his father is described 'shifting into Tamil to make the point more strongly' (p. 34). Tamil kinship terms are also widely used in the novel when reference is made to the elders. Abraham's father is referred to as 'Appa' and his mother 'Amma'.

As discussed in the outset, Tamil Christian families observe many customs that were similarly observed by the Hindu community, one of which was the traditional Tamil cultural practise of arranging for prospective suitors to meet prospective brides, through a formal social introduction by either a family member or a close friend of the family. Such scenes are played out within the novel, with the most detailed being Mercy's first introduction to a prospective suitor, where we witness the dialectics of the intersections of Tamil Christian identity:

> Mother's sister had made contact through one of her own friends with a good Jaffna Tamil family, Methodists, who lived in Johore, across the Causeway. Their son, having entered the priesthood and taken charge of his first parish, was in search of a good Christian wife. … I was dressed in my Sunday best. … Mercy had been taken by Mother a few days before to find a new length of material for a sari. … Mother began to fuss and toil over her daughter's appearance: oiling and plaiting her hair, helping her to apply her makeup and, later, adjusting her sari. (p. 61)

Note the reference to Christian groundings, in the vocation of priesthood and the expectations of the good Christian wife and its subsequent intermingling with the cultural signifiers of Tamil identity (Good Jaffna Tamil family), the sleekly oiled and plaited tresses and the sari that must be worn with modest decorum. Likewise, the prospective suitor's mother is clad in a 'red sari', and presumably so is Abraham's mother. Almost every Indian woman character in the text is seen at one time or another clad in a sari. In one of Abraham's most vivid recollection of Rose he fantasises 'unwinding her sari' (p. 52). The men however appear at such social gatherings in their Western suits. Abraham is dressed in his 'Sunday best', the father of the prospective suitor, and the suitor himself are similarly clad in formal Western suits. It thus becomes increasingly evident that the Indian female body becomes the vessel of Tamil culture, swathed by the enfolding yarn of tradition and customs. However, in the younger generation of the Tamil Christian women, this yarn flutters in the winds of individual aspiration and catches at the emerging corners of liberation and modernity. Mercy ends up scalding the suitor with hot tea and instead of meekly apologizing, transgresses all form of cultural and feminine decorum by roaring with laughter at the sight of the screaming priest. The departure of the incensed guests is threaded through with Biblical allusions to Lot's wife and to Sodom and Gomorrah (p. 64), bearing witness to the rays of Christian consciousness that frequently illumine cultural space and the disavowal of Mercy's place in the scheme of both Christian and Indian sensibilities. This conflict within the younger Indian woman is best encapsulated in Rose's letters to Abraham. Both Rose and Mercy were sent to Colombo, the cultural homeland of their parents during the Japanese Occupation of Malaya to keep them safe from physical harm. The following excerpts depict the emerging intellectual aptitude in Mercy that Rose is cognizant of and which she fears might be stifled by traditional expectations of the Indian woman, of succumbing to the family pressure of keeping to the covenant of the good Indian Christian wife:

> *My thoughts, dear Abraham turned especially to Mercy. She is spirited and stubborn, for knowledge of qualities I must thank the time we spent together in Colombo. She proved herself very able in her studies there, and I was given to understand that the teacher of literature at the convent had the highest regard for her.*
>
> *I mention this, dear Abraham, because I am convinced that it would be a shame if she were not encouraged in her studies, or worse, discouraged or prevented from their continuance. I remember that you told me that she had not fussed, or shown any real anxiety, when your parents indicated that she had studied all she needed in order to become a good wife, but, Abraham, forgive me, you must learn that people, especially women, do not always express how they feel.* (p. 58, Italics original)

While the girls studied at a Christian mission school in Colombo, in the eyes of the family, it was predominantly a haven that would eventually return their daughters safely ensconced in their homes once again, in time for their venture into the arena of the good wife. However, as relayed in Rose's letters, the intersections between traditional Tamil and Christian expectations of gender roles, especially with regards to women, often leave little space for the articulation of individual aspirations. Rose escapes this when she marries Charles and migrates to England. Mercy however, when she eventually does get married, finds that the seemingly modern Indian Christian persona in her husband that is presented to her before the marriage is usurped by a traditionalist who allows his mother full reign over the household and consequently over his wife. Extremely distressed with the stifling circumstances of her marriage, Mercy takes her own life. However, moments before she does so, she appeals to her brother Abraham to understand and to protect her, perhaps even save her from her ordeal. This is relayed to us in the last conversation between the siblings: 'Annai, I can't stand it … he won't let me smoke … and his mother … keeps on and on and on about a baby' (p. 87). However, this outpouring of emotions is curtailed by Abraham's demand that she refrain from transgressing cultural norms by being disrespectful to her husband:

'You shouldn't talk like that, not about your husband' (p. 87). The last words that Mercy utters to her brother reveals an interesting dichotomy between tradition and modernity, for hemmed in by traditional expectations that seek only to stifle her very being, she in turn indicts her brother for breaking the covenant of protection that every male member of a Tamil cultural household partakes from birth: 'Annai you're my brother, my elder brother but you never look after me' (p. 87). Soon after, Mercy commits suicide, the act of penultimate sin in the eyes of Christians. As her father-in-law expresses to a dazed Isaac family 'Mercy has shamed us … she has killed herself' (p. 93). Yet, the church, we are told 'was sufficiently enlightened to accept the funeral', thus contravening the customary practise of denying those who commit this grievous sin a full church funeral service. Abraham appears to be the only one who feels anger at the tragic end of his sister's life and is even more incensed that to his family 'the dishonour bound up in Mercy's choice of death caused to them the profoundest pain' and that they insisted on 'shouldering their burden of humiliation without a word of anger against him who was the true cause' (p. 92). Added to this is his recognition of the denunciation that he sees in many of the congregation, epitomized in the scene where Rose's elder sister, Lily Chinappa half-heartedly extends her hand in condolence as 'her body seemed to back away, seemingly wary of contagion' (p. 92). Into this scene of the dissonant dialectics of a fundamentally Christian dilemma, we are reminded of the cultural identity of this group of mourners, through the depiction of the 'women who had accompanied the hearse, all of them clad in elegant saris and flimsy slippers'. Immediately we witness the reterritorializing of a mainly Christian experience into a Indian culture-scape, a synchronicity of custom and theological rites into the narrative space. However, there appears to be a sense of distance between the narratorial voice and the narrator as speaker, a technique that Jeyaretnam uses as he moves from third person narration to first-person narrations. Subramaniam, in a reading of the ideological stylistics in *Abraham's Promise*, speaks of this strategy as 'the viewing position' where 'the transitivity process reveals that all the propositions are determined by, and belong to, the narrator, Abraham … (of) how the narrator's mental processes embed processes, which have others in actor/agent position' and thus often reveals his 'reading and rationalising of other's thoughts, beliefs, and actions' (2008, p. 223). Abraham's view of the ladies reveals a scornful undertone, and can be linked to his awareness of the judgement that is passed on the manner of the passing of his sister. While Abraham clearly blames David for the death of his sister, Rose on the other hand includes him in this equation, though the manner in which she does so is grounded in Christian discourse, this time pointing to the need for repentance and forgiveness: 'Do not blame David. Still less yourself, Abraham … . Perhaps it was God's plan to remove her from a suffering she could not endure. Repentance and prayer are important but they should not consume your life' (Jeyaretnam 1995, pp. 94–95). The impact of her words on Abraham is colossal, as it strikes at the tenets of the tablet of his role as the elder brother, a role that Mercy herself had questioned in her last conversation. In a diatribe that fuses both the Indian and Christian principles, Abraham expresses his thoughts of her lack of responsibility to family and her breaching of the code of conduct of her role as the metaphorical ecclesiastic cleric in the verbal confessional box: 'The audacity! Writing from thousands of miles away, having long since abandoned her own family in Singapore, she dared to apportion blame, grant dispensation and offer encouragement like some distant deity' (p. 94). Soon after we see the introduction of Rani, who replaces Rose in Abraham's affections, and who he marries.

The meeting between Rani and Abraham is arranged by his parents, eager for him to settle down after the tragedy of Mercy's demise. The entrance of Rani into the narrative space is ensconced within the traditional Tamil setting of matrimonial initiation occasions:

> Rani emerged from the back of the house, accompanied by the tinkling of her bangles and of an anklet hung with tiny chimes. Her sari was a pleasant mix of greens, a stylised pattern of leaves and vines. As I stood up to greet her I caught a waft of her fragrance, sandalwood, yes, but mingled another scent that seemed to tickle me between the eyes. (p. 104)

Her depiction is accompanied with images of audible and visual splendour that are predominantly Indian and specifically traditionally feminine, traditional emblems of Indian womanhood in the bangles, the belled anklet, the ubiquitous sari and the scent of sandalwood. However, at the background of this cultural ensemble there is a perceptible dialogical conflation of Christian allusion. This we see especially in the imagery of the pattern of leaves and vines on the sari, the latter of which we connect to the Biblical metaphor of Christ as the vine: 'I am the true vine, and my Father is the gardener', John 15. Added to that is the name Rani, which though Tamil in origin could also be linked to the Queen Bathsheba in the *The Holy Bible* (nd), especially significant for her seduction by King David. The parallels can be seen in the unfolding of the story of Abraham and Rani and her seduction by Krishna, Abraham's friend, a name also symbolic in the Hindu pantheon for its romantic associations. Yet, Abraham is not entirely blameless for Rani's indiscretion is most plausibly tied to her awareness of the ghost of Abraham's love for Rose.

As the narration progresses, the trail of the commingling Indian Christian sensibility follows suit, especially with strong references to food and its accompanying symbolic overtones of lost sustenance. No more privileged to come home to the 'welcoming smell of sambar bubbling on the stove' and the preparation of his 'favourite rava *dosai*' Abraham frequents the various Indian restaurants in Singapore's Little India, Seranggoon Road. In the concluding chapters however, the focus turns to his relationship with his son, Victor and it is here that the parallels with the parable from which the novel takes its name emerges, synchronized to the personal conflicts that Abraham faces as he begins to question the true paternity of Victor. We see the appearance of Rose, in much the same manner as the Angel in the Biblical story, to prevent the sacrifice of his son on the jagged tablet of his wife's broken commandment. Simultaneously we are reminded too of the covenant between Abraham and God as Rose asks 'Who are you to think that your seed could not produce such as he' (p. 172). The novel ends soon after, with Abraham seeking atonement for the betrayal of his son and the concluding lines: 'What more could be asked of me? And what more could I ask of my son' (p. 178), affirming the Apostolic creed of the forgiveness of sins.

The second testament in this pageant of Indian Christian creative articulations is the short story, 'The Kiss' by Malachi Edwin Vethamani (1995). The story reveals an intricate symbiosis between the religion, customs and the language of the Tamil Christian community. The initial moments of the story appear to present a typical Indian diasporic family, and with the strong cultural markers evident, one might be most inclined to imagine a Hindu household:

> When Periappa died a few minutes before midnight, Periamma stood by his hospital bed crying quietly. … Poor Periamma, I thought. I had seen her in tears so many many times. Periappa, now lying on the bed, very dead, had been the cause of much of her sorrow and physical pain. There she was crying. I knew she was crying for him, her husband. Even if he had been her husband and had hit her many many times. Yet, she wanted him alive.

As the narrator is thrown in the midst of the funeral arrangements, memories of his uncle flood his consciousness. These memories are presented to us through a creative imagination that effortlessly navigates the transitions in narratorial voice, moving from third person to first person points of view, with all the modulations of nativized speech patterns of the Malaysian Indian community. For instance there is the recollection of rides in his uncle's car: '"Appa's back from work. You want to go for drive or not?" Malar, one of my cousins, would ask. … As we got into the car, he (Periappa) would usually ask my brother and me, "Dei, your mother knows you're going for a drive with Periappa?"'

Then there is also the nativized social setting, for as the narration moves back into the present, we encounter another scene that is characteristically Indian, 'As they brought the coffin into the small hall, women wailed loudly.' Such a strong display of grief is said to be culturally grounded in Hindu death rites, whereby it is the cultural duty of the women to lament loudly at the passing of the deceased. The deceased is also laid in his coffin 'dressed in a white long sleeved shirt and a well ironed vesti'. However, soon after, we are made aware of the religious leanings of the family: '"Pastor's coming, Pastor's coming," my cousins started announcing', thus interpellating the Christian into the narrative space. As soon as this element is introduced, the dialogics of the text take on a significantly different trajectory and the following scene encapsulates this fact quite prominently:

> Hymn books appeared from nowhere and soon almost everyone had one each. … Soon page numbers were being suggested and Tamil hymns were being sung rather solemnly and this was better than listening to the weeping.

The enactment of the liturgy of the funeral rites within the home illustrates the fusion of Christian and Indian signifiers. The hymn book, which is central in all sacramental Christian worship and praise, is here reconstellated to illumine the Indian identity of the congregation. Also important is the reference to the wailing women in the background. While on one level, as mentioned above, it shares a connection with Hindu funeral customs, on another level it might be possible also to read a subliminal allusion to the biblical episode of the wailing women in the Gospel of Luke 23: 26–32: 'And there followed him a great multitude of the people, and of women who bewailed and lamented him.' We are subsequently told of Periappa's penchant for Tamil hymns:

> Periappa actually had a powerful singing voice. When he attended church services, which was not often, his loud voice could be heard when Tamil hymns were sung. Most choir members could not read Tamil. They held the hymn books in front of them and pretended to sing. He outdid them handsomely.

This depiction can be read as a signifier of the sonorous projection of ethnic identity within a mainly Christian space, much like the Indian material interpellated and cemented on the interior walls of the St Andrew's church in Singapore.

Simultaneously the recollected episode also brings home the point that number of Indian Christians might have lost touch with their linguistic roots through their attendance of services held in English or a tendency to converse in English both at home and in church. As the narrator continues to describe the observance of the Christian funeral rites as well as his encounters with various family members, we witness other similar interpellations recurring in the narrative space. Take the following scene for example:

> The Pastor decided to say a prayer and heads were soon bowed. Just as I was about to do the same, someone touched me on my shoulders. It was Athan, my brother-in-law.

Here we see the shifting between ecclesiastical discourse and cultural propriety of strong Tamil kinship ties. This is again apparent towards the close of the story:

> My younger brother emerged from a group of cousins and sat next to me. He did not look very well.
>
> 'What's wrong with you?' I asked, not really wanting to know.
>
> 'Akka said we have to kiss Periappa before they close the coffin,' he informed.
>
> 'What?' I almost shouted. This was our first family funeral. Kissing living members of the family would have been an ordeal enough. Kissing our dead Periappa was a definite no, no.
>
> 'I'm not kissing anybody, dead or alive,' I hissed back.
>
> 'You've no choice,' he insisted.

The act of kissing the deceased is a predominantly Christian practise, according to Hastings and Selbie (1915), 'Joseph kissed his dead father and the custom is retained in our civilization of imprinting a farewell kiss on dead relatives' (p. 742). This last exchange reveals the adoption of Western funeral rites within this Indian Christian community. The intermingling of both Western and Indian cultural practices in the story effectively reveals the intricacies of the Indian Christian existence, wreathed in the vines of theological doctrine and ethnic practices.

The third enactment of Indian Christian identity politics is the novel *Love's Treacherous Terrain* by Shoba Mano (2003). Like the two texts discussed above, this too reveals the commingling of Indian Christian myths and metaphors, in doctrine, rituals and custom. The main protagonist within the story, Tanusha Koshi, is a devout Christian and often relies on the figure of Christ to soothe and answer her prayers. The reader is made aware of her strong devotion within the first few pages of the novel where she finds herself in the midst of a comprising situation, the victim of a cruel joke administered by a number of misguided university students. In the midst of this confusion and fear, we witness the ascension of the figure of Christ within the narrative space:

> Jesus, I'm so sorry I did not consult you about joining this club. I was so sick and tired of not fitting in. I just wanted to belong to the coolest group in university. Forgive me Lord. You did not fit in yourself, and it never bothered you. I'm so sorry for my foolishness. (p. 15)

Her prayers indicate both her devotion to the religion and her grounding in biblical knowledge. Throughout the text, such Christian inflections within Tanusha's life become readily apparent. She attends mass weekly, is the lead singer in the choir and volunteers at the church. She also converses with Jesus through prayer on a daily basis and practises the word of God within her life. However, although the novel appears to be strongly located within such Christian tenets, it simultaneously intertwines ethnic cultural identity, located within the Indian Christian household of the Koshi family, seen especially in the playing out of the cultural habitus of the preparation of daily meals and the adornment of significant cultural items, specific to the Tamil community.

Our introduction to the Koshi family household offer interesting revelations. We first see Tanusha at the stove 'stirring chicken curry' in preparation for lunch. Shortly after, Techu, her brother, is described playing gospel music on his electric guitar, and Tanusha is urged to join him by singing the verses from 'Everyday it's you I live for' a Christian hymn. As soon as their mother arrives home, the family sits down to partake of the Indian meal that Tanusha has prepared. Here, grace is said, offering praise yet again to the almighty (pp. 43–45). In this way, the everyday habitus reveals an ensemble Christian exaltation and Indian sustenance. As De Certeau (1984) asserts, the space of the everyday is a site that does not garner much attention although the small details and behaviour of the individual attest to a larger sense of the community that the person is located within, thereby making visible the 'ways of operating' (p. xi). Highmore (2007) is more specific in his definition:

> Everyday life is not simply the name that is given up to a reality readily available for scrutiny; it is also the name for aspects of life that lie hidden. To invoke an ordinary culture from below is to make the invisible visible, and as such has a clear social and political resonance. (p. 1)

The resonances from the Koshi household clearly invoke the modulations of Indian Christian culture-scapes. This is again made evident in the depiction of the Christmas celebrations. Christmas morning is heralded with 'the blaring of Joy to the world, the Lord has come', a recognizably Western hymn and the ensuing praise and worship at Christmas service in English. However, as they return home to prepare for the arrival of guests for the customary 'open-house', in the Malaysian tradition of inviting neighbours and friends to the house to partake in the festive meal and share in the joy of celebration, we see the return of the ethnic into the personal space. While dominant images of the yuletide season are often located within a Western context, of the traditional roast for instance, within the Koshi household the Christmas spread reveals a hybrid array of dishes:

> Mrs Koshi recruited Tanusha into the kitchen. The oven had been turned on low to keep the roast hot and crisp on the outside. When Tanusha tried to transfer the mutton *perattal* from the pressure cooker into a Pyrex bowl, Mrs Koshi stopped her. (p. 128)

The presence of both roast and mutton *perattal,* a spicy Indian dish with a dry gravy base, is a clear indication of the porous boundaries of ethnicity and religion. As Ganguly (2001) puts it, 'Indian food functions metonymically in relation to immigrant identity because the whiff of belongingness, nostalgia, or hope is carried along by the taste and aromas of a wide range of dishes' (p. 126).

Apart from food, cultural emblems too play an important role in the novel and this is evident in the following passage:

> Mrs Koshi paused a moment to scoop her thali and drop it inside the neck of the maxi. It was popular for Catholics of Indian ancestry to wear a thali or wedding chain and ring at their wedding to maintain Indian tradition with religion. The only symbol left of her marriage now was the thali. The ring, had been taken off for fear of chastisement from her community. The thali was mostly hidden like now. (p. 54)

It is interesting that the traditionally Western marriage emblem of the ring is dispensed off, while the Indian signifier is maintained. Although the thali is hidden from the view of the reader and the public, Mrs Koshi's maintenance of it around her neck indicates her attachment to the religious and cultural item. The symbol of the thali does not merely connote her attachment to her departed husband, but also the influence of the dominant culture that is practiced in her everyday. As Steven Vertovec (2009) asserts:

> By way of illustration, in some places outside India basic Hindu ritual procedures have become truncated … refashioned … or eclectically performed … much of the style or corpus of rites has been virtually 'invented' in conjunction with social change in the community … and in still other places, basic rites have been mutually 'negotiated' so as to provide a kind of socio-religious bridge. (p. 142)

Seen in this context, the thali that is used by Mrs Koshi is reappropriated to accommodate both its cultural signifier of marriage, and its sentimental value, of negotiating resonances of the memory of her late husband. Similar eclectic negotiations on the socio-religious bridge are also evident in another Indian Christian family that we are introduced to in the novel, the Fernandez family. When Tanusha visits the family, she notices 'Mr and Mrs Fernandez's wedding photo. Mrs Fernandez was in a sari but wore a veil and white gloves, holding a bouquet. There was no doubt they had a Christian wedding' (p. 71). The veil and white gloves are predominantly Christian signifiers, the veil symbolizing the modesty and chastity, while the whiteness of the gloves indicating purity. The attire of the sari however reveals the refashioning of the traditional wedding gown with the yarn of culture. In this way, the wedding photograph itself becomes a visual symbol of Indian Christian eclecticism. The novel continues in a symphony of Christian biblical verse and phrases, oftimes interspersed with visualizations of the ethnic habitus of food, traditional attire and ritual items. An interesting aspect of this novel is that while it ends with the marriage of Tanusha to Ashwin Fernandez, the porous boundaries of ethnic and religious space allow for the integration of other worlds, as the marriage takes place in a chapel in Bali with Tanusha's wedding apparel a 'traditional Balinese wedding costume' (p. 252). This ultimately points to the creative capacity of diasporic communities to reorient sacred space and anoint the cultural habitus with the acceptance of diverse cultural legacies, and the Indian Christian community as we have shown in the discussion above is no exception.

Conclusion

The main aim of this paper has been to highlight the syncretism of the identity politics of the Indian Christian community in Malaysia and Singapore through the transfiguration of Christian experience into Indian culture-scapes. It hopes that the illumination of the numerous creative pageants of this community that has remained on the fringes of the garment of discussions about writings from the Malaysian and Singaporean diasporic Indian community can witness a shift from periphery to centre, in recognition of heterogeneous ethnic spaces.

Acknowledgements

The authors would like to acknowledge the kind assistance of P. Sakthivel, of the Library & Archives, Seminari Theoloji Malaysia, Seremban in obtaining some of the research material.

Notes on contributors

Shanthini Pillai is a senior lecturer at the School of Language Studies and Linguistics, Universiti Kebangsaan Malaysia. Her main teaching areas are Literary and Cultural Theory, Nativization in Literature, Literature and the Media, while research interests include Diaspora and Transnationalism in Literary and Cultural Texts and Multimodality and Higher Education Literature Learning. She is author of *Colonial Visions, Postcolonial Revisions: Images of the Indian diaspora of Malaysia* and has numerous articles in various areas of Literary Studies. She is a recipient of the 2006–2007 Australia–Malaysia Institute Fellowships and Director of Research and Development for the Malaysian English Language Teaching Association (MELTA).

Sharenee Philomena Paramasivam is currently pursuing her Masters in Postcolonial Literatures in English at University Kebangsaan Malaysia. She has a BA in English Literature from the University of Winnipeg. Her research interests are Feminism, Diaspora and Graphic novels. She is the co-creator of the blog site http://www.thecocoatoyourpuffs.wordpress.com, a space that examines the representation of brown women within the everyday.

References

Daniel, J.R., 1992. *Indian Christians in Peninsular Malaysia.* Kuala Lumpur: City Reprographic Services.

De Certeau, M., 1984. *The practice of everyday life.* Berkeley: University of California Press.

De Mendonca, D.J., 2002. *Conversions and citizenry: Goa under Portugal, 1510–1610.* New Delhi: Concept Publishing.

Dirks, N.B., 2001. *Castes of mind: colonialism and the making of modern India.* Princeton, NJ: Princeton University Press.

Frykenberg, R.E., 2010 [2008]. *Christianity in India: from beginnings to the present.* Oxford: Oxford University Press

Ganguly, K., 2001. *States of exception, everyday life of postcolonial identity.* Minneapolis: University of Minnesota Press.

Hastings, J. and Selbie, J.A., 1915. *Encyclopedia of religion and ethics,* part 14. New York: Charles Scribner's Son.

Highmore, B., 2007. *The everyday life reader.* London: Routledge.

Jacobsen, K.A. and Raj, S.J., 2008. *South Asian Christian diaspora: invisible diaspora in Europe and North America.* Aldershot: Ashgate.

Jeyaretnam, P., 1995. *Abraham's promise.* Singapore: Times Books International.

Ludden, D., 1985. *Peasant history in south India.* New Delhi: Oxford University Press.

Mano, S., 2003. *Love's treacherous terrain.* Secunderabad: OM Paperbacks.

Oddie, G., 2001. Indian Christians and nationalism 1840–1947. *The Journal of Religious History,* 25 (3), 348–366.

Poon, M., 2005a. *A historical note on William Topley Humphrey: insight into the beginnings of Saint Andrew's mission in Singapore.* Available online from: http://www.ttc.edu.sg/csca/poon/wth.pdf [Accessed 21 August 2010].

Poon, M., 2005b. *Indian contribution in the founding of Saint Andrew's Church, Singapore.* Available online from: http://www.ttc.edu.sg/csca/rart_doc/ang/sing/sac-h2.htm [Accessed 21 August 2010].

Subramaniam, G., 2008. *Ideological stylistics and fictional discourse.* Newcastle Upon Tyne: Cambridge Scholars Publishing

The Holy Bible, nd. King James version. Electronic Text Center, University of Virginia Library. Available online from: http://etext.virginia.edu/etcbin/toccernew2?id=KjvGene.sgm&images=images/ modeng&data=/texts/english/modeng/parsed&tag=public∂=all

Thomas, C.D., 1978. *Diaspora Indians: Church growth among Indians in West Malaysia.* Penang: Malaysian Indian Evangelism Council.

Vertovec, S., 2009. *Transnationalism.* New York: Routledge.

Vethamani, M.E., 1995. 'The Kiss' Sunday style. *The New Sunday Times.* Kuala Lumpur. Available online from: http://edwinvethamani.com/modules/tinycontent/index.php?id=26 [Accessed 21 August 2010].

Vethamani, V.J., 1987. A study of the Methodist Tamil work in Malaysia with particular reference to the formation of the Tamil annual conference. Unpublished thesis. Biblical Seminary Yavathmal, Maharashtra.

Celebrating 'the sons of Jats': the return of tribes in the global village

Anjali Gera Roy

Department of Humanities and Social Sciences, Indian Institute of Technology, Kharagpur, India

While critics of globalization had apprehended that its homogenizing wave would erase ethnic, cultural and sectarian difference to produce cosmpolitanized identities, the counter movement towards fragmentation in the present global process has paradoxically led to the thickening and intensification of boundaries and the return of 'the tribes', which converge on primordial essences such as language, culture, region, religion, ethnicity and caste. The return of the tribes in the global era appears to confirm Samuel Huntington's apprehensions about the future civilizational realignment of the world along the lines of religion and ethnicity (1997). The thickening of boundaries noted by theorists of globalization in the contemporary world has been particularly visible along lines of religion. While Islamic identity narratives have received considerable global attention, particularly after 9/11, a transnational consolidation of Sikh ethno-religious identity post 1984 has gone relatively undocumented. This essay traces the production and mobilization of a transnational unified sacral Sikh narrative after 1984 to argue that it reveals deep fissures along class, caste and sectarian differences.

Introduction

Edward Shils distinguished between the public, civil ties of the modern state and the primordial ties of family, religious and ethnic groups and argued that primordial ties of kinship and religion were integral even to modern secular society (Shils, in Smith 1998, p. 151). The present global process, apprehended as a homogenizing narrative eroding ethnic, cultural and religious difference, revealed a paradoxical intensification of primordial ties across the world. Roland Robertson and JoAnn Chirico noted the 'near-worldwide resurgence of religious fundamentalism, the extensive development of new religious movements (including liberational-theological movements within conventional churches and denominations), and the proliferation and sharpening of church–state tensions across much of the modern world' as early as the mid 1980s (2000, p. 93). A decade later, Benjamin Barber coined a catchy metaphor in his book *Jihad vs McWorld* to describe the contradictory trends within globalization that have entered the vocabulary of globalization (1995). Defining McWorld as a 'product of popular culture driven by expansionist commerce', he contrasted it with Jihad, a term which 'betokens religious struggle on behalf of faith, a kind of Islamic zeal' in its mildest form and 'bloody holy war on behalf of partisan identity that is metaphysically defined and fanatically defended' in its strongest political manifestation (1995, p. 24). Asserting that 'the fundamental source of conflict' in the new world 'would not be primarily ideological or primarily economic' but that 'the great divisions among humankind and the dominating source of conflict will be cultural', Samuel Huntington put forward his now famous hypothesis about the clash of civilizations a couple of years later, which proved to be eerily prophetic in the wake of events that followed (1997, p. 22). Showing that civilizations are 'differentiated from each other by history, language, culture, tradition, and, most important, religion', he argued that 'the conflicts of the future will occur along the cultural fault lines separating civilizations' (1997, p. 25). While Huntington's definition and typologies of civilizations have been contested, his point about people defining their identity in ethnic and religious terms is corroborated by a virtually worldwide eruption of religious and quasi-religious concerns in the era of globalization. Huntington made a specific mention of the intensifying religious strife within India between increasingly militant Hindu groups and India's substantial Muslim minority resulting in the destruction of the mosque in Ayodhya (1997, p. 34). While Hindu fundamentalism has undoubtedly been on the rise since the 1990s, Huntington overlooked the transnational mobilization and consolidation of Sikh religious identities beginning more than a decade earlier that culminated in the demand for a separate Sikh nation. Sikh religious identity or *Sikhi* has evolved into a transnational phenomenon in the twenty-first century produced through extensive Sikh social, political and economic networks that co-opted print and electronic media, popular cultural genres, educational and religious institutions in the propagation of the Sikh cause. However, while the mobilization of a Sikh identity through Sikh religious symbols following the violence against Sikhs in the 1980s has facilitated the production of a unified discourse of *Sikhi* or Sikh ethnocultural identity, the resurgence of suppressed Sikh movements in the new millennium reveals the homogenous Sikh discourse to be fissured by the overlapping discourses of class, caste and sect. This essay traces the production and mobilization of a transnational unified sacral Sikh narrative after 1984 to argue that the reemergence of dera sects since 2007 foregrounds deep-rooted fissures along class, caste and sectarian differences within Sikhism that were historically repressed. Beginning with an overview of the origins of Sikhism and its gradual separation from Hinduism, it proceeds to analyze the events leading to the production of a transnational Sikh identity through the Sikh diaspora's appropriation of a sacral origin and trace its disruption by casteist identity narratives before concluding with the implications of primordialist returns in the politicization of ethno-religious identities.

The origins of Sikhism

Sikhism is a religion based on the teachings of its founder Guru Nanak that emerged in Punjab in North India in the fifteenth century. The disciples of Guru Nanak, 'who belonged to a community of *sants* (saints) who propagated the worship of a shapeless (*nirguna*) world soul and the gurus as a manifestation of transcendent reality', formed together a community or *panth* (spiritual path), which came to be known as Sikhs (*Sikh* disciple). Although the history of Sikhs is one of constant struggle with the Mughals, the Hindu Sikh identities reveal frequent overlaps and crossovers until the end of the nineteenth century (Van der Veer 1994, p. 54, Kaur 2003, p. 283). While Hinduism responded to the birth of Sikhism through incorporating Sikhism as a sect by resignifying the Sikhs as 'the sword arm of Hindus', a view shared by certain Sikh factions, the Sikhs put forward their claim to a separate religious identity at different points in time.[1] The contentious issue of Sikhism's positionality vs Hinduism acquired political dimensions with the rise of Sikh nationalism at the end of the nineteenth century in response to the emergence of Islamic and Hindu nationalism, particularly with the birth of the Singh Sabhas and the articulation of their standpoint on Sikh identity as unique and separate from Hindu in Bhai Kahn Singh Nabha's *Hum Hindu Nahin* (1889).[2] The Sikh call for a separate nation at the beginning of the twentieth century and the Sikhs' self-representation as a separate community culminated in the storming of the Sikh shrine the Golden Temple at Amritsar by the Indian army to flush out Sikh militants led by their religious leader Sant Jarnail Singh Bhindranwale. While the 'desecration' of the Sikh holy shrine permanently alienated the Sikh community, the anti-Sikh riots that followed the assassination of the Indian Prime Minister Indira Gandhi by her Sikh bodyguards in 1984 completed the rupture between Hindus and Sikhs. Since 1984, the Sikh 'demand' for a separate nation, Khalistan, has been buttressed by the claim of a separate Sikh identity substantiated by Sikh religious and historical texts.[3] The separatist claim is propped on what Tony Ballantyne calls the Khalsacentric approach to Sikh history predicated on the *tat khalsa* ideology, which privileges the Khalsa over other understandings of Sikhism (Ballantyne 2006, p. 4). Sikh historians cite the fluid nature of Punjabi identifications and the strong imbrication of Sikh with Hindu thought and practices to argue against such a reading (McLeod 1990, Grewal 1990, Oberoi 1994). While historians continue to battle over the relationality of Sikhism and Hinduism based on their interpretations of Sikh religious and historical texts, Sikhism's appropriation of Punjabi cultural practices in their self-constitution in the present has led to a disturbing synonymy of Punjabi and *Punjabiyat* [Punjabi identity] with *Sikhi* divesting other Punjabi ethnicities of a shared Punjabi heritage. The contemporary mobilization of a Sikh identity through recourse to language and culture has a historical basis in the Akali Dal's call for a Sikh nation in 1925 and its couching of the demand for a Sikh homeland, a religious community, as a linguistic demand (Axel 2001). The imagining of a transnational Sikh community along religious lines has largely been enabled through the Sikh appropriation of the victimhood narrative of the Jewish diaspora, which is sanctified by rituals of blood.

Sikh scholars of various ideological and academic affiliations have been engaged in a debate on Sikhism's claims to being an independent religion, which are, in turn, tied to the political Sikh secessionist movement. The Sikh separatist narrative is undermined by Sikh leadership's historical couching of its religious demand as a linguistic demand over the years in view of post-colonial Indian state's secular ideological pressures and the eventual award of a separate linguistic state in 1966 following the linguistic reorganization of states after Independence (Axel 2001). The publication of Harjot Oberoi's *The Construction of Religious Boundaries* introduces a note of disjuncture in the Sikh production of a separate Sikh narrative (1994). Through examining the porous, penetrating, fluid religious boundaries of Punjab at the village level until the end of the nineteenth century, Oberoi argues that the construction of formal religions closed these overlapping boundaries through the instrument of script and destroyed the undivided memory of Punjab. Oberoi traces the destruction of the fluid religious boundaries at the village level in Punjab to the emergence of formal, organized religions, which were appropriated in religious nationalisms at the end of the nineteenth century. He also establishes the complicity of script in the destruction of the overlapping boundaries of Punjab in the fifty years prior to partition when Hindi, Urdu and *gurmukhi* emerged as the ethnocultural signifiers of Hindu, Muslim and Sikh identity respectively. It is this fissuring of the undivided Punjabi speech community that facilitates the identification of *gurmukhi* with Punjabi and *Sikhi* and its mobilization in the production of a transnational Sikh discourse since the 1970s. As the privileging of Hindi and Urdu led to Punjabi's marginalization and disappearance from the Indian and Pakistani nation state respectively, Punjabi was attached to *Sikhi* through the combined efforts of Sikh political and religious leaders, schools, gurdwaras and so on. While Hindu and Muslim Punjabis submitted to the authority of the national language in their self-constitution as Indian or Pakistani citizen subjects, Punjabi was left in the custody of Sikhs.

Oberoi returns to an earlier period in the history of Punjab that reveals the interpenetration of Hindu, Muslim and Sikh religious practices until the end of the nineteenth century. The Hindu Sikh boundaries appear to have been particularly permeable until the formal organization of Sikh religious practice by Guru Gobind Singh in 1699 with the formation of the Khalsa (Kaur 2003, p. 283). Peter van der Veer regards 'the formation of the Khalsa as a major development that later enabled the Sikhs to formulate their own nationalism, distinct from that of the Hindus' (1994, p. 54). Citing the Sikh case as an 'excellent example of the influence of British colonial policies on the development of a communal identity', van der Veer argues that through the British promotion of the Khalsa identity, 'a loosely integrated culture, in which "Sikhs" had a variety of multiple, overlapping identities, was replaced by a more strongly integrated Khalsa culture based on "Khalsa" identity, which formed the basis for religious nationalism' (1994, pp. 55–56). The changing composition of the Sikh population owing to the fluid, porous identities of Punjab has been corroborated by Pettigrew and Kaur (Pettigrew 1991, p. 169, Kaur 2003, p. 270).

The etymology of the word Sikh has its roots in the Sanskrit *shisya* or disciple. Not only was the founder of Sikh religion, Guru Nanak, born a Hindu Khatri but also a number of Sikh gurus succeeding him had a Hindu parentage while most of the lay members derived from a larger social category of the Jats (Kaur 2003, pp. 270–271). The Adi Granth, the collection of the teachings of Guru Nanak and the first five Gurus, includes the sayings of other bhakti saints such as Kabir, Farid and Ravidas and the *Dasam Granth*, compiled by Bhai Mani Singh in the *braj* dialect with a mixture of Sanskrit, Persian and Arabic, specifically refers to Hindu gods and goddesses. The practice of raising the first male child as a Sikh in Hindu families, the fluidity of religious practices among followers of certain Sikh sects, the institution of Hindu shrines in the Sikh gurdwaras and the widespread Hindu practice of worshipping at Sikh gurdwaras suggest a gradual thickening rather than the closure of religious boundaries between Hinduism and Sikhism particularly after their formalization in the Khalsa in which bodily signifiers, scriptural authority and ritual practices constructed Sikhs as a visible religious community (Axel 2001). As van der Veer points out, the abolishment of the line of succession of spiritual leaders, while laying the authority in the hands of the entire brotherhood, by Guru Gobind Singh made the boundaries between Sikhs and non-Sikhs much easier to maintain (1994, p. 56). The post 1984 production of a separate Sikh identity is made possible only by the privileging of the Khalsa narrative over other narratives of Sikh identity (Kaur 2003, p. 271).

The production of a transnational Sikh identity

The consolidation of a transnational Sikh identity after 9/11 in the diaspora reveals the resignification of a martial or economic diaspora into a religious diaspora imagined after the Jewish model through the myth of persecution and the invention of a sacred narrative sanctified by suffering. The myth of the persecution of Sikhs by Hindus in the post-national discourse of *Sikhi* or Sikhism traces continuity between the persecution of Sikh religious leaders in the past and the present. Sikh representations of atrocities perpetrated on innocent Sikhs in the decade of 'the Punjab problem' and the anti-Sikh riots in 1984 invoke the martyrdom of Sikh saint leaders during the Moghul and the British rule to invest Sant Jarnail Singh Bhindranwale, who was killed in Operation Bluestar, with the status of the ethno-religious signifier of Sikh martyrdom. Contemporary Sikh hagiographies frame the acts of Indira Gandhi's assassins and those of Sikh militants against the Sikhs' historic role in opposing the persecution of minorities during the Moghul rule. The circulation of the images of 'the tortured bodies' of Sikhs in the production of these narratives invokes the sacrifices made by Sikh leaders from Guru Tegh Bahadur to Gobind Singh in order to protect the rights of the minorities (Axel 2001). Strong evidence of the persecution of innocent Sikhs in the aftermath of Indira Gandhi's assassination confirms charges of atrocities on the Sikhs by Hindus and the complete rupture between Hindus and Sikhs. While moderate Sikhs had been divided in their loyalties to the separatist Sikh cause, the 'defiling' of the Golden Temple during Operation Bluestar that deeply hurt Sikh sentiments antagonized them and the massacre of innocent Sikhs after 1984 led many of them to ally themselves with the militant Sikh movement.

The Sikh diaspora's appropriation of the sacred narrative of Sikh martyrdom in the production of a transnational discourse of *Sikhi* through its convergence on the persecution of Sikhs by the Indian state was a strategic move that gave voice to the Sikhs globally. The intervention of international institutions in the alleged human rights violations triggered another wave of Sikh migration overseas through the route of asylum. However, the transnational mobilization of *Sikhi* was once again couched as a linguistic demand through a call for the preservation of Punjabi language and culture. The production of a unified Punjabi discourse by Sikh institutions and organizations ironically triggered Punjabi returns in India as well as in Pakistan among Hindu as well as Muslim Punjabis. Although *Sikhi* was represented as synonymous with *Punjabiyat*, the affirmation of Punjabi ethno-cultural and ethno-linguistic identity, pointed towards the dissolution of religious boundaries by shared cultural memories. The unified discourse of *Punjabiyat*, however, revealed fissures along the lines of caste, place of origin and gender through its domination by the landowning Jat caste. Therefore, the transnational mobilization of Sikh religion and identities, couched as a linguistic rather than sectarian nationalism, indirectly unified the ethno-linguistic Punjabi community while leading to the intensification of caste, class and gender boundaries.

The transnational sacral narrative of *Sikhi* patterned after the Jewish diaspora could be produced only through historical inaccuracies and distortions as the economic motive of Sikh migration at the end of the nineteenth century was reinscribed as a sacral one. While the exile of Prince of Duleep Singh to England and of Bhai Maharaj Singh to Malaya after the annexation of Punjab following the Anglo-Sikh wars might be framed within the historical context of exile or martyrdom, the larger movement of Sikh artisans, cultivators and soldiers in the service of the British Empire belongs to the history of labour in British imperialism that is entrenched in the social, political and geographical reengineering of Punjab by the imperial government. As Ian Talbot, Darshan Singh Tatla and others have pointed out, the establishment of the canal colonies in Punjab and imperial Land Reform acts that subdivided the lands and altered the revenue system increased rural indebtedness forcing migrations from Punjab (Talbot 2007; Talbot and Thandi 2004; Tatla 2004).

The production of Punjab as the granary of India increased pressure on landholdings leading families to encourage younger sons to migrate overseas and of Sikhs as a martial race in British imperialism led to their preferential recruitment in the imperial army. The porousness of religious boundaries is confirmed as late as this period through the phenomenal increase of Sikh population within a year following the preferential recruitment in the army through a large number of Hindus assuming a Sikh identity (van der Veer 1994, p. 55). The Sikh migration to East Africa began with the recruitment of blacksmiths, carpenters and other skilled artisans in the construction of the railways at the end of the nineteenth century. The Sikhs moved to South-east Asia through their recruitment in the army and the police force. It is the Sikh soldiers posted in Hong Kong who initiated the migration to Vancouver and California around the same time. The Sikhs in UK include both direct migrants who chose to migrate immediately before or after 1947 as well as 'twice migrants' from East Africa. It is only after 1984 that a large number of Sikhs exploited the openings for migration offered by asylum through genuine or fabricated stories of persecution by the Indian state. However, this wave of migration of Sikhs enabled a transnational Sikh community to converge on Sikh shrines and the Holy Book to reimagine themselves as a sacral community through the transnational circulation of images of the tortured bodies of Sikhs thus transforming an economic diaspora into a religious diaspora (Axel 2001).

The sacral narrative could be produced only in retrospect as the homeland was imagined as a small place in the imperial history of Sikh migration predating the making of nation states in which identarian narratives of caste, region, dialect dominated those of a larger Sikh religious affiliation. Two dispersed stories – one from East Africa and the other from Australia confirm the subordination of religious identity to village kinship networks. Hansraj Aggarwal, the son of Munshi Ram Aggarwal, the partner of the first migrant to East Africa, Kala Singh, pointed out that distinctions between Hindus and Sikhs were not important until the end of the nineteenth century while confirming the bonding between his Hindu *bania* father and the Sikh pioneer (Aggarwal, nd).[4] Similarly, the female protagonist is continuously exhorted to cultivate good Punjabi, rather than Muslim or Pathan, values in Meena Abdullah's *Cry the Peacock*, which is regarded as the first Australian Afghan novel. The overlapping boundaries in this phase not only between religions but also languages led to a confusion of Afghan, Mirpuri, Seraiki and Punjabi identities. Small region, caste or dialect based identities appear to have superseded religious identities in the early phase of migration from Punjab. It was the formation of post-colonial nation states that led to the classification of these diasporas as national diasporas with Punjabis identifying themselves with India or Pakistan.

While religious identifications might have been accretive or relative in the past, the rise of Hindu, Islamic and Sikh fundamentalism in the present redistributes the old and new diasporas along religious lines enabling the formation of a transnational Sikh imaginary. Yet, the persistence of small place identities in the older diasporas and the domination of certain groups leads to a reassertion of linguistic, caste and regional identities. The Sikh discourse is fissured along lines of caste, gender, region and place of origin as the domination of Jat Sikhs in the diaspora based on their historical position in Punjab is resisted by the 'twice migrant' *lohana*, *ramgarhia* or *chamar* Sikhs from Africa through their professional upward mobility.[5] Similarly, the Sikh discourse is fractured along the lines of region such as Malwa, Majha and Doaba with their distinctive *malwai*, *majholi* and *doabi* dialects. The class angle is accentuated through the difference between the new high-skilled and the old low-skilled migrants. While these fissures were visible until 2007 only in the social and intimate space, the emergence of new Sikh sects along caste markers and the revival of syncretic Sikh *panths* has acquired a political dimension through exclusionary religious practices and attacks on rival sects.

Casteist fragmentation of the Sikh identity

The thickening of caste lines in Sikh identity is propelled by the resistance to the domination of the Jat 'caste' in Sikh identity narratives.[6] Surinder Jodhka points out that the Punjabi caste hierarchy deviates from those in other regions in its elevating the Khatri or warrior over the Brahmin who is regarded as a menial figure (2001).[7] Peter van der Veer believes that Jats 'are peasants with a tradition of militancy who, according to a hypothesis of the historian Irfan Habib, were originally pastoralists' and speculates that 'their changeover to a sedentary way of life may have been accompanied by parallel processes of Hinduization and Sikhization' (1994, p. 53). Joyce Pettigrew avers that 'the Jats, whether Hindu, Sikh or Muslim, have formed the backbone of the agricultural community in Punjab, the neighboring provinces of Rajastan and Sind, and in the western portion of the Gangetic Doab' (1991, p. 163). While they claim to have an Indo-Scythian origin,[8] the Jats are regarded as Kshatriyas or the warrior class according to the *Varna* (caste) system.[9] Although they are placed lower than Khatris or *bhapas* in the social hierarchy, their domination as a cultivator caste in Punjab's agrarian economy positions them above all other castes, including the trading castes of *banias* and the artisan castes such as *ramgarhia*, *lohana* and so on. Jats, who have the longest tradition of adherence to Sikhism, considered themselves to be 'born Sikhs' and felt tremendous pride in having built up the military organization, which led to the establishment of the Sikh rule in the Punjab (Pettigrew 1991, pp. 168–169). While the Jats have conventionally imagined themselves as a separate group, their contemporary domination is traced back to Sant Bhindranwale's privileging of Jat Sikhs over others to form an alternative power base to the Akali Dal, the bastion of upper class Sikhs. The emergence of a Jat consciousness has been visible since the 1970s with the Jat synechdochically serving as the signifier not only of Sikh but also of Punjabi identity. Cultural forms such as film, music and fiction were co-opted in the mobilization of a specifically Jat identity and disseminated over transnational print and electronic media. In particular, Bhangra music became the prime tool in the production of a Jat Sikh identity.

Traditionally Bhangra was performed by the hereditary performing caste of bhands or *mirasis* for the entertainment of higher castes, including the Jats. In the Punjabi caste hierarchy, the performing castes or tribes such as the *mirasi* or bhand occupied the lowest strata in society and earned their living through royal or aristocratic patronage or through the support of the community. However, the contemporary Bhangra scene displays the reinvention of the Jat as a singer with Jat singers dominating the Bhangrascape. In view of the stigma attached to feminine pursuits such as singing and dancing in the hypermasculine Punjabi society, the Jat's arrogation of the role traditionally occupied by the lower caste *mirasi* should have been a cause for concern rather than jubilation. In Gurdas Mann's film *Yariaan* (2009), dealing with a young unemployed Punjabi Jat lawyer who is forced to migrate to Canada in search of better opportunities and ends up becoming a caterer or a *halwai*, Mann's character humorously bemoans this fact: 'Once the Jats ruled the world; then they turned into singers and now they have to turn into caterers'. As a Jat singer who has won national and international acclaim, Mann's character's statement reflects the Jat Sikh singers' cognizance of the irony of the altered professional landscape that disturbs traditional caste hierarchies.

Although hereditary *mirasi* performers continue to be consecrated through honours, awards and state patronage by both state and commercial institutions and organizations, the commercial Bhangrascape is dominated by singers of Jat origin. Allegations of the marginalization of talented *mirasi* and lower caste singers by the Jat coterie in the Bhangra industry transforms the Bhangra performing space into a microcosm of broader social and political conflicts. For instance, the unofficial ban of one of the most talented and acclaimed singers of the *mirasi* caste, Daler Mehndi, confirms the clout of the Jats in the Bhangra sonic landscape and accentuates Jat/non-Jat, rural/urban, regional/national divisions. While *mirasi* legends such as Kuldip Manak might still continue to be eulogized and younger *mirasis* such as Sardool Sikandar and Noori be given their due recognition, Bhangra has come to acquire a distinctive Jat location in contemporary Punjab and the Punjabi diasporas owing to its domination by Jat Sikhs. The best names in Bhangra boast of a Jat origin and use it for the celebration of a Jat identity. With the British Queen conferring the highest honours on him, the Birmingham based folksinger Malkit Singh is elevated to the status of a transnational signifier of Jat pride and identity. Similarly, Gurdas Mann is officially consecrated as the ethno-cultural signifier of Jat values in Punjab and the youth icon Jazzy B, shuttling between Canada, the UK and Punjab, becomes the emblem of a transnational Jat youth identity. Their international visibility and recognition has reversed the pejorative associations of singing and dancing in traditional Punjabi society. Instead, Jat performers view themselves as custodians of Punjabi culture and identity and take pride in the upward mobility that their performance of 'lower caste' occupations has brought them.

The Bhangra performer's transformation of the signifier of Jat pride and values is accomplished through the circuits of production, dissemination and consumption. Out of the three best known Bhangra singers, two – Gurdas Mann and Malkit Singh – have a common Jat origin and take great pleasure in claiming their Jat Sikh identity. Not only Bhangra producers but also their consumers have a distinctively Jat Sikh location. The Bhangra space is dominated by Manns, including Gurdas Mann, the brothers Harbhajan and Gursevak Mann, Babbu Mann, Bhagwant Mann and so on. The Mann clan is believed to be the purest of the Jat clans who are offspring of a warrior race and were constructed as the martial race by the British. Bhangra performers such as Gurdas Mann continuously affirm Jat values and identity in their interviews, which are presented as synonymous with *Punjabiyat* or Punjabi identity. 'I couldn't have dreamt in my wildest imagination that one day I would be speaking to journalists. I am basically a happy-go-lucky type of person from a Jat household, whose livelihood was through agriculture', Gurdas Mann told Madhur Tankha (Tankha 2002) unlike Mann, who is unambiguous in his self-description as a Jat Sikh, others like Jazzy B, Malkit Singh and others switch between Jat, Sikh and Punjabi self-identifications that often appear to be synonymous.

While Jat identity is mapped on the bodies of Jat singers, the Bhangra text becomes the prime instrument in the consolidation of Jat identity. Bobby Friction from BBC Radio 1's Asian underground music programme notes: 'There are many songs about Jat pride, about the life of a Jat … Jat nationalism is running rampant in bhangra music now to the point where every bhangra album that comes out in Britain has at least one track that alludes to the power of the Jats' (quoted in Puri 2003). A large number of Bhangra songs, even those performed by hereditary *mirasi* singers posit Jats as their imagined subjects and their apparently innocuous nonsense lyrics invoke Jat pride and affirm Jat nationalism. The pervasive Jat imagery dominating Bhangra texts transforms Bhangra into a Jat song in which the rusticity associated with Jats becomes a source of its appeal and the rustic Jat comes to embody Punjabi materiality and authenticity.

As *mirasi* bards were traditionally employed in the service of the Jat landowners, the convention of eulogizing the Jat patron is continued by the *mirasi* legend Kuldip Manak. While Manak, born Latif Mohammed, whose grandfather and father sang at Sikh shrines, embodies the fluid sectarian boundaries mentioned by Oberoi, many of Manak's songs extol Jat values. One of his best known songs '*Jat ho gaya sharabi pike poori vodka* [the Jat got drunk after swigging a whole bottle of vodka]' has been a favourite on the Bhangra circuit for several generations. Surinder Shinda, of *tarkhan* or carpenter caste, is reported to be happy to praise Jats in his songs as he believes that the Jats are keeping the Punjabi culture alive. Similarly, Gurdas Mann's best known song 'apna Punjab hove' centralizes the Jat as a nawab or princeling. While Malkit Singh celebrates the Jats dancing the Bhangra in '*hai shava jat bhangray paonday*' [The Jats are dancing the Bhangra], Jazzy B has him wooing his beloved with the song '*put Jatan da sohniye tere te marda*' [the son of Jats is crazy about you]. Not only Bhangra music but also Punjabi films have been appropriated in the mobilization of Jat pride and a Jat Sikh identity. The protagonist of Punjabi films from *Mitti Vajan Mardi* (2007), *Mera Pind* (2008), *Yaariyan* (2008), played by one of the Manns – Gurdas or Harbhajan – becomes the prime instrument for the romanticization of Jat values and glorification of the sons of Jats or *put jatan de*. The remarkable success of Punjabi films among diasporic populations notwithstanding their low production values, stereotyped plots and characters, must be attributed to their celebration of Jat values with which a large number of their audience identify.

While a casual listener views the content of Bhangra texts as mere entertainment, the arrogation of superior values by Jat Sikhs alienates other castes from the narratives of *Punjabiyat* produced in Bhangra and leads them to produce similar identity discourses. '*Put Chamaran de*', a video uploaded around 2009 on *YouTube*, presents an interesting case study of the schisms between Jat and other Sikhs, particularly the lower castes. The video displaces the Bhangra formulaic lyric '*put Jatan de*' [the sons of Jats] with '*put chamaran de*' [the sons of *chamars*] and superimposes the images of Akshay Kumar, a Hindi film actor of the Khatri caste, dancing to the rhythm of Nusrat Futeh Ali Khan's '*tu cheez badi hai*' from his film *Mohra* (1994) to parody the celebration of Jat identity in Bhangra songs. A seemingly innocuous substitution, the music video, underlines deep historical chasms between Jat cultivators and lower castes, particularly the untouchable caste of Chamars, which are reinforced through Bhangra albums. The economic prosperity of twice migrant Punjabis of this caste who form the professional Punjabi diasporas in the UK enables them to proudly acknowledge their marginalized caste status in order to challenge the Jat domination. Kathryn Lum believes that the Ravidasia movement has stimulated the growth of both collective and individual self confidence with members taking pride in their caste identity: 'I am proud to be a Chamar [historical, derogatory term for the leather-working caste]. I tell everyone, I don't feel any shame. This is who I am and I want others to know' (Lum 2009). Similarly, Ravish Kumar in a special report on NDTV in June 2010 titled

'Ravish ki Report' threw light on a growing trend of the articulation of pride in Chamar identity in Punjabi music through Chamar singers' parodic repetition of Jat songs to reinforce Chamar pride (2010).

A visit to Sikh, Punjabi and Jat chatrooms reveals how deeply entrenched caste difference is among diaspora Sikhs, even among new generations of youth. In these chatrooms, caste hierarchies are preserved more religiously than at home with Jat Sikhs marginalizing and even ridiculing other castes. A discussion thread titled 'Why are Jats so Obsessed with their Caste' has interesting responses:

By Sunny Singh on Tuesday, 27 March 2001 – 9:34 pm:

> All I know is whether Hindu, Sikh, or Muslim, a Jat will let you know he is one! Meaning they take more pride in themselves then their respective religions, i.e Jat first, religion next. No amount of religious brainwashing will erase this trend. Am I wrong????

By desi Jati on Tuesday, 27 March 2001 – 8:20 pm:

> i think that everyone should stop giving us Jat a hard time, we are proud to be Jat and so should you be, it doesn't matter if your TK, chura or chamar.

By Jatandein putt Jatatein on Wednesday, 4 April 2001 – 11:58 pm:

> hi i just wanna say to all you Jat this issue was solely designed to make chammar look better it's like us indian wanting to become english nationality as well as look white i mean so there is no difference in colour so let the chammar do the hard work (after all they should be used to it) and try to become to the top of the caste ranking like they will ever.

The proliferation of websites exclusively dedicated to Jat issues such as Jatworld, the debates on Jat's position on Punjabi and Sikh websites point to the consolidation of a Jat identity. These narratives of Jat values and identity produced in cultural forms such as music, dance and film, internet chatrooms and social networking sites often draw on colonial and post-colonial historical documents to assert Jat supremacy in the present. The consolidation of Jat identities through which non-Jat Sikhs are excluded from the fold of *Sikhi* in turn leads to the mobilization of other Sikh identities along caste lines, such as the convergence of Dalits on 'the untouchable' saint Ravidas who rose to spiritual leadership with forty one of his *banis* being included in the Sikh religious book.

The consolidation of Jat identity in real and virtual spaces might have gone unnoticed and the clashes between Jat and non-Jat youth in neighbourhoods, clubs and parties contained through the vocabulary of deviance had the factionalism underlining Sikh identity in the new millennium not taken a political colour. Violent confrontations between Sikhs and followers of deras at home and abroad beginning in 2007, which were played up by the national and international media, reveal the renewal of primordial caste-based identities and their historical antagonisms (Raman 2007). An advertisement issued by the leader of the Dera Sachha Sauda in which he was attired in a fashion similar to Guru Govind Singh provoked the ire of the orthodox Sikhs leading to violent clashes in Punjab. Similarly, the killing of the leader of another Dera in a Vienna Gurdwara following violent clashes between rival Sikh factions on 24 May 2009 received international attention and underlined the caste, class, sectarian divide threatening to disrupt the unified narrative of Sikhi produced by higher caste Sikhs.[10]

Reporting the Vienna incident, Satwinder Bains related the rise of the dera sects in Punjab to the lower castes and the lower strata of Punjabi society 'trying to carve out a distinct identity for themselves' and called attention to other confrontations such as those between Sikhs and Dera Sacha Sauda, the Dera Sach Khand of Jalandhar Sikh fundamentalists, Divya Jyoti Jagran Sansthan and Baba Bhaniarewala. Bains attributed the incident to 'a simmering undercurrent of animosity between the dominant Jat Sikh community of Punjab and the largely Dalit Sikh dera-goers' (2009).

The followers of *deras* come from the lower caste and economically disadvantaged groups who are not considered pure Sikhs by conservative Sikh factions. The rise of the dera sects in Punjab and the diasporas has its origins in a narrative of migration with the increase in economic power of the 'twice-migrant' Sikhs, belonging to the artisan and lower castes, from Africa to the UK who have been instrumental in the establishment of deras and Ravidasia gurdwaras. Initially motivated by their exclusion by Jat Sikhs, the Ravidasias set up their own gurdwaras in India and abroad and have proceeded to the assertion of an independent, religious identity with its own symbols. Jodhka (2009) and others have pointed out that the economic mobility of the diaspora Chamar*s* and lower castes gives them greater power in gurdwara politics through the means of donations and also in homeland politics as deras and gurdwaras funded by them proliferate all across Punjab.

Jodhka (2009) traces the history of the Ravidasi movement to the Adi Dharm movement in the early 1920s in Punjab, its dissolution through its absorption in Hindu Dalit discourses and revival through the setting up of a Ravidas temple in 1965. He regards the 1990s as a second wave in Ravidasi revival when Non Resident Indian (NRI) capital collaborated with local underprivileged castes to begin a transnational Ravidasi movement through the setting up of deras and gurdwaras in Punjab and overseas. While the Adi Dharm movement remained a political rather than a religious movement, the Ravidasi movement displays an interesting example of the development of a religious identity for attaining social and political goals.

The incidents at Dera Sachcha Sauda and the Vienna gurdwara revealed not only the transnationalization of identity narratives but also the deep imbrication of the socio-economic with the political. They called attention to the fact that the Sikh dominated state had perhaps the largest number of Dalit*s* or untouchables and that despite Sikhism's doctrinal rejection of the caste system, Punjabi Sikhs, like Punjabi Hindus, continue to be divided against caste lines even in the twenty-first century.[11] The Sikh example proves that the homogenizing narrative of globalization is disrupted by increasing fragmentation through the global return of ethnicity and religion in the present that affirm primordial ties.

Conclusion

Although Geertz did not use the term, his celebrated 1963 essay became the fulcrum of heated debates on the concept of 'primordialism' (Geertz 1996). He claimed that the new states in Asia and Africa were abnormally susceptible to serious disaffection based on primordial attachments and cited Ambedkar's frank defence of the sense of primordial ties in articulating his concern about subnationalism in the new states. In 'The Inexpungeable Tie of Primordiality', Steven Grosby had held that though primordiality might be socially constructed and largely 'an affect issue', human beings 'do make classifications of the self and the other in accordance with such criteria' (1996, p. 74). The return of caste based Sikh identities and movements affirm the power of 'the inexpugnable ties of primordiality' and return of the tribes in the global village. Illustrating the fragmentary countermovement that neutralizes the effects of globalization's homogenizing drive, they exhibit the unexpected resurgence of the premodern in the postmodern. They also confirm Huntington's apprehensions about the wars in future over identity and religion. The eruption of dera sects in the twenty-first century reveals deep chasms in the unified narrative of Sikh identity and calls attention to the erasure of multiple competing Sikh identity spaces in the production of the Sikh master-narrative. Returning to an ancient history of caste antagonisms and the historical suppression of Dalit Sikh discourses by dominant Jat Sikh narratives over several centuries, they foreground the tensions within the Sikh religious formation purportedly founded to end Hindu social hierarchies.

Notes

1. The Hindu view is substantiated by passages such as the following:
   kahaiya Hinduan daro na ab tum
   aim likho pathon dil sain Guru Nanak ki gadi par
   ab hain Tegh Bahadur Unko jo Muhummadi kar lihoon
   to ham hain sab sadar Arya Dharma rakhak pragatiyo hain
   [Hindus, do not fear Guru Tegh Bahadur is Guru Nanak's successor
   If Muslims bother you I'll take care of them.
   For I am the protector of Hinduism.
   Guru Tegh Bahadur].
2. Bhai Kahn Singh's pamphlet, in the form of a dialogue between a Hindu and a Sikh, was written in response to a publication entitled *Sikh Hindu Hain* [*Sikhs Are Hindus*] (1899) by a Sanatan Sikh, Thakur Das.
3. For a detailed discussion on different approaches to Sikh history, see Ballantyne (2006). The separatist claim is propped on a Khalsacentric approach to Sikh history, which privileges the Khalsa over other understandings of Sikhism. Other historians cite the interweaving of Hindu and Sikh thought and practices.
4. 'Munshi Ram and Kala Singh got to be friends in India and came over together. You know in those days there was no difference between Hindus and Sikhs. We were all called Hindus even the Sikhs. It was only when the Muslims began attacking the Hindus that some became warriors under the guidance of Guru Nanak Devji (Guru Gobind Singh Ji [Kanwal]). In my grandfather's time even now in India it wasn't only the Sikhs who wore turbans; all the older men wore turbans' (Aggarwal, nd).
5. The Sikh movement to Africa was largely that of the lower castes of *lohana*, *ramgarhia* or *chamar* Sikhs who gained upward mobility through education and entrepreneurship and form the educated, professional diaspora in the UK. For a detailed discussion of the persistence of caste boundaries among twice-migrants and understanding of the differences in the imaginings of Sikh community, Eleanor Nesbitt's research among Sikh youth in Britain is extremely educating (2000, 2004).
6. The claims of Jats to be a caste is contested by historians as they do not fulfill the conditions for the formation of castes. It might be more accurate to describe the Jats as a tribe than a caste but as it is commonly used, I have used the term caste rather than tribe.
7. 'Originally and in general the Siques (Sikhs) are zemindars (landowners) or cultivators of land, and of that tribe called Jats (Jats) which, in this part of India, are reckoned the best and most laborious tillers, though at the same time they are also noted for being of an unquiet and turbulent disposition. This tribe of Jats (Jats) is very numerous and dispersed in all the country from the Sind (presently, a province of Pakistan or river Indus) to the southward far beyond Agra (a city in northern India) (Polier 1974).
8. 'It is from these Scythian immigrants that most of the Jat tribes are at any rate partly descended. They thus colonized the Punjab, Northern Rajputana (modern Indian state of Rajasthan), and the western half of the Gangetic Doab (western part of the modern Indian

state of Uttar Pardesh in northern India), and a considerable proportion of the inhabitants of these countries are undoubtly of Scythian origin'.

9. As they were outside the rigorous brahmanical social order, this position was not emphasized till the growth of the Arya Samaj among the Jats.
10. Sikh fundamentalists attacked a congregation of the followers of Dera Sach Khand headed by Sant Niranjan Dass. His deputy Sant Ramanand was killed during the attack leading to widescale protects in Punjab. 'Dera Sach Khand was set up over 70 years ago in Ballan village near Jalandhar by Sant Pipal Singh. The sect follows the ideals of Sant Ravi Dass, a late 15th century preacher. Over the ages, it has become a power centre for members of the lower castes' (Bains 2009).
11. According to the census of 2001, scheduled castes constituted 28.95 % of the total population. Although exact figures are not available, the percentage of dalits has risen to 30–35% of the population of Punjab in 2010 (Singh 2010).

Notes on contributor

Anjali Gera Roy is Professor in the Department of Humanities and Social Sciences at the Indian Institute of Technology, Kharagpur. She researches in the areas of literary, cultural, media and diaspora studies with particular interests in South Asian popular culture, Partition 1947 and Punjabi diaspora. She has published nearly 80 journal essays and book chapters. Recent publications include *Partitioned Lives: Narratives of Home, Displacement and Resettlement* (Pearson 2008) and *Bhangra Moves: From Ludhiana to London and Beyond* (Ashgate 2010). Her latest project investigates Bollywood's transnational flows and its role in promoting India's soft power.

References

Aggarwal, H., nd. Why Kenyan Sikhs are called 'Kalasingas'. Sikhs of East Africa: Untitled Document. Retrieved from: http://www.sikh-heritage.co.uk/heritage/sikhhert%20EAfrica/sikhsEAfrica.htm [Accessed 3 October 2010].

Appadurai, A., 1996. *Modernity at large: cultural dimensions of globalization.* Minneapolis: University of Minnesota Press.

Axel, B.K., 2001. The *Nation's tortured body: violence, representation, and the formation of the Sikh 'diaspora'.* Durham, NC: Duke University Press.

Bains, S., 27 May 2009. Vienna incident: Jat-Dalit divide flashpoint. *Punjab Newsline.* Retrieved from: http://www.punjabnewsline.com/content/vienna-incident-jat-dalit-divide-flashpoint [Accessed 15 August 2010].

Ballantyne, T., 2006. *Between colonialism and diaspora: Sikh cultural formations in an imperial world.* Durham, NC: Duke University Press.

Barber, B., 1995. *Jihad vs. McWorld: how globalism and tribalism are reshaping the world.* New York: Times Books.

Das, L.T., 1899. *Sikh Hindu Hain.* Hoshiarpur: Khatri Press.

Geertz, C., 1996. Primordial ties. *In:* J. Hutchinson and A.D. Smith, eds. *Ethnicity.* Oxford: Oxford University Press, 42–43.

Grewal, J.S., 1990. *The Sikhs of Punjab.* Cambridge: Cambridge University Press.

Grosby, S., 1996. The inexpungeable ties of primordiality. *In:* J. Hutchinson and A.D. Smith, eds. *Ethnicity.* Oxford: Oxford University Press.

Huntington, S.P., 1997. *The clash of civilizations and the remaking of world order.* New York: Simon & Schuster.

Jodhka, S.S., 2001. Caste in the periphery. *Seminar,* 508: 41–46.

Jodhka, S.S., 26 May 2009. Making sense of the Ravi Dasis. *Kafila.* Retrieved from: http://kafila.org/2009/05/26/making-sense-of-the-ravi-dasis-surinder-s-jodhka/ [Accessed 15 August 2010].

Kaur, R., 2003. Jat Sikhs: a question of identity. *In*: B Chakrabarty, ed. *Communal identity in India: its construction and articulation in the twentieth century.* New Delhi: Oxford University Press.

Lum, K., 2009. Face to Faith. *The Guardian,* 8 May. Retrieved from: http://www.guardian.co.uk/commentisfree/ belief/2009/may/08/kathryn-lum-face-to-faith [Accessed 15 August 2010].

M[c]Leod, W.H., 1990. *The Sikhs.* New York: Columbia University Press.

Nabha, K.S., 1889. *Ham Hindu nahin.* Amritsar: Khalsa Press.

Nesbitt, E., 2000. *The religious lives of Sikh children: a Coventry-Based study.* Leeds: Community Religions Project, University of Leeds.

Nesbitt, E., 2004. I'm a Gujarati Lohana and a Vaishnav as well: religious identity formation among young Coventrian Punjabis and Gujaratis. *In:* S. Coleman and P. Collins, eds. *Religion identity and change.* London: Ashgate, 174–190.

Oberoi, H., 1994. *The construction of religious boundaries: culture, identity and diversity in the Sikh tradition.* New Delhi: Oxford University Press.

Pettigrew, J., 1991. The Jats of Punjab. *In:* D. Gupta, ed. *Social stratification.* New Delhi: Oxford University Press.

Polier, A.L.H., (Colonel and died in A.D. 1795). 1974. *An account of the Sikhs, in early European accounts of the Sikhs.* Ganda Singh, ed. New Delhi: Today & Tomorrow's Printers & Publishers, 192–193.

Puri, N., April 2003. The caste divide. BBC Radio 4.

Raman, S., 17 May 2007. Thursday, July 25 2002. India tensions over Sikh protests. BBC News. Retrieved from: http://news.bbc.co.uk/2/hi/south_asia/6667219.stm. [Accessed 3 October 2010].

Ravish Kumar. NDTV 25 June 2010. Ankhi Putt Chamaran De. Ravish ki Report. *YouTube – Ankhi Putt Chamaran De – NDTV Report – Part 2.* Retrieved from: www.youtube.com/watch?v=Fi-LCSZvbfI [Accessed 15 August 2010].

Robertson, R. and Chirico J.A., 2000. Humanity, globalization, and worldwide religious resurgence. *In:* F.J. Lechner and J. Boli, eds. *The globalization reader.* Oxford: Blackwell, 93–98.

Singh, J., 2010. Institutions, modernity and caste atrocities: a critical analysis of special laws for social change. Paper presented at Seminar on *Modernity and Changing Social Fabric of Punjab and Haryana,* 27–29 September 2010, Indian Institute of Advanced Studies, Shimla.

Smith, A.P., 1998. *Nationalism and modernism.* London: Routledge.

Talbot, I., 2007. The Punjab under colonialism: order and transformation in British India. *Journal of Punjab Studies,* 14 (1): 3–10.

Talbot, I. and Thandi, S., ed. 2004. *People on the move: Punjabi colonial and post-colonial migration.* Oxford: Oxford University Press.

Tankha, M., 2002. Turning a new leaf with hope. *The Hindu.* Retrieved from: http://www.hindu.com/thehindu/mp/2002/07/25/stories/2002072500900200.htm [Accessed 15 August 2010].

Tatla, D.S., 2004. The rural roots of the Sikh diaspora. *In*: Ian Talbot and Shinder Thandi, eds. *People on the move: Punjabi colonial, and post-colonial migration.* London: Oxford University Press.

Van der Veer, P., 1994. *Religious nationalisms: Hindus and Muslims in India.* Berkeley: University of California Press.

Multiple modernities and the Tibetan diaspora

John Whalen-Bridge

English Language and Literature, National University of Singapore, Singapore

In response to Chinese claims that Tibet has been liberated from feudal power structures and is undergoing a process of modernization, members of Tibet's Government-in-Exile are developing a discourse of Tibetan modernity to counter China's version. For the Dalai Lama, Director of the Library of Tibetan Works and Archives Geshe Lhakdor, and Prime Minister of Tibet's Government-in-Exile Samdhong Rinpoche, 'modernity' is not just a triumph of innovation over tradition. As the government of Tibet's Government-in-Exile cannot exert itself within the Chinese borders that now contain Tibet, the discourse is intimately linked to the diasporic migration of Tibetans into countries such as India, Nepal and Bhutan. This modernization is part of a broad cultural survival strategy in which the main actors must alter tradition in order to preserve it.

As a diasporic community, Tibetans in exile have been fighting a two-front war. On the one hand, they are defined by their attempts to preserve traditional culture, which has been attacked by the PRC for being an impediment to modernization. Defined as they are by the PRC as feudal and anti-modern, the 'Dalai clique' also struggles to define their vision of what Tibetan life should be, asserting that they have a suitable approach to modernization that does not depend upon the obliteration of traditional Tibetan culture. The concept of 'multiple modernities'[1] can help to highlight an emergent discourse of modernity within the Tibetan diaspora.

Like all aspects of the study of Tibet,[2] the question of 'modernity' is heavily conditioned by the ideological struggle between the PRC and those who believe that the Chinese invasion of Tibet in 1950 was the beginning of an especially oppressive form of colonization. From Beijing's point of view, the Western sentimentalization of Tibet ignores the oppression of Tibet's previous underclass and has functioned as part of a hegemonic way of imagining China–Tibet relations. According to Chinese critics, Tibetan sympathizers are anti-modern reactionaries who do not wish to recognize Tibet as part of China because they are conditioned by Western imperial ideology. While it is true that fantasy-constructions of Tibet as a land untouched by war have proliferated with Western popular culture, current scholarly descriptions of Tibet are quite mindful of the role of orientalist fantasy. Donald Lopez's edited volume *The Curators of the Buddha* (1995) and his *Prisoners of Shangri-La* (1998) help to dissociate myths and demonstrable realities. Martin Brauen's *Dreamworld Tibet* (2000) and Orville Schell's *Virtual Tibet* (2000) provide rich portraits of the continuous border violations between the dream world and the quotidian one. Critics like Lopez,

Brauen and Schell have argued that the 'romance of exile' (Buruma 2001) and other sentimental appropriations of the Tibetan diaspora may prevent us from recognizing the difference between huggable lamas and stateless people who suffer indignities most people do not have to imagine. Such fantasies also obscure the dilemma faced by Tibetans in exile, for whom opportunities for modernization must be balanced against the aim of preserving a culture under attack.

The Chinese modernization of Tibet: the eradication of feudalism

According to Chinese narrative constructions, Tibet has been part of China at least since the eighteenth century, and Tibet's tangled relationship with China can be traced back at least to the meeting of Genghis Khan and Tsangpa Dunkhurwa (Gtsang pa Dung khur ba) in 1215 (Petech 1990, p. 6, Shakabpa 1967, p. 61). In the eighteenth and nineteenth centuries, a number of imperial scrimmages were fought over Tibetan sovereignty, but Tibet enjoyed *de facto* independence between the fall of the Qing Dynasty in 1912 and the Communist victory over the nationalists after the Second World War.

The idea that Tibet was 'feudal' well into the twentieth century is not contested, although there is debate about quality of life of non-landholders before the Chinese invasion and the degree to which the invasion improved living conditions, if at all.[3] Smith reports in *Tibetan Nation* (1996) that China organized a propaganda campaign while building up 30,000 troops on the border of the Kham region of Tibet: 'Tibetans from all areas reported the same version of Chinese justifications for having entered Tibet: they had come to Tibet to help Tibetans and they would leave when Tibet had "improved" and Tibet was capable of self-rule' (Smith 1996, pp. 273–274). The Chinese liberation effort was portrayed as a triumph against imperialism in 'Support Agreement on Measures for Peaceful Liberation of Tibet':

> In the last hundred years and more, imperialism penetrated into China and at the same time also into Tibet. ... Following the victorious development of the great revolution of the Chinese people and the people's liberation war, the imperialists and their lackeys became still more frantic like mad dogs, and hastily manufactured the so-called 'Tibetan independence' and various 'anti-communist' plots in an attempt to make the Tibetan people to be completely cut off from their motherland, to lose their independence and freedom completely and become their complete slaves. (Smith 1996, p. 302)

The Chinese left the Dalai Lama nominally in power but began to eradicate practices that A. Tom Grunfeld describes in *The Making of Modern Tibet* as 'feudal' (1996, p. 8). Melvyn C. Goldstein concurs in *A History of Modern Tibet* (2007), developing the analogy between Tibet's premodern estate system and European feudalism:

> Tibet's estate system was roughly analogous to the manorialism found in medieval English and western continental Europe in the sense that both were characterized by lands held by lords who were supported by a legally bound peasant population. (p. 9)

Estates in this system 'could be held by aristocratic families, monasteries, incarnate lamas, or the government itself' (p. 9). According to Goldstein, 'the Tibetan government, as of 1951, consisted of a system of hierarchically arranged offices staffed by a bureaucracy of roughly five hundred officials, about half of whom were monk officials and half lay aristocratic officials' (p. 2). The lay officials were 'recruited from a hereditary aristocracy that consisted of about two hundred families. Each aristocratic family held at least one manorial estate with attached peasant families' (p. 2).

Justifications of the Chinese presence in Tibet (beginning with the invasion of 1950 and the repression of Tibetan revolt in 1959) depend upon the argument that Tibet was an anachronistically feudal state. According to a BBC report on the sixtieth anniversary of Tibet's failed 1959 revolt, 'China says its troops freed Tibetans from effective slavery in a feudal society. It is planning to mark 28 March – the day in 1959 on which the Communist Party dissolved the existing local government in Tibet – as Serfs' Emancipation Day' (BBC 2009). Tibetans who were enslaved by the social system, the argument goes, were liberated by the Chinese, and Tibetan living conditions have been undergoing improvement since the 1950s (BBC 2009).[4]

Historians such as Grunfeld and Goldstein agree that social relations in pre-1959 Tibet resembled those of medieval Europe in some ways and that social inequities regularly benefited entrenched hereditary elites – but so does the Dalai Lama.[5] The question is whether Tibetan culture is undergoing a program of modernization or destruction. Tibetan culture within what is now China has undergone several attacks by Chinese modernization policies (Bass 1998, p. 3).[6] Tibetans within China-occupied Tibet have been given educational opportunities but often in Chinese rather than Tibetan. Temples are allowed to present religious iconography that makes them more suitable as exotic tourist sites, but it is forbidden to post an image of the Dalai Lama. The most developed area of Tibet is Lhasa, former seat of the Dalai Lama, and it has been flooded with Han Chinese migrants to such a degree that Tibetans are a minority group within their own land.[7]

Most damaging to China's claims that its activities are progressive steps for the benefit of (ethnically Tibetan) Chinese citizens are the claims that sinicization policies are predicated on human rights abuses and lead, ultimately, to cultural genocide. Vincanne Adams writes in 'Suffering the Winds of Lhasa' that in

> most thorough accounts, human rights violations are presented as taking the form of cultural genocide: the complete eradication of a distinctive Tibetan way of life. During the Cultural Revolution, it is argued, the Chinese government practiced cultural genocide in Tibet and throughout China by attempting to eliminate all traces of the Tibetan religion and the folk culture associated with it. Accounts today confirm that Tibetans who demand the right to practice Buddhism as they wish, who have in their possession images of the Dalai Lama, or who advocate at any time a non-Chinese Tibet are often imprisoned. Cultural genocide is portrayed by advocates of an independent Tibet as taking place through massive sinicization programs. (1998, p. 77)

From the Tibetan point of view, China invaded Tibet in the 1950s to firm up its borders for various geo-political reasons, and they have been taking advantage of Tibet's national resources ever since – which has required the violent repression of Tibetan language, religion and of course political authority.

Tibet-in-Exile's discourse of modernization

On 31 March 1959, the Dalai Lama fled the Chinese clamp-down in Lhasa and crossed the border into India. On that day, he was accompanied by an entourage of 20 men, including six cabinet ministers, and in the weeks to come tens of thousands joined him in exile. According to the government-in-exile's web page, there are 145,150 Tibetans in exile, mainly in India, Nepal and Bhutan, with some 25,000 in the rest of the world, outside of Tibet (Office of Planning Commission, nd).[8] Since 1959, any Tibetan within China's political borders has had to choose between silence, co-optation and punishment. Tibet's fledgling efforts at self-modernization, completely frustrated as they were by aristocratic and monastic elites (Bass 1998, p. 2), faced the additional burden of political exile.[9]

Having placed the Tibet situation, both politically and discursively, in context, I would like to proceed to discuss modernism as espoused by three Tibetan leaders, all of whom are robed monastics in leadership positions.[10] Prime Minister Samdhong Rinpoche, the Dalai Lama and Geshe Lhakdor have addressed the education of Tibetan monastics and lay refugees in relation to exile. The three informants in this essay refuse such a division. They specifically avoid potentially schismatic self-representations by finding ways to foreground commonalities of modernity and Buddhism, articulating an approach to Buddhism that both appeals to modern psychological and pedagogical values while allowing space for religious practices that many would identify as the antithesis of modernity.

It could be said that Samdhong Rinpoche is very much the product of systems that many Westerners would call 'pre-modern'. He was born on 5 November 1939 and given the name Lobsang Tenzin, and he was recognized as a reincarnation of the fourth Samdhong Rinpoche five years later.[11] In 1959, 20 years after his birth, he fled Tibet with the Dalai Lama and 80,000 other refugees, crossing the Himalayan Mountains to reach India. He has also been described as a modernizer within the context of the Tibetan diaspora:

> Samdhong Rinpoche was an educator and former Principal and Director of the Central Institute for Higher Tibetan Studies (CIHTS) in Varanasi-Benaris, the first successful higher educational institution to combine Tibetan, Sanskrit, and modern languages, cultures, and education systems. He was also a key author of the new education policy, which reasserts a primary role for Tibetan language and cultural practices and contents in Tibetan secular education in exile. (MacPherson *et al.* 2008)

On 25 October 2009, I interviewed Samdhong Rinpoche. The interview focused on the cooperative programs between Tibetan Buddhist monasteries and Emory University designed to provide monks and nuns with a basic understanding of scientific methods, goals and findings.

Tibetan education policies are adaptive responses to diaspora. In response to my question as to whether there was a tension between preserving traditional Tibetan society and developing adaptive strategies for modernization, Samdhong Rinpoche referred to the 'Basic Education Policy for Tibetans in Exile' (nd), which begins by referring to a foundational aim to produce 'an ideal education policy meeting the basic needs of Tibet' (Samdhong Rinpoche, Interview with author, 25 October 2009).[12] Section 1 of the Tibetan Government-in-Exile's educational policy, makes clear that education is part of a wider adaptive response to refugee life, but the adaptation is not merely an accommodation to the hopefully temporary condition of exile:

> As no such policy has yet been formulated, it is felt that the time is ripe to review the current situation of education of Tibetans in exile and to resolve upon a basic education policy that is better suited to the current needs of Tibetans in exile and that may serve as a basis for the education policy of Tibet in [the] future when a self-governing status is attained .... (Basic nd, p. 1)

That modern, secular education is not merely a survivalist accommodation is asserted in sections 2.1–2.6, which form the second chapter of the document, entitled 'The Meaning of Education'. Education 'is to be recognized as a human quality that enables understanding of external objects and phenomena, and that leads to the awakening, maturing and completion of the potential of the inner consciousness' (section 2.1). The language of this section is deeply enmeshed with the metaphysics of Vajrayana Buddhism. Embedded in these descriptions are references to Vajrayana Buddhist *lojong* or 'mind training' disciplines, as we see in section 2.3: 'Education is to be recognized as a unique inner quality in which the discriminative wisdom and mind-pacifying techniques are conjoined into close partnership'.[13] Education should, according to the views limned by this document, do more than offer a way to give the individual a competitive advantage. The bodhisattva ideal of placing self before others is fore-grounded in section 2.5: 'Education is not to be recognized merely as a means of livelihood. Instead it is to be recognized as a means of achieving temporary as well as long-term welfare for the self and others. In particular, it is to be recognized as a vehicle of social welfare and service.' The relationship between 'temporary' and 'long-term' welfare is vague and could accommodate, at its most elastic, the *very* long-term welfare of multiple lifetimes.

Provisions are made in this document for the protection of Tibetan culture, but distinctions are made so that the effort to protect cultural assets will not preclude modern educational practices in the way that, as discussed above, monastic and aristocratic elites were able to block modernization during the rule of the thirteenth Dalai Lama. Section 3 asserts the necessity of preserving Tibetan culture as a form of 'wealth' that can benefit all peoples, and section 4 divides 'Tibetan' and 'Modern' forms of education, tracing Tibetan educational traditions to the animistic Bon religion and to the Buddhadharma as transmitted from India. 'Wealth' is, again, vague enough to accommodate religious practices that might conflict with a program of modernization.

The balance between modernization cultural self-preservation also marks Tibetan language policy. Tibetan has been under attack at various points within the Chinese program of modernity, whereas the Government-in-Exile's conception specifically privileges Tibetan. 'The Tibetan language', section 4.3 states, 'is, in fact, the only standard base of all Tibetan studies.' Alternatively, 'Modern Education' is not tightly connected with a linguistic-cultural system in the same way. As 'a system that was developed in recent centuries by human beings through investigation and experimentation, primarily, on external objects and phenomena', it mainly includes 'the study of science and technology, mathematics, social sciences, economics, management and planning, and most arts subjects' (section 4.5). In other words, 'Modern Education' refers to the construction of knowledge we find in contemporary secular universities. The system of education outlined by this document resembles the more progressive programs one might encounter in Western contexts. For example, section 7.4 states that 'Until a new system suitable for Tibetans is introduced for the three-year pre-primary level, the Montessori system shall be followed'. All Tibetans shall have the right to a free education through Class XII without discrimination based on gender, race, religion, place of origin, 'being rich or poor, being ordained or lay' (section 13.1), and parents shall not have the right to refuse children access to education.

Western conceptions of modernization typically entail the separation of spheres within civic space such that religious authority no longer has mastery and the section on Moral Conduct asserts the centrality of religious texts but in a carefully modulated way. Section 8.11 states that 'Morality is not to be taught as a separate subject' but, instead, is to be connected closely to the 'central theme of all educational activities'. Excerpts from religious writings including 'biographies of ancient and contemporary great personalities' are to be included 'within the content of school textbooks or supplementary writing' (section 8.11). One does not suppose that 'great personalities' is meant to imply celebrities; the linkage between 'moral conduct' and 'great personalities' does not exclude strictly secular leaders but, given the patterns of Tibetan history, it does not seem that such a group would be very large.

Modernity is not presented as valuable in and of itself. At several points the document defines Tibetan education and even 'sciences' against the unhealthy extremes that characterize modernity:

> In order to instill into pupils the principles of wholesome thought and conduct from the pre-primary school level, the quality and role of teachers, formation of school curriculum, and methodology of teaching shall be framed mainly in accordance with traditional Tibetan principles and sciences, rather than the modern system. (Section 6.7)

The Dalai Lama regularly says, even in Buddhist teaching contexts, that those religious beliefs that are disproved by science should be dispensed with, which would seem to be at variance with section 6.7, although it is hard to tell. The passage states specifically that 'Tibetan principles and sciences' trump 'the modern system', but it is unclear from the passage how Tibetan science and the modern system differ. What is explicitly clear is that a system that is clearly modern in comparison to that of pre-1959 Tibet is discursively constructed in such a way that the modern element does not displace the 'traditional' element.

This document has been translated into English, but it was originally written in Tibetan for Tibetans and the policy was announced in *Kashog* (Parliament) on 14 May 2005.[14] The text embraces modernity at many points, clothing itself in the language of technological progress, human rights, democratic forms and so forth, but at other junctures, it seems an attempt to limit the damage wrought by the uncritical embrace of technological modernity. At these moments, the text is not 'counter-modern' but rather a conception that does not measure its own authenticity by the degree to which it conforms to a prior Western conception, or, of course, to a Chinese conception.

I mentioned to Samdhong Rinpoche, an ex-monk I had come to know in Boulder, Colorado who was now studying for the G.E.D. (high school equivalency test), but who did not even know his times-tables. Samdhong Rinpoche:

> Unfortunately the general training level for monks is not really strict, particularly in the cases of those monks who strongly wish to relocate to Western countries. They are often immature monks – not very properly trained ones. Thoroughly trained monks do not wish to go out. Most of those ones want to develop meditation skills, and the rest remain in the monasteries to teach people there. (Samdhong Rinpoche, Interview with author, 25 October 2009)

However, there has been a 'mushroom growth of religious centers' in the West between 1995–2010, which has led to a 'scarcity of well-trained teachers'.

Earlier efforts at self-modernization such as those by the thirteenth Dalai Lama met with failure because they were considered a threat to tradition, and this concern remains even if its shortcomings are quite clear in retrospect.[15] Given the historical fact of monastic resistance to modernization, I asked Samdhong Rinpoche whether foreign education might have deleterious effects on monastic culture. When someone has been educated in a strictly monastic context and then leaves either for formal study or to live and teach in a Western dharma center, disruptions often occur. Samdhong Rinpoche would not generalize to say that exposure of this sort would cause disturbance.

> Basically we think that people who study Dharma in depth must have an exposure to Western education as well, particularly modern science. Without exposure to modern science, you may not be able to understand the Dharma in an appropriate way, particularly in today's world. So exposure is generally good, but I can't say that there is no danger of disturbance. If someone who is not very well-grounded in the Dharma or religious studies in general, and they are exposed to Western, modern education, modern science, then instead of clarity, they might accumulate confusion and doubts. (Samdhong Rinpoche, Interview with author, 25 October 2009)

Samdhong Rinpoche frankly conceded the possibility of tension between the worldviews of scientific materialism and Tibetan Buddhism, but expressed the concern about a lack of exposure to Western or modern ideas, which, according to Goldstein, has been quite costly for Tibet.

The dystopian and utopian possibilities of 'science' – the potential of science to be used for utterly selfish aims and without empathy for the life forms coalesces with its capacity to ameliorate suffering – are distinguished in the early, autobiographical sections of Dalai Lama's *Universe in a Single Atom: the Convergence of Science and Spirituality*. In the first sentence of the book, the Dalai Lama rhetorically situates himself outside – 'I was never myself trained in science' (Gyatso 2005, p. 1). The book itself measures the gap between Buddhism and science, presenting itself as 'a result of that long period of thinking and of the intellectual journey of a Buddhist monk from Tibet into the world of bubble chambers, particle accelerators, and fMRI'. The next three sentences interweave associations having to do with physical exile with ideas about the science/religion binary. 'Many years after I went into exile in India,' the second paragraph begins, 'I came across an open letter from the 1940s addressed to the Buddhist thinkers of Tibet' (p. 2). In this letter the dissident modernist thinker Gendün Chöphel outlines possible lines of dialogue between Buddhism and science – but the Dalai Lama does not mention that the letter-writer was a radical who loathed the Lhasa hierarchy and was jailed three years for sedition. The documentary *Angry Monk* tells Gendün Chöphel's colorful story.[16] Next, the Dalai Lama reports 'a disturbing conversation I had … a few years earlier with an American lady who was married to a Tibetan' (p. 2). Having heard of his 'active engagement in dialogue with scientists', she warns him that science is a direct threat to Buddhism as it is usually a 'killer' of religion, and so he supposes that he has 'stuck [his] neck out' in maintaining such dangerous friendships. Undeterred, the Dalai Lama writes: 'My confidence in venturing into science lies in my basic belief that as in science so in Buddhism, understanding the nature of reality is pursued by means of critical investigation', adding the stricture that 'if scientific analysis were conclusively to demonstrate certain claims in Buddhism to be false, then we must accept the findings of science and abandon those claims' (pp. 2–3). What could be construed as a concession to modernity or a gambit to entice the skeptical-materialist reader is presented by the author as a necessity of survival. Once again, the pressures of diasporic existence are a fundamental condition of the identity shaped in response:

> The motivation for my interest in science is more than merely personal. Even before I came into exile, it was clear to me and others in the country that one of the underlying causes for

> Tibet's political tragedy was its failure to open itself to modernization. As soon as we arrived in India, we set up Tibetan schools for refugee children with a modern curriculum, which included scientific education for the first time. (p. 3)

There is a humorous moment in Martin Scorsese's biographical film *Kundun* (1997) when one of the tutors of the young Dalai Lama says, approvingly, 'He's a modern man, just like he was last time.' The ironic juxtaposition here is between the fact, on the one hand, that the thirteenth and fourteenth Dalai Lamas were both much more progressive than the bureaucratic hierarchies with which they had to negotiate and the belief, on the other hand, that the fourteenth Dalai Lama is in some sense a reincarnation of elements of the mindstream of his predecessor the thirteenth. If we have an either/or approach to modernity in which a mindset or belief is either scientific or religious, then anyone who professes belief in the continuity of mindstream elements across life-spans will very likely fail the modernity test.

The Universe in a Single Atom specifically contests this construction of modernity and it is part of a comprehensive, coordinated discourse. There have been dozens of Mind/Life Institute meetings since the first one in 1987, and these dialogues between representatives of contemplative practices (especially the Dalai Lama) and scientific students of cognition and neurobiology (such as world-class expert on human emotions, Paul Ekman) have produced a rich stream of publications that range from the more academically rigorous kind of research to popularizing texts designed to help people change their lives, e.g. Daniel Goleman's *Emotional Intelligence* (1997).[17] In addition to the speculative and summative dialogue sessions, the Buddhism/science conversation is being made part of monastic training and is directly promoted by the three modernist-monastics under discussion, Dalai Lama, Geshe Lhakdor and Samdhong Rinpoche. With the assistance of foreign universities, especially Emory University, science courses are being taught in a number of Tibetan Buddhist monasteries. This de-segregation of what typically is called secular knowledge and spiritual training is taking place throughout the Tibetan-speaking world, even at the level of secondary schools.[18]

Intellectual and cultural leaders of the Tibetan diaspora, in which ordained monks figure quite prominently, have also worked to reconfigure the concept of 'Modernity' itself. The degree to which their positions coincide with those of other cosmopolitan thinkers has not been sufficiently recognized. One of these leaders is Geshe Lhakdor, the Director of the Library of Tibetan Works and Archives; he is primarily responsible for preserving Tibetan texts, getting them translated into other languages, and creating a widely distributed library of authoritative texts. Geshe Lhakdor must preserve Tibetan culture, but his cultural mission is to find ways to keep living traditions sustainable under the pressure of modernity – a museum conception of the Tibetan past is not what Tibet's Government in Exile wishes to promote. Not only are traditional texts selected for promulgation, translation and dissemination – the cultural leadership must also work actively to develop the optimal relationship with the discourse of modernity.

In our interview, Geshe Lhakdor describes modernism (in the valorific sense) as the movement toward equality and meritocracy and not the advancement of technological progress. 'Although science and technology – the modern shiny gadgets and so forth – are external indicators of modernization, the real indication of modernization is the presence of the most cultivated ideas about equal rights and human responsibility' (Geshe Lhakdor, Interview with author, 23 September 2010). Geshe Lhakdor distinguishes between internal and external motivations in ways that align with the Basic Education Policy, both of which conform to the Buddhist notion that motivation is prior to all else. Section 2.3, as we have seen, distinguishes between education as 'a unique inner quality in which the discriminative wisdom and mind-pacifying techniques are conjoined into close partnership' and a behaviorist (perhaps we could say Pavlovian) kind of learning in which the stimulations from the outside entice the student to move through a series of steps.

In defining modernity as a progressive movement toward equality, Geshe Lhakdor's adjustment to the unreflective notion of modernity as technological progress resonates with Amartya Sen's notions in *The Idea of Justice.* Sen writes that 'every normative theory of social justice that has received support and advocacy in recent times seems to demand equality of *something* – something that is regarded as particularly important to that theory' (2009, p. 291). Geshe Lhakdor insists that modernism in this sense must refer 'more to the human being than to what he has produced'. Like Amartya Sen, Geshe Lhakdor protects his conception of modernity against materialist reductions in which metrics supporting of an overall standard of living often mask a serious decline in something like human *caring.* Both Sen and Lhakdor admire the priority given to human cultivation in the Western enlightenment but find that modernization, defined as progress toward equality or movement away from arrogance, are powerfully expressed in the Buddha's teachings, which shows that modernism is not a European monopoly or invention, or a 'provincialism'. Sen writes,

> It is not my claim ... that there is some radical dissonance between 'Western' and 'Eastern' (or generally, non-Western) thinking on these subjects. ... It is my claim, rather, that similar – or closely linked – ideas of justice, fairness, responsibility, duty, goodness, and rightness have been pursued in many different parts of the world, which can expand the reach of arguments that have been considered in Western literature and that the global presence of such reasoning is often overlooked or marginalized in the dominant traditions of Western discourse. (p. xiv)

Sen acknowledges that 'Athens certainly has an excellent record in public discussion' but points out that 'open deliberation also flourished in several other ancient civilizations, sometimes spectacularly so. For example, some of the earliest open general meetings aimed specifically at settling disputes between different points of view, on social and religious matters, took place in India in the so-called Buddhist "councils", where adherents of different points of view got together to argue out their differences, beginning in the sixth century BC' (p. 331). Sen's move in locating a form of proto-modernity within Buddhist civilization is a challenge to monolithic, Eurocentric conceptions of modernity.

The future of Tibetan modernity

At whatever pace, there is no doubt that Tibetan people, including both those who live within the historical boundaries of Tibet and those in refugee communities in countries such as India and Nepal, are undergoing some form of modernization, but to assume that there is only one kind of modernization in play would oversimplify the process and would tend to exclude the voices of those Tibetans who are in the best position to challenge the imposed modernization from China. If we were to approach the matter with a singular conception of modernization, it would be difficult to avoid the conclusion that the Chinese disruption of the 'lamaist state' is a form of modernization, but we would also have to conclude that this modernization fails to measure up to expectations if the Western conception of modernization is the yardstick. For Göle, 'science and technology and, on the other hand … individual emancipation, which meant getting away from traditions and religiosity' are the two primary ways in which Western societies have charted their progress from pre-modernity into modernity' (n.d.), but this measure of modernity would clearly be self-defeating for the intellectual leadership of Tibetans in exile.

Acknowledgements
I would like to thank Bill Mihalopoulos, Andrea M. Pinkney, Rajesh Rai and Chitra Sankaran for suggestions with this article.

Notes

1. In 'Multiple Modernities' (2000), the introductory essay to a collection of essays popularizing this concept, S.N. Eisenstadt argues that the plural notion of modernity goes against the 'classical' theories of modernization that drew on the work of Marx, Durkheim and Weber and which held sway through the 1950s. Until the Second World War historical conditions supported a unified conception of modernity in which 'the cultural program of modernity … developed in modern Europe … and would ultimately take over in all modernizing and modern societies' (p. 1), but then, Eisenstadt argues, things changed: 'the actual developments in modernizing societies have refuted the homogenizing and hegemonic assumptions of this Western program of modernity' (p. 1). Calling attention to patterns which were 'distinctively modern, though greatly influenced by specific cultural premises, traditions, and historical experiences', these forms of modernization 'developed distinctly modern dynamics and modes of interpretation, for which the original Western project constituted the crucial (and usually ambivalent) reference point' (p. 1). Even though many of the defining features of what we call 'modernity' arose in Europe, the modernities that developed in non-Western societies have 'articulated strong anti-Western or even anti-modern themes', and so Eisenstadt and other proponents of multiple modernities believe that the story of modernity is best told as a 'continual constitution and reconstitution of a multiplicity of cultural programs' (p. 2). Eisenstadt sees this project as a conscious effort carried out 'by specific social actors in close connection with social, political, and intellectual activists' (p. 2), along with various social movements and programs that are not necessarily aligned in their specific goals.

   The project of 'multiple modernities' is an attempt to recognize forms of modernization as adaptations to particular conditions without assuming at the outset that Western, European modernity is the only measure of what modernity might be. Nilüfer Göle, in 'Snapshots of Islamic Modernities,' makes this point explicitly: '… I will try to highlight some of the patterns that carry a potentiality through which modernity is not simply rejected or readopted but critically and creatively reappropriated by new religious discursive and social practices in non-Western contexts' (2000, p. 93).
2. Although ethnic Tibetan populations have a considerable presence in other Chinese provinces, 'Tibet' in this paper shall refer to the Tibetan Autonomous Region (TAR).
3. Warren Smith cites a letter from the former abbot of Gyantse monastery and governor of the Gyantse district Thupten Nyenjik that was sent to *The Statesmen* newspaper in New Delhi, the Indian and Pakistan premiers, and to President Eisenhower and other officials in the USA: 'To us Tibetans the phrase the 'liberation of Tibet,' in its moral and spiritual implications, is viewed as deadly mockery. The country of a free people was invaded and occupied under the pretext of Liberation. Liberation from whom and what? Ours was a happy country with a solvent government and a contented people till the Chinese invasion in 1950 since when we have been so exploited that we have been reduced to a state of intellectual, spiritual, and economic bankruptcy' (Smith 1996, p. 410).

   The letter, dated 20 July 1956, also mentioned the bombing of temples, the importation of 'large numbers of Chinese settlers' and the plan – attributed to Mao Tse Tung – to increase the population from 'two–three million' to over ten million. To Thupten Nyenjik, 'this can only mean genocide, the complete disappearance of an ancient culture and people through the importation of Chinese on a gigantic scale. Such is the meaning of Chinese autonomy for Tibet' (411).

As Buruma (2008) points out, more than population is at stake: 'The Chinese have exported their version of modern development to Tibet not only in terms of architecture and infrastructure, but also people – wave after wave of them: businessmen from Sichuan, prostitutes from Hunan, technocrats from Beijing, party officials from Shanghai and shopkeepers from Yunnan. The majority of Lhasa's population today is no longer Tibetan. Most people in rural areas are Tibetan, but their way of life is not likely to survive Chinese modernization any more than the Apaches' way of life survived in the United States.'

4. BBC, 'Tibetan People "Put Through Hell"', 9 March 2009. In this report, the Dalai Lama reiterates his complaint that, owing to sinicization policies, Tibet's religion, culture, language and identity were 'nearing extinction'.
5. See Buruma (2008): 'The Chinese have much to answer for, but the fate of Tibet is not just a matter of semi-colonial oppression. It is often forgotten that many Tibetans, especially educated people in the larger towns, were so keen to modernize their society in the mid-twentieth century that they saw the Chinese Communists as allies against rule by holy monks and serf-owning landlords. In the early 1950s, the young Dalai Lama himself was impressed by Chinese reforms and wrote poems praising Chairman Mao.'
6. In *Education in Tibet: Policy and Practice since 1950* Catriona Bass traces the development of China's educational policies and practices from 1950 to 1998. During the Cultural Revolution (1966–1976) 'all aspects of Tibetan culture in the curriculum came under attack, including the Tibetan language' (1998, p. 3).
7. Grunfeld includes an appendix on the population of Tibet with estimates between 50,000 and 12,000,000 Han Chinese civilians within the Tibet Autonomous Region. Andrew M. Fischer agrees that 'it is difficult to come to an exact agreement about the numbers of Chinese in Tibetan areas' but adds that 'it is as much a political battle over the representation of the crisis as a more straightforward statistical procedure' (Blondeau and Buffetrille 2008, pp. 145–146). Fischer points out that many Han Chinese leave Tibet in the winter and that tourism inflates the Han population during the summer months. Even if the Han population is small in the rural parts of Tibet, Fischer believes an accurate 'appraisal of the Han population of the TAR' would probably surpass '50 percent in the cities year around' (p. 151).
8. The Office of the Planning Commission projects this number based on its 2007 estimates, figuring in average estimated population growth.
9. Bass writes that the thirteenth Dalai Lama attempted unsuccessfully to introduce 'a modern secular education system in Tibet', but 'these foreign secular establishments had faced considerable opposition from traditional conservative groups among the clergy and aristocracy' since 'it was believed that the schools would be vehicles for introducing Western ideas into Tibet, and would undermine Tibet's cultural and religious traditions' (1998, p. 2).
10. From this point onward, 'Tibetan' shall refer to Tibetans-in-exile unless otherwise stated.
11. This means that he was found to be, at age five, the reincarnation of a highly realized teacher and that he was the '5th Samdhung Rinpoche' tells us that this succession of rebirths had gone back five generations. The current Dalai Lama, the fourteenth, is thus the reincarnation of the thirteenth, and so on.
12. This language carries over from another document, from the 'Charter of Tibetans in Exile', which is described in this way by the web page of the Office of the Dalai Lama: 'In 1963 His Holiness presented a draft democratic constitution for Tibet that was followed by a number of reforms to democratize our administrative set-up. The new democratic constitution promulgated as a result of this reform was named "The Charter of Tibetans in Exile". The charter enshrines freedom of speech, belief, assembly and movement. It also provides detailed guidelines on the functioning of the Tibetan government with respect to those living in exile' (A Brief Biography, nd).
13. For a modern translation of the 'mind-training' genre of Buddhist teachings, see Jinpa (2005). Jinpa's introduction provides an in-depth historical framework for understanding the cognitive psychology of a thousand years ago. A recognized reincarnation of this sort is usually called a 'tulku' and that word is sometimes included as a formal title.

14. It would be instructive to compare the Tibetan and English versions of this document to see whether modernization is characterized in roughly the same ways for English and Tibetan speakers.
15. Goldstein writes that the thirteenth Dalai Lama's attempts at self-modernization 'sent shock waves through the monastic and aristocratic elites who held most of the land in Tibet in the form of feudal estates' (1997, p. 35). New tax levies were required 'to support military buildup' and educational practices were felt to be a threat to Buddhism. Conservative officials convinced the Dalai Lama that modernization was a threat to Buddhism and to his authority. Goldstein presents this resistance to modernization as a complete disaster: 'By the mid-1920s their efforts had succeeded, and in one of the pivotal policy decisions of modern Tibetan history, the thirteenth Dalai Lama gutted the heart of the reform program by demoting the entire group of promodernization officers and closing the English school. Overnight, Tibet lost its best chance to create a modern polity capable of coordinating international support for its independent status and defending its territory.'
16. See Lopez (2007) for the fullest account of the 'mad monk'.
17. See for example, Begley (2007) and Hayward and Varela (1987). For more academic exchanges between university researchers and the Dalai Lama, see Harrington and Zajonc (2006).
18. When Geshe Tsewang Dorje, who is currently the gekü (chief disciplinarian; akin to Dean or Provost) at Sera Je Monastery in Bylakuppe, Indian, proposed to the Dalai Lama to start a small monastic school in his home village of Saboo, Ladakh, the Dalai Lama strongly urged Geshe Dorje to mix secular and religious education. From an appeal letter sent out by the school-building project: 'There are plans for a secular school to educate children who otherwise would not have access to education; the Ngari Institute will also train monks and nuns, but the monastic education will be combined with social service (e.g. teaching); and, finally, the institute will create avenues for inter-cultural exchange based on educational sharing rather than mere tourism-based consumption.'

Notes on contributor

John Whalen-Bridge is Associate Professor of English at the National University of Singapore. He is the author of *Political Fiction and the American Self*, co-editor with Gary Storhoff of *Emergence of Buddhist American Literature* and *American Buddhism as a Way of Life*, and editor of *Norman Mailer's Later Fictions*. With Tan Sor-Hoon he co-edited *Democracy as Culture: Deweyan Pragmatism in a Globalizing World*. He is completing a study of Engaged Buddhism and countercultural writing in postwar America, focusing on Gary Snyder, Charles Johnson and Maxine Hong Kingston.

References

A Brief Biography, nd. Retrieved from: http://www.dalailama.com/biography/a-brief-biography [Accessed 22 September 2010].

Adams, V., 1998. Suffering the winds of Lhasa: politicized bodies, human rights, cultural difference, and humanism in Tibet. *Medical Anthropology Quarterly,* NS, 12 (1): 74–102.

Basic Education Policy for Tibetans in Exile. Available on the *Tibetan children's educational and welfare fund.* Retrieved from: http://www.tcewf.org/publications/edupolicy/index.html [Accessed 28 July 2010].

Bass, C., 1998. *Education in Tibet: policy and practice since 1950.* London: Zed Books.

BBC, 2009. Unsigned report. Tibetan people 'put through hell'. Article updated 10 March 2009. Retrieved from: http://news.bbc.co.uk/2/hi/7933207.stm [Accessed 28 October 2010].

Begley, S., 2007. *Train your mind, change your brain: how a new science reveals our extraordinary potential to transform ourselves.* New York: Ballantine.

Blondeau, A.-M. and Buffetrille, K., eds, 2008. *Authenticating Tibet: answers to China's 100 questions,* foreword by Donald Lopez. Berkeley: University of California Press.

Brauen, M., 2000. *Dreamworld Tibet: western illusions.* Authored in collaboration with Renate Koller and Markus Vock, translated by Martin Willson. Trumbull, CT: Weatherhill.

Buruma, I., 2001. The romance of exile. *The New Republic,* 12 February 2001: 33–38.

Buruma, I., 2008. The last of the Tibetans. Retrieved from: http://burmadigest.info/2008/04/07/the-last-of-the-tibetans/ [accessed 28 October 2010] (originally published as 'The Tibetans last stand' in *The Guardian,* 14 April 2008).

Eisenstadt, S.N., 2000. Multiple modernities. *Daedalus,* 129 (1), 1–29.

Goldstein, M.C., 1997. *The snow lion and the dragon: China, Tibet, and the Dalai Lama.* Berkely: University of California Press.

Goldstein, M.C., 2007. *A history of modern Tibet: the calm before the storm: 1951–1955,* Vol. 2. Berkeley: University of California Press.

Göle, N., 2000. Snapshots of Islamic modernities. *Daedalus,* 129 (1): 91–117.

Göle, N., nd. Interview with *Frontline.* Retrieved from: http://www.pbs.org/wgbh/pages/frontline/shows/muslims/ interviews/gole.html [Accessed 28 October 2010].

Goleman, D., 1997. *Emotional intelligence.* New York: Bantam.

Grunfeld, A. T., 1996. *The making of modern Tibet, rev.* ed. New York: M. E. Sharpe.

Gyatso, T., (the fourteenth Dalai Lama), 2005. *Universe in a single atom: the convergence of science and spirituality.* New York: Morgan Road Books.

Harrington, A. and Zajonc, A., eds, 2006. *The Dalai Lama at MIT.* Cambridge, MA: Harvard University Press.

Hayward, J.W. and Varela, F.J., 1987. *Gentle bridges: conversations with the Dalai Lama on the sciences of mind.* Boston, MA: Shambhala Publications.

Jinpa, (Geshe) Thupten., trans., 2005. *Mind training: the great collection.* Boston, MA: Wisdom Books.

Kundun. 1997. Film. Directed by Martin Scorsese, written by Melissa Mathison. De Fina-Cappa.

Lopez, D.S., ed., 1995. *Curators of the Buddha: the study of Buddhism under colonialism.* Chicago, IL: University of Chicago.

Lopez, D.S., 1998. *Prisoners of Shangri-La: Tibetan Buddhism and the West.* Chicago, IL: University of Chicago Press.

Lopez, D.S., 2007. *The madman's middle way: reflections on reality of the Tibetan Monk Gendun Chopel.* Chicago, IL: University of Chicago Press.

MacPherson, S., Bentz, A.-S., and Ghoso, D.B., September 2008. Global nomads: the emergence of the Tibetan diaspora. Retrieved from: http://www.migrationinformation.org/Feature/display.cfm?id=693 [Accessed 30 October 2010].

Office of Planning Commission Estimates, nd. Retrieved from: http://www.tibet.net/en/index.php?id=9 [Accessed 22 September 2010].

Petech, L., 1990. *Central Tibet and the Mongols* (Serie Orientale Roma 65). Rome: Instituto Italiano per il Medio ed Estremo Oriente.

Schell, O., 2000. *Virtual Tibet: searching for Shangri-La from the Himalayas to Hollywood.* New York: Metropolitan Books/Henry Holt.

Sen, A., 2009. *The idea of justice.* Cambridge, MA: Belknap Press of Harvard University Press.

Shakabpa, T.W.D., 1967. *Tibet: a political history.* New Haven, CT: Yale University Press.

Smith, W.W., Jr., 1996. *Tibetan nation: a history of Tibetan nationalism and Sino-Tibetan relations.* Boulder, CO: Westview Press.

'Forget not your old country': absence, identity, and marginalization in the practice and development of Sri Lankan Buddhism in Malaysia

Jeffrey Samuels

Department of Philosophy & Religion, Western Kentucky University, Kentucky, USA

This article examines various linkages through which Sri Lankan diaspora communities in Malaysia sought and still seek meaning. Taking my cue from Engseng Ho's work on the Hadrami in which he notes how absence shapes diasporic experiences, I investigate the constructive role that feelings of loss have played in the imagining and reimagining of the Sri Lankan community's identity in Malaysia. More specifically, this article considers the role that particular sites of memory – Buddhist institutions, rituals, and cemeteries – play in the production of an ethnic and religious identity. Finally, I explore how such produced identities may become threatened by competing communities and by the nation state as well as how interreligious and interethnic alliances produced through temple networks provide the means by which state control could be challenged and feelings of marginalization overcome.

In studying diasporic communities, attention is often paid to the factors that draw groups of people abroad. While it is important to consider what motivates people to leave the familiarity of their own homes and family and face uncertainty in a new land, understanding the movement of people across geographical regions, Engseng Ho argues, also requires us to 'appreciate the degree to which absence shapes diasporic experiences. To be in one place', Ho maintains, 'is to be absent everywhere else. Moving between places, mobility leaves in its wake a trail of absences' (2006, p. 18).

Those who have been away from home and their family for any length of time may come to understand what Thomas Haynes Bayly meant when he said in his poem 'Isle of Beauty' that 'Absence makes the heart grow fonder'. However, what role does absence play for those who remain away? While it may make any experience of return a poignantly powerful event, what effect does it have on groups of people who choose not to return? Does experiences of absence simply find expression in feelings of self-pity, profound loss, or the glorification of the past? Or, does it play a positive role in the diasporic experience?

Turning to the Sinhalese communities in Malaysia, this article reflects on these very questions. Focusing specifically on the Sri Lankan Buddhist community of Kuala Lumpur, I first examine the constructive role that absence has played in the founding of religious institutions and in the maintenance of the group's ethnic identity. Then, examining more recent demographic changes taking place at the two Sri Lankan temples in Kuala Lumpur, I consider how absence, memory, and identity have resulted in inter-caste and inter-ethnic tensions. Finally, I propose that the desire of the Sinhalese to overcome meaninglessness and marginalization in the Malay-Muslim nation state of Malaysia has resulted in unique forms of institution-building and community alliances. However, before turning to how absence shapes the Sri Lankan diasporic experience in Malaysia, it is first necessary to set the scene by examining briefly the different types of Sinhalese communities that came to Malaysia.

Sri Lankan migrants in Malaysia

Sri Lankan migrants came to Malaya in multiple waves. Although census data before 1871 include no mention of Sri Lankans living in Malaya, they were present in the port cities of Penang, Melaka and Singapore well before then. Besides trade between the Malayan peninsula and Sri Lanka dating back as far as 1828, Melaka and Singapore were treated as penal colonies (established first under the East India Company) for convicts from India, Sri Lanka and Burma.[1] Prior to the 1870s, we also know that groups of Christian missionaries migrated to Penang from Sri Lanka, most notably from around Jaffna, one of 'the earliest centres of Christian missionary work' (Raja Singam 1968, p. 19).

Starting in the 1860s we find different types of Sinhalese immigrants. Rather than being forced to migrate for retributive reasons (i.e. convicts) or encouraged to migrate for ideological reasons (i.e. missionaries), businessmen began to arrive on their own accord. With the transfer of the Straits Settlements to the Crown Colony in 1867, flow between the two British colonies was made easier and even encouraged. Many of Sri Lankans who came around this period were 'traders in jewellery and gems, goldsmiths and confectioners. Many of them chose the port cities of Singapore, Penang and Melaka as their home, a place from which they could easily keep in contact with their families in Ceylon and from where they could send over remittances' (Arseculeratne 1991, p. 16). The discovery of tin deposits in the nineteenth century as well as the development and expansion of rubber estates and other plantations (most notably tea and coffee) spurred additional waves of Sri Lankan migrants to Malaya.

The signing of the Pangkor Engagement or Treaty in January 1874 between the Sultan of Perak and the governor of the Straits Settlement, Sir Andrew Clarke, allowed for an expanded British involvement in the Peninsular states which, in turn, paved the way for the next wave of immigrants from Ceylon. The Engagement provided the British access to the hinterlands and with that the possibility of developing the country, with attention first given to the states of Perak and Selangor. To develop what was, up until then, thick jungle, the government of the Straits Settlements needed a new and different type of immigrant: those who could build and manage a much needed infrastructure (Samarawickrama 2003, p. 7f). Looking westward, Sri Lanka was an important place from where recruits could be sent as their knowledge of English and, more importantly, familiarity with the British colonial machinery made them a valuable workforce. It may also be argued that the migration of Sri Lankans to Malaya was politically motivated as it counter-balanced what some people, such as Sir Frederick Weld (governor of the Straits Settlements from 1880 to 1887), believed to be an overwhelming number of Chinese immigrants in Malaya.

Indeed, in one dispatch from the Settlements to the Secretary of State in England, Weld wrote that 'I am anxious for political reasons that the great preponderance of the Chinese over any other race in the Settlements and to a larger marked degree in some of the Native States, under our administration, should be counter-balanced as much as possible by the influx of Indian and other nationalities.'[2]

With the development of Malaya and the tin industry came the need for a system of transportation. The British, turning to their own civil servants already working abroad, asked J.W.W. Birch to move from Sri Lanka to Malaya in the 1870s. With him came two divisions of the Ceylon Pioneer Corps who were charged with building the first rail line in Malaya. That line was completed in 1884, and linked the tin town of Taiping in Perak to Port Weld on the Larut River. More Sri Lankans came to work on the railway after 1891 when C.E. Spooner, a man who would later become the first General Manager of the Malay States Railway, arrived to Malaya from Sri Lanka. Like Birch, Spooner brought with him a large numbers of Sri Lankan Sinhalese and Tamils from the Ceylon Public Works Department where he previously worked. Along with continuing work on the railway, Spooner and his so-called 'Spooner men' devoted themselves to developing the state of Selangor by designing and constructing the Klang Water works, Pudu Gaol and the government building in Selangor. Following Spooner's decision to establish, in 1901, a single railway administration – the Federated Malay States Railways – a central workshop to service the entire network of trains was established in Sentul, Kuala Lumpur to where a number of Sri Lankans – Sinhalese as well as Tamils – moved.

Many Sri Lankans were recruited through the colonial offices in Sri Lanka and Malaya. Along with them, Sri Lankan traders and businessmen – tempted by stories about the *El Dorado* or the Land of Gold (*Svarnabhumi*) lying just eastward – continued to make it over on their own accord. Attracted to what they saw as opportunities for wealth, many Sinhalese immigrants gravitated toward the port cities of Penang and Singapore as well as the larger cities of Taiping, Ipoh, Kuala Lumpur, Melaka and Klang. These cities experienced rapid growth during the late nineteenth and early twentieth centuries and there was ready employment in a number of different occupations.

The forces motivating people to migrate can rarely be reduced to a single factor. While economic opportunities were alluring to many who risked much to travel across the Indian Ocean, it is also worth bearing in mind that moving to a new country often offers people freedom from their past. S.N. Arseculeratne's book on *Sinhalese Immigrants in Malaysia and Singapore 1860–1990*, for instance, mentions several people who came to Malaya from Sri Lanka to escape repercussions from their involvement in the Sinhalese–Muslim riots of 1915. Other people came simply to break free from Sri Lanka's more conservative social culture as well as from their own inherited past, including their social status. As no documents were needed to travel from Sri Lanka to Malaya, people were freely able to seek different types of employment than was available to them in Sri Lanka and, by changing their names – a clear marker of their caste status – overcome certain social liabilities that previously hindered their chances for self-betterment.

The founding of Sri Lankan temples in Malaya

The first Sri Lankan temples were established in Malaya in the late nineteenth century. These temples were built to serve the religious and social needs of Sri Lankan immigrants who chose to remain permanently in the Land of Gold. The decision to remain in Malaya brought new sets of challenges, particularly finding comfort during more difficult times when a sense of uncertainty and meaninglessness filled the minds and hearts of the diasporic community. We read in the history of Buddhist Maha Vihara in Brickfields that 'The pioneer Sinhala Buddhist immigrants also faced many shortcomings in Malaya in the early days particularly with regard to the performance of their religious obligations. There were no Theravada Buddhist temples and no monks. Cases had occurred where certain Sinhala Buddhists had died and were interred without even the proper last religious rites being administered' (de Silva, 1998, p. 23). Although Sri Lankan Buddhists living in other areas in Malaya (e.g. Kedah and Kelantan) tended to seek solace in Thai temples that dotted the region, the absence of such temples in Kuala Lumpur,[3] as well as the seeming foreignness of Chinese temples there (with their focus on ancestral worship and the prevalence of Chinese deities) – led the Sinhalese in Kuala Lumpur and Taiping to found more familiar places of worship.

Following the establishment of the first Sinhalese Buddhist temple in Malaya in 1889 – Bodhi Langka Ram Vihara in Taiping, Perak – a second temple was built to serve the growing number of Sri Lankans living in Kuala Lumpur. The location chosen for the temple – Buddhist Maha Vihara – was the cosmopolitan section known as Brickfields, an area of Kuala Lumpur where the Public Works Department factory was located and where a number of Sri Lankan Sinhalese and Tamil civil servants lived (Baxstrom 2008). As the community did not have sufficient funds to buy, outright, a piece of land, it was decided that the community would petition the colonial government. The Sri Lankan community sent their request to the British government through C.E. Spooner, the State Engineer from the Public Works Department who, fond of the Sinhalese, supported their petition. Spooner's hope, according to the history of the Brickfields temple, was that a Sri Lankan temple in Kuala Lumpur would encourage other Sri Lankans to emigrate to Malaya (see de Silva 1998, chap. 3). In response, the British wrote that land intended for public service could only be granted to an organization. A decision was then made among the Sri Lankan Buddhist community there to form an organization which they called the *Sāsana Abhiwurdhi Wardhana Society*.

The foundation stone for the shrine room was laid on 25 August 1894; however, it was only completed 'some time during the first decade of the 20th Century' (de Silva 1998, p. 96). Prior to that, modest living quarters were built to house the first incumbents – Venerable (Ven.) Patthalagedera Dhammananda Thera and his student, Ven. Godagama Sobhita Thera – who arrived from Sri Lanka in May 1895.

The temple in Brickfields was soon followed by a second one in Kuala Lumpur: the Sri Lankan Buddhist temple in Sentul.[4] With the establishment of the central workshop for the Federated Malay States Railways in Sentul, 100 quarters were constructed for the railway workers. A large number of Sri Lankans occupied the quarters, thus creating a need for a closer place of worship. In 1917 a piece of land in Sentul was reserved for the Sinhala Buddhist community and in 1921 the Sri Saddharma Wardhana Society was formed and charged with the duties of collecting funds to build a temple. In 1930, a larger plot of land next to the railway workshop was delineated for the temple. The old temple was taken down and rebuilt on the new site.[5]

There is another factor – besides the eleven or so kilometers between Brickfields and Sentul – that led to the formation and development of the Sentul temple: caste and class biases that existed among certain Sri Lankans living in the diaspora at the time. Before we examine that, however, we first need to understand the role that the temples played in preserving Sri Lankan culture and identity.

Temples as sites of collective memory

Although feelings of absence led certain Sri Lankans in Malaya to return home, the same emotions compelled some of those who stayed to find ways not only to make the unfamiliar familiar, but also to keep the collective memory of the community's past inscribed on the hearts and minds of future generations of Sinhalese. Maurice Halbwachs (1992, see also Coser 1992) has pointed out in his work on social memory – and Jun Jing (1996) and Jean DeBernardi (1994, 2004) have illustrated with regarding to the Chinese communities in China and Malaysia – that one social institution that often plays a key role in the social construction and maintenance of a group's collective memory is religion.[6] Complete with its calendrical rites, rituals, festivals, celebrations, as well as religious and language schools, the Sri Lankan Buddhist temples in Malaysia provided its devotees with the social context from which the group's social memory about Sri Lanka and their own collective identity as Sri Lankans living in the diaspora could be preserved.

Like for many Chinese communities in Malaya (DeBernardi 1994), many Sri Lankans living on the peninsula drew a close connection between their own ethnicity and their religion. In that regard, then, it is not surprising to find that the Sinhalese temples in Malaya and the recently arrived Sinhalese monks attracted the interest of the diaspora community as they were seen, in the words of one prominent layman in Kuala Lumpur, Vijaya Samarawickrama, as an embodiment of all that was Sinhalese. The important role of temples and their resident monks in the lives of the Sinhalese community in Malaya was further accentuated by the belief – then and now – that the Sri Lankan Christian community living in Malaya has largely lost their Sinhalese identity as a result of their religious conversion. It is in regard to this that Arseculeratne's comment about the cultural role that Sri Lankan Buddhist temples played for immigrant Sinhalese begins to make sense:

> The Sinhalese Buddhist temples and their monks in the Malay peninsula also served a surrogate role in the cultural and social life of the Sinhalese; they were inextricably intertwined with the customs, traditions and language of the Sinhalese and helped in the sustenance or revival of their religious and secular customs … . Social life amongst the Sinhalese was invigorated through the temple, which became a fountain of Sinhalese culture and a catalyst for social coherence [which] provided some cultural anchorage to the Sinhalese youth who tended to drift towards Christianity through education in missionary schools. (1991, pp.163, 164)

Along with being a gathering place for the Sri Lankan Buddhist community, the Sri Lankan temples played a part in organizing important religious *cum* cultural celebrations such as Vesak and the Sinhala New Year. By being home to several Sinhalese associations and clubs (such as the Malaysian Sinhalese Association) and by fostering Sinhalese heritage through sponsoring music events, dramas, sports meets and literary activities, the temples became lively sites where those living in the diaspora could overcome feelings of absence while, at the same time, remember their past and their own ethnic distinctiveness. While some performances held at the temples had specific Buddhist themes, others were based on the community's Sri Lankan heritage, such as the drama organized by Ven. Siriniwasa Thera that was held in conjunction with Sri Lanka's independence from Britain.

One important way that the Sri Lankan temples were able to preserve the community's cultural identity was through language instruction. In 1929 a Buddhist Sunday school (*daham pasala*) was established at the Brickfields temple for a small number of *Sri Lankan* students. Drawing on the Sunday school curriculum created by the Young Men's Buddhist Association (Taruṇa Bauddha Saṅgamaya) in Sri Lanka, the Sunday school at Brickfields focused not only on teaching religious doctrine, but also the Sinhala language. Around 10 years later, the head monk of the Sentul temple at the time – Ven. Siriniwasa Thera – began conducting Sinhala language classes at the nearby Methodist Boys' School until a special building was constructed for that purpose in 1947.[7]

Engseng Ho (2006, p. 3) has argued that 'In a society of migrants, what is important is not where you were born, but where you die. This, if nothing else, makes a diaspora entirely different from a nation.' It was, perhaps, this particular concern that led the Sri Lankan community in Kuala Lumpur to establish a Sinhalese cemetery in 1903. Like other cemeteries which, as Lynn Rainville (2008, p. 2) notes, are 'particularly well suited for recovering the constructed memories of the past', the Sinhalese cemetery functioned as an important 'site of memory (*lieu de mémoire*)' (Nora and Kritzman 1996, p. xvii) for the Sri Lankan diaspora community in Malaysia. With the dead being unable to speak for themselves, their bodies, graves and tombstones became signifiers on which meaning and memory could be projected, particularly by those experiencing absence, uncertainty and meaninglessness.

Given the role that cemeteries may play as sites of memory, it becomes clearer why many Sinhalese Buddhists in Malaya chose to bury their dead. Vijaya Samarawickrama, for instance, noted in an interview with S.N. Arseculeratne (1991, p. 164) that families tended to bury their dead 'because of the immigrant mentality … the need for something physical of their kin to hold on to'. Discussing this further with me, Samarawickrama explained how the earliest generations of Sinhalese in Malaya 'must have felt terribly isolated in a largely hostile environment: disease, loneliness, financial woes and so on. If they had cremated them, then there would not be a physical contact with their loved ones, thus increasing the sense of isolation from the familiar.'

The rituals performed regularly in the cemeteries also became an important strategy for constructing and maintaining the diasporic community's memory at the collective and individual level, as well as for 'attaching and rooting the immigrant community to the soil of the new homeland' (Francis *et al.* 2000, p. 42). Thus, it is no wonder that after the Sinhalese cemetery was neglected in 1915, the temple in Brickfields – particularly the resident monk at the time (Ven. Wanaratana Thera) and the temple's association (Sasana Abhiwurdhi Wardhana Society) – decided to take over the task of maintaining it. Although the upkeep of the cemetery was later transferred to a different committee, the Brickfields temple continued to play role in the mortuary landscape of the Sinhalese community by organizing clean-up days and by performing annual merit-transference rituals at the cemetery.[8] What is important to mention with regard to those events is the date on which they occurred each year. Often held on the Sunday before the Sinhala new year each year, the event was a way of reminding the Sinhalese community to 'Forget not your old country'[9] while, at the same time, of helping them feel a closer connection to their new homeland by highlighting their unique place there over the *longue durée*.

Sri Lankan temples as sites of difference: caste/class divisions, ethnic tensions, and marginalization

There are both positive and negative consequences of temples being 'inextricably intertwined with the customs, traditions and language'. As a positive, the temples – as locales of Sinhalese identity – are believed to have stemmed the drift of Sri Lankans to other religions as well as to have slowed the pace of westernization. At the same time as holding the Sri Lankan community together, the temples also became sites of fracturing. One such tradition or custom that crept into – perhaps infected is a better term – temple life and prevented the Sinhalese Buddhists from realizing its need to work together as a single diasporic community was caste and class.

Sri Lanka has a caste-based society, though some have argued that it is slowly changing to a class-based society. In Sri Lanka, the highest common caste (apart from the noble or radaḷa caste) is the agriculturalist or goyigama caste. With help from kings and local rulers, the goyigama subjugated the other castes – referred to derogatively as lower castes (*aḍukula*) or service castes – through a system of taxation and forced labor or service. By marking their difference from the lower castes by dress, behavior, and language, as well as by limiting their contact with the lower castes, the radaḷa and goyigama sharply divided Sri Lankan society. Although we find a more ambivalent attitude toward caste during the British period – especially with the passing of the Colebrooke–Cameron reforms of 1833 – caste and class divisions did not disappear. Indeed, John Rogers (1994, p. 13) has aptly noted that during the British period, caste was 'still recognized by courts enforcing customary law, and was sometimes taken into account for administrative appointments'. Even though some low caste members, particularly those along the west coast of Sri Lanka, were able to use their increased economic status to affect social change, caste biases continued to fragment society, including monastic society (see Roberts 1982, Samuels 2007).

While some of the Sri Lankans that Arseculeratne discusses may have come to *Svarnabhumi* to escape from Sri Lankan's more conservative social order that continually reinforced their social standing, Malaya was not a shimmering Land of Gold for everyone. The very fact that some low-caste Sinhalese had to change their surnames when they came to Malaya or that some Sinhalese preferred to associate, almost exclusively, with the Chinese and Thai communities there suggests that caste and, later, class biases remained somewhat prevalent within the community. While it may be true that the breakdown of traditional caste-determined occupations in Malaya as well as the importance placed on social cohesion in a country where their numbers are quite small eventually drew the community together, caste prejudices affected the Sinhalese communities in Malaya and Singapore for several generations.[10] One Sinhalese firm in Malaya, for instance, maintained 'separate tables for the staff of different castes' in the 1920s (Arseculeratne 1991, p. 96), and caste continued to play an important role among some Sinhalese social institutions (e.g. marriage).

With Sri Lankan temples functioning as sites of cultural heritage and identity, it is not surprising to find that caste biases also infected monastic culture in Malaya. Ven. Ananda Mangala Thera (1977, p. 117f.), a Sri Lankan monk who lived in Malaysia and Singapore from 1961 until his death in 1986, discussed caste divisions with regard to the Sri Lankan communities and temples in Kuala Lumpur when he wrote that

> Several buddhist [*sic*] missionaries laboured under great handicaps, even suffering scorn and insults by the very Sinhalese migrants who got them down to be their spiritual guide. The motley crowd of Sinhalese in Kuala Lumpur were rather petty because they allowed

> their differences of clansmanship (caste) to influence their thinking. The loosely knit group of people managed to form the Sasana Abhiwurdhi Wardhana Society in 1895 with each clan holding to their own prejudices .... However, it took a long long time for the Sasana Abhiwurdhi Wardhana Society to transcend the pettiness of clansmanship (caste). Through a process of trial and error the Sinhalese community came to their senses and formulated a policy of togetherness.

Along with affecting the lay communities at each temple, such prejudices may have driven a wedge between the Brickfields and Sentul temples. While some, including Arseculeratne (1991, p. 96, see also p. 168), have argued that caste biases at Brickfields compelled certain patrons to establish a separate temple at Sentul, others disagree. Vijaya Samarawickrama, a Sinhalese Malaysian who has been actively involved in both temples, maintained that low-caste Sinhalese were actually quite involved in the development of Buddhist Maha Vihara over the years. Nonetheless, Samarawickrama did acknowledge the presence of certain class divisions: among the Sinhalese in Malaysia, Brickfields was (and still is) known as the 'rich man's temple'.[11]

Greater social mobility and educational achievements have certainly lessened and may have even eliminated caste prejudices among subsequent generations of Sinhalese living in Malaysia. At the same time, my own fieldwork in Malaysia suggests that the 'policy of togetherness' that Ven. Ananda Mangala mentioned has not yet become a complete reality. With Sri Lankan temples functioning as sites of identity for Sinhalese Buddhists living in the Southeast Asia diaspora, new conflicts and divisions have arisen. One such conflict pertains to certain demographic changes that have affected the Sri Lankan temples in Malaysia.

There had been, before the 1960s, a growing interest in Theravada Buddhism among certain Chinese communities living in Malaysia (Liow 1989, Nagata 1995).[12] Feeling cut off from Chinese sources related to Buddhism, many English-educated Chinese Buddhists began frequenting Theravada temples in ever increasing numbers, particularly Sri Lankan temples where English was more widely spoken.[13] Although such shifts in patronage affected the Sri Lankan temple in Penang during the late 1940s (Liow 1989, p. 62), it had an effect on the temples in Kuala Lumpur only in the 1960s when Chinese patrons began surpassing those of Sinhalese descent (see Koh and Yeoh 1989, p. 47).

One key reason behind the demographic changes at the temples in Kuala Lumpur is leadership, particularly the arrival of Ven. Dhammananda to the Brickfields temple in the 1950s and Ven. Saranankara to the Sentul temple in the 1980s. Quite similar to monks along the southwest coast of Sri Lanka who, in responding 'to new social demands among the laity' (Roberts 1982, see also Kemper 1980, p. 29) opened the *sangha* to other caste groups living there,[14] Venerables Dhammananda and Saranankara creatively responded to the social needs of other lay communities shortly after their arrival. Unlike the previous head monks who specifically catered to the religious and cultural needs of the Sri Lankan community in Kuala Lumpur, Dhammananda and Saranankara began to focus on the needs of Chinese Malaysians. By learning about their customs and beliefs, by preaching a rational form of Buddhism that resonated well with their educational levels, and by appealing to their penchant for making merit through ambitious social service projects, these progressive head monks opened their temples' doors to the Chinese and, in the process, permanently changed the face of Sri Lankan monastic culture in Malaysia.

The shifts in patronage taking place at the temples in Brickfields and Sentul were not welcomed by everyone. Seeing how similar shifts affected other ethnic Theravada temples in Malaysia, some Sinhalese argued that opening *their* temples to Chinese Malaysians would expose the temples to Chinese Buddhist iconography (e.g. statues of Amitabha and Kuan Yin), to new rituals (e.g. car-blessing rituals), and to new celebrations (e.g. Chinese New Year). Although many of the Sinhalese who opposed opening their temples' doors to other ethnic communities were unable to challenge Ven. Dhammananda's or Ven. Saranankara's vision outright, they were indirectly able to address their concerns about retaining the temples' Sri Lankan heritage.

Egil Lothe (1986), in his thesis *Mission in Theravada Buddhism*, has aptly noted that the main difference between the Sinhalese temples in Sri Lanka and those in Malaya is that while the former are owned by the monks themselves, the latter are owned by lay associations.[15] What further distinguishes the temples in Kuala Lumpur from other Sri Lankan temples in Malaysia is that the governing boards of the temples in Brickfields (Sasana Abhiwurdhi Wardhana Society) and in Sentul (Siri Jayanti Association) are restricted to Malaysian citizens of Sri Lankan descent.[16] Although there have been several instances of Chinese Malaysians sitting on the board of the Brickfields temple and some Chinese Malaysians sitting on the Board of Advisors of the Sentul temple,[17] their role in the temple's management has remained quite limited. Needless to say, the current governing structures there have not only led to occasional ethnic tensions, but also to claims of chauvinism and racism.[18]

In my own fieldwork in Malaysia and Singapore I came to understand that the system of ownership of Sri Lankan temples has somewhat limited the ability of reformist monks, such as Ven. Dhammananda and Ven. Saranankara, to make sweeping changes. While Ven. Saranankara, for instance, acknowledged that the temple's bye-laws were unfair, I came away from my conversations with him and his senior students with the sense that there was little that could be done to change it. The inability to make sweeping changes was even more acutely felt by monastic leaders who are not yet Malaysian citizens or permanent residents, as they must placate the temples' management boards with the hopes of receiving their continued sponsorship.

Rather than deal with the problem of governance head on, some monks have been able to work around their temples' bye-laws in other, more creative, ways. One tactic that some head monks have used to allow Chinese Malaysians to participate in their temples' administrative affairs while remaining sensitive to the temples' Sinhalese heritage is to create new organizations and associations that are specifically oriented to and run by Chinese patrons. Through the formation of the Buddhist Missionary Society and the Ti-Ratana Welfare Society at the Brickfields temple, as well as the Siri Jayanti Welfare Organization and the Maha Karuna Buddhist Society at the Sentul temple, Ven. Dhammananda, Dhammaratana,[19] and Saranankara have partially circumvented their temples' racially exclusive policies.

The earliest society to involve the Chinese community in an administrative capacity at the Brickfields temple was the Buddhist Missionary Society, created under Ven. Dhammananda's leadership in 1962. From its inception, the Society, which consisted mainly of Chinese Buddhists, sought to further the propagation of Buddhism in Malaysia. Through a plethora of publications (including its own periodical, *Voice of Buddhism*), frequent lecture tours (especially to Buddhist university groups), regular seminars, leadership training programs, correspondence courses, youth sections, as well as branch societies and – later – community centers, the Society provided the means through which 'several Chinese devotees who were patronising the Temple, yet who were strictly barred from direct involvement by the Sasana Abhiwurdhi Wardhana Society' to take a leadership role (Ananda Mangala 1977, p. 118).[20] Similarly, through the creation of the Maha Karuna Society in 2001 at the temple in Sentul, Ven. Saranankara was able to involve the Chinese patrons there in various welfare projects (e.g. educational relief, a mobile free clinic, an orphanage, and an old age home with hospice services), thus providing them with a sense of pride and ownership while, at the same time, allowing the temple's main governing body to continue feeling as if the temple belongs to them.

The temples' changing demographics have certainly helped both the Sri Lankan and Chinese communities in a several ways. On the one hand, most Sinhalese Buddhists recognize the role that the Chinese have played financially; most temple building projects completed from the 1980s to the present were the result of keeping 'the rich Chinese and their financial props within the [temples'] fold'.[21] On the other hand, the establishment and running of the temples' welfare organizations by the Chinese have increased their own social capital within their communities, where there already exists a penchant for relating generosity to social standing and honor.

Another point to consider when thinking about how the temples' changing demographics have affected both communities pertains to the Malay-Muslim nation state of Malaysia. As many scholars have noted, the entanglement of race and religion that was part of post-colonial policies favoring Malay-Muslims with regard to economic well-being, education and religion adversely affected minority communities in Malaysia. While all communities that are not labeled 'sons of the soil' or *bumiputera* feel the negative effects of such policies as the New Economic Policy, the university-quota system (not to mention making Malay the primary medium of instruction at the primary, secondary and tertiary levels), and the *Rukunegara* or national ideology (which effectively excludes religious belief systems that are not monotheistic),[22] smaller and less prosperous minority communities (such as the Tamil and Sinhalese) feel the effects much more tangibly.

With that in mind, then, it is not difficult to imagine the role that the Chinese community – by virtue of its sheer size and economic prosperity – played in transforming the Sri Lankan temples from closed off ethnic zones to cosmopolitan spaces. Although it may be true that such spaces remain marginalized *vis-à-vis* the dominant Malay-Muslim nation state, it is equally the case that the presence of the Chinese at the Sri Lankan temples helps generate a larger sense of community from which Sinhalese anxieties, fears, and hopes could be expressed and acted upon.

As with the Sinhalese, being considered the 'cultural other' in Malaysia has driven the Chinese community there to find other ways of feeling a sense of citizenship and belonging (see DeBernardi 1994, 2004, see also Ong 1993, 1996, 1999). While the Chinese in Malaysia may have questioned their 'ties to a single nation-state, or even to a single imagined community' (Ong 1993, p. 747), the Sri Lankan temples – with their expanding networks – may be playing an important role in providing Chinese Buddhists with the opportunity to envision themselves as part of multiple 'imagined' communities of Buddhists in South, East and Southeast Asia. Although the Chinese have had other ways to seek legitimation – such as through their economic prosperity (Duara 1997, Ong 1999), through 'family biopolitics' (Ong 1993, p. 755f.), or through uniting the ethnically and linguistically diverse Chinese community through shared Chinese rituals (DeBernardi 1994, 2004) – their involvement in a world religion such as Buddhism (with its sacred texts, moral codes and cachet of modernity) has helped link the Chinese community 'into networks of wide extent' (deBernardi 2004, p. 224f).

While all Buddhist traditions may have provided Chinese Malaysians with the means to overcome their feelings of marginalization, the Sinhalese Theravada temples played a particularly crucial role in this process for anglicized, university-educated Chinese. By minimizing the various cultural accretions that often envelop the Buddhist traditions through packaging it as a rational, progressive religion or philosophy, as well as by playing down Buddhism's sectarian divisions through working alongside Mahayana and Vajrayana Buddhists, monastic leaders such as Ven. Dhammananda and Ven. Saranankara were able to construct a much larger, united Buddhist community. Finally, by joining forces with members of other minority religious communities through their participation in such organizations as the Malaysian Consultative Council of Buddhism, Christianity, Hinduism and Sikhism,[23] the Sri Lankan monks were able to work against state control in a much more effective manner, thus providing the Sinhalese and Chinese communities with multiple planes of reference through which they are able to challenge state control and Malay *cum* Islamic hegemonic policies.

Conclusion

Feelings of absence have had a profound effect on the Sinhalese diasporic community in Malaysia. The desire to retrieve what was absent has led the Buddhist community living in Kuala Lumpur to establish temples that would provide comfort during times of uncertainty and loneliness. As institutions that were and still are simultaneously rooted in two different cultures, the temples not only fulfilled the community's religious requirements, but their ethnic and cultural needs as well. With the close connection made between ethnicity and religion, the Buddhist temples in Kuala Lumpur became the means by which Sinhalese ethnic identity, cultural heritage, and collective memory could be preserved and transmitted to subsequent generations.

While the temples in Kuala Lumpur have brought groups of Sinhalese together, it has also torn the community apart. The early histories of the two temples suggest that they functioned as the arena in which different groups Sinhalese migrants vied with one another, particularly with regard to caste and class. More recently, intra-cultural strife has given way to inter-ethnic tensions. Demographic changes with regard to temple patronage has threatened the temples' role as preserving Sinhalese culture and identity.

Some progressive Sri Lankan monks in Kuala Lumpur have embraced the changes that living in a different country bring by searching for creative ways to reach out to new audiences. As other ethnic communities become involved in the temples' events and programs, new alliances are formed. Although tensions may emerge, there are also certain benefits that result from the creation of larger inter-ethnic and inter-religious networks. Whereas the temples may benefit financially from the wider webs of monastic patronage, the temples' patrons benefit emotionally as they come to feel a growing sense of pride and a greater degree of prestige. Finally, through interethnic and interreligious alliances, the Sri Lankan temples provide their patrons with multiple planes of reference through which they are able to challenge state control and, in the process, overcome their minority status and feelings of marginalization.

Acknowledgements

An earlier version of this article was presented at National University of Singapore as part of the Migration and Religion Research Clusters within the Faculty of Arts and Social Sciences. I benefitted from numerous comments and suggestions that followed the present–ation as well as from further conversations with Irving Chan Johnson and Pattana Kitiarsa. I also acknowledge the very helpful reviewer's comments that has not only strengthened this article but has encouraged me to think differently about my longer term project on Theravada Buddhism in Malaysia. Finally, I would like to thank Rajesh Rai who encouraged me to submit an article to *South Asian Diaspora*, as well as Monica Smith and Rodney Sebastian who made my earlier visit to National University of Singapore possible.

Notes

1. Not surprisingly, under the Dutch East India Company, convicts from Malaya were sent to Sri Lanka where they were imprisoned.
2. Dispatch from Straits Settlements to Secretary of State, No. 307, 24 September 1887; cited in Raja Singam (1968, p. 29f.).
3. Currently (2010), there are two Thai temples in Kuala Lumpur: Wat Meh Liew (est. 1929) and the much larger royal-sponsored temple, Wat Chetawan (est. 1957). While S.N. Arseculeratne (1991, p. 154) notes that the former temple was established by a Chinese woman who married a Sinhalese man, temple records indicate that the woman was Thai (personal communication, Phrakhru Sirik Panjavud, head monk of Wat Meh Liew). Kedah, Kelantan, Perlis and Terengganu belonged to Thailand prior to 1909; thus, there are many Thai communities (and Thai temples) there (see Ismail 1983, 1990). There were a number of Sinhalese living in Kelantan and Kedah during the nineteenth and early twentieth century, and some Sinhalese men married Thai wives (see Arseculeratne 1991, p. 131).
4. Between the founding of the temple in Brickfields and the one in Sentul, a Sri Lanka temple was established in Penang in 1914 when a Sri Lankan monk – Ven. Pemaratana—en route from Sri Lanka to Thailand via Singapore, decided to stop over in Penang for a few days. During his stay at the Batu Lanchang Hokkien Cemetery, he preached sermons and several within the Sinhalese and Chinese communities asked him to set up a temple on the island (see Indaratana *et al.* 2004). There is another temple in Malaysia that has some connections to Sri Lanka: Seck Kia Eenh (Lord Buddha's Monastery) in Melaka. This temple, however, is Mahayana in origin. With the arrival of the temple's first resident monk – Ven. Ananda Mangala – from Sri Lanka in 1963, Theravada Buddhism and Pali chanting was introduced. Today, the temple blends Mahayana and Theravada Buddhism and remains under the administration of a Sri Lankan monk (see Tan Kim See 2010).
5. This is discussed in the temple's history, *The Sri Lanka Buddhist Temple: A Historical Overview, 1900–2000* (Anon 2000b; see also Anon 2000a and 1991).
6. See, especially, Halbwachs (1992, chap. 6). In another of Halbwach's works, *The Collective Memory*, he writes 'While the collective memory endures and draws strength from its base in a coherent body of people, it is individuals as group members who remember … . Every collective memory requires the support of a group delimited in space and time' (1950, pp. 48, 84, cited in Coser 1992, p. 22).
7. In the *70th Anniversary of the Sri Lanka Buddhist Temple, 1991* it is noted that Ven. Siriniwasa began teaching Sinhala language classes at the temple as early as the 1920s.
8. This ritual is described in Gombrich (1971) – see also Keyes (1983).
9. This statement, 'Forget not your old country (*wuwang guguo*)', is inscribed on one of the boulders in the gardens of the famous Kek Lok Si temple in Penang. It was written by Kang Youwei who encouraged the Chinese community in Malaysia to remember their own roots and ethnic identity (see DeBernardi 2004, p. 24).
10. Writing about similar biases among the Sinhalese of Singapore, Y.D. Ong (2005, p. 55) notes that 'When Sinhalese Buddhists arrived in Singapore, they kept to their caste groups. Each caste tended to support monks from its own Nikaya but monks from different Nikayas did come together for communal and religious celebrations'.
11. Personal communication with Vijaya Samarawickrama on 9 July 2010. Several lay people I spoke to said that under its current administration, the Brickfields temple – with its

current ambitious welfare agenda – favors wealthy patrons. Venerable Ananda Mangala (1977, p. 119) also noted that one of the former head monks of the Sentul temple – Ven. Dhammeswara – was known as 'the missionary of the middle-classes'.

12. By 1928, for instance, several Theravāda temples in Penang already began celebrating the Chinese new year and by 1948, 'there were more Chinese Buddhist devotees at all these Theravāda temples [on the island of Penang] than the Thais, Sri Lankans or Burmese' (Liow 1989, p. 62).
13. In general, the level of English is much lower at Thai temples with the monks there largely catering to the Thai and Thai–Chinese communities in Malaysia. For a further discussion of Thai Buddhism in Malaysia, see Ismail (1990, 1983) and Johnson (2008).
14. Because of feelings of religious disenchantment as a result of the *sangha* being restricted to goyigama, members of the three principal lower castes of the southwest coast – the Karāva (fisher), Durāva (toddy tapper) and Salāgama (cinnamon peeler) – were able to use their increased economic status to challenge, to some degree, the high caste hegemony by importing new ordination lineages from Burma in 1799 (Amarapura Nikāya) and in 1864 (Rāmañña Nikāya).
15. The system of temple-ownership in Sri Lanka – particularly monks owning temples with large tracts of land that is leased out to farmers – has sometimes been viewed as rupturing the delicate monk–patron relationship by creating a class of land-owning monastics who are no longer dependent on the laity for their requisites (see, for instance, Evers 1972, p. 16, Gunawardana 1979, and Bechert 1970). At the same time, however, there are also some benefits that result from monks owning temples. As several laypeople in Sri Lanka mentioned to me, monks who own temples are more likely to take a leadership role and to be committed to the temple's development (Samuels 2010, p. 105).
16. The Sinhala governing board at Bodhi Lankarama Buddhist Temple in Taiping made sweeping changes by opening up membership to devotees of all ethnic backgrounds in 1999 and by amending the temple's bye-laws to allow non-Sinhalese to occupy places on the temple's governing board. Since that time, the 'office bearers and committee members of Taiping Bodi Langka Ram Buddhist Association have predominantly been Chinese' (see http://www.bodhilankarama.net/History/History.htm for more detail). With much smaller Sri Lankan communities in Penang and Melaka, Mahindarama Temple (Penang) and Seck Kia Eenh (Melaka) have had to rely on the support and governance of the Chinese community from the very beginning. Today, there are no Sri Lankans on the management committee of either temple.
17. There are two instances in the history of the Sasana Abhiwurdhi Wardhana Society in which a non-Sinhala person was a patron of the Society: once in 1948 with the appointment of L.Y. Swee (who was also Vice-President of the Society from 1935 to 1948) and another in 1969 with the appointment of Teh Thean Choo. Another non-Sinhalese person to sit on the Society's board of trustees was Yeoh Cheng Hock who served as Treasurer from 1935 to 1948 (see de Silva 1998, p. 363f.). With regard to Sentul's Board of Advisors, see *70th Anniversary of the Sri Lanka Buddhist Temple, 1991* (Anon 1991).
18. The Sinhala-only policies of the Sentul temple governing board – Siri Jayanti Association – has, in fact, had negative repercussions for the Association's current President, Mervyn Weerasena. For instance, before retiring from the Royal Malaysian Police, Weerasena was accused of being a racist. The claimant argued that as Weerasena is a President of an Association that bars the participation of certain ethnic groups, he is not fit to be a civil servant. Although Weerasena claims that the charges actually came from a jealous Sinhalese patron of the temple, the fact that he was encouraged to step down as the Association's President until he retired from the police force suggests that the current bye-laws are not regarded as being fair and open (personal communication, Mervyn Weerasena, June 2010).
19. Venerable Dhammaratana became the head monk of Buddhist Maha Vihara in Brickfields in 2006 when the previous head monk, Ven. Dhammananda passed away. While Dhammananda was still alive, Ven. Dhammaratana created the Ti-Ratana Welfare Society which ran several of the temples social service projects.
20. Since the 1980s, a number of community Buddhist centres and associations (e.g. Buddhist Gem Fellowship, Subang Jaya Buddhist Association, Bandar Utama Buddhist Society, Shah Alam Buddhist Centre, and so on) have been formed with the goal of bringing Buddhism from the temple into the community. Many of the community centres' founders

were earlier students of Ven. Dhammananda and, according to some of them, were encouraged by him to create these local centres. This is discussed in Ananda Fong's (1999) article; see also Liow (1999) titled 'The Millennium Challenge'.

21. This is quoted in Arseculeratne (1991, p. 168).
22. The effects of such policies on minority communities are discussed in DeBernardi (2004). The *Rukunegara* is further discussed in Gan (1980) and Ariffin Omar (1980).
23. The organization, which was established in 1983, was later expanded into the Malaysian Consultative Council of Buddhism, Christianity, Hinduism, Sikhism and Taoism in 2006.

Notes on contributor

Jeffrey Samuels is Associate Professor in the Department of Philosophy of Religion and Coordinator of Asian Studies at Western Kentucky University. His research interests center on the intersection of religion and culture in South and Southeast Asia. He has published several journal articles on Buddhist monastic culture, pedagogical practices and research methods. Along with co-editing *Approaching the Dhamma: Buddhist Texts and Practices in South and Southeast Asia* with Anne Blackburn in 2003, he has published *Attracting the Heart: Social Relations and the Aesthetics of Emotion in Sri Lankan Monastic Culture* (University of Hawaii Press, 2010). He is currently writing a social history of Theravada Buddhism in Malaysia.

References

Ananda Mangala Thera, 1977. Sri Lanka Monks in Malaysia and Singapore. *The Young Buddhist* 117–124.

Anon, 2000. Official Opening, 10 June 2000 (2455 B.E.): Sri Lanka Buddhist temple, Sentul, Kuala Lumpur, Malaysia. Siri Jayanti Association.

Anon, 2000. *The Sri Lanka Buddhist temple: a historical overview 1900–2000.* Kuala Lumpur: Siri Jayanti Association, Sri Lanka Buddhist Temple.

Anon, 1991. *70th Anniversary of the Sri Lanka Buddhist temple, 1991.* Sentul Pasar (Kuala Lumpur): Siri Jayanti Association, Sri Lanka Buddhist Temple.

Arseculeratne, S.N., 1991. *Sinhalese immigrants in Malaysia and Singapore 1860–1990: history through recollection.* Colombo: K.V.G. De Silva and Sons.

Baxstrom, R., 2008. *Houses in motion: the experience of place and the problem of belief in urban Malaysia.* Stanford, CA: Stanford University Press.

Bechert, H., 1970. Theravada Buddhist Sangha: some general observations on historical and political factors in its development. *Journal of Asian Studies,* 29 (4), 761–778.

Coser, L., 1992. Introduction: Maurice Halbwachs, 1877–1945. *In: Maurice Halbwachs, On Collective Memory.* Chicago, IL: University of Chicago Press, 1–34.

DeBernardi, J., 1994. Historical allusion and the defense of identity: Malaysian Chinese popular religion. *In:* C. Keyes, L. Kendall and H. Hardacre, eds *Asian Visions of Authority.* Honolulu: University of Hawaii Press, 117–139.

DeBernardi, J., 2004. *Rites of belonging: memory, modernity, and identity in a Malaysian Chinese Community.* Stanford, CA: Stanford University Press.

de Silva, H.M.A., 1998. *100 Years of the Buddhist Maha Vihara (1895–1995).* Kuala Lumpur: Sasana Abhiwurdhi Wardhana Society.

Duara, P., 1997. Nationalism among transnationals: overseas Chinese and the idea of China, 1900–1911. *In:* A. Ong and D.M. Nonini, eds *Ungrounded empires: the cultural politics of modern Chinese transnationalism.* New York: Routledge, 39–60.

Evers, H., 1972. *Monks, priests and peasants: a study of Buddhism and social structure in central Ceylon.* Leiden: E.J. Brill.

Fong, A., 1999. The millennium challenge. *In:* B. Liow ed. *K. Sri Dhammananda felicitation: essays in honour of his 80th birthday.* Petaling Jaya (Kuala Lumpur): Buddhist Gem Fellowship, 240–252.

Francis, D., Kellaher, L., and Neophytou, G., 2000. Sustaining cemeteries: the user perspective. *Morality,* 5 (1), 34–52.

Gan, T.C., 1980. A Buddhist view. *In:* Y.K. Khoo, ed. *One god, many paths.* Penang (Malaysia): Ganesh Printing Works, 35–42.

Gombrich, R., 1971. 'Merit transference' in Sinhalese Buddhism: a case study of the interaction between doctrine and practice. *History of Religions,* 11 (2), 203–219.

Gunawardana, R.A.L., 1979. *Robe and plough: monasticism and economic interest in early medieval Sri Lanka.* Tucson: The University of Arizona Press.

Halbwachs, M., 1950. *The collective memory.* New York: Harper-Colophon Books.

Halbwachs, M., 1992. *On collective memory,* trans. Lewis Coser. Chicago, IL: Chicago University Press.

Ho, E., 2006. *The graves of Tarim: genealogy and mobility across the Indian Ocean.* Berkeley: University of California Press.

Indaratana, E., Ven., Witanachchi, C., and Lim, L., eds, 2004. *Mahindarama Buddhist Temple: 85 Years of history (1918–2003).* Penang: Mahindarama Dhamma Publications.

Ismail, M.Y., 1983. *Buddhism and ethnicity: social organization of a Buddhist Temple in Kelantan.* Singapore: Institute of Southeast Asian Studies.

Ismail, M.Y., 1990. Buddhism among the Siamese of Kelantan: minority religion in a Muslim state. *Jurnal Antropologi Dan Sosiologi,* 18: 55–69.

Jing Jun, 1996. *The temple of memories: history, power, and morality in a Chinese village.* Stanford, CA: Stanford University Press.

Johnson, I.C., 2008. The mobility of stories and the expansive spaces of Kelantanese Thai religiosity. *In:* M. Montesano and P. Jory, eds *Thai South and Malay North: ethnic interactions on a plural peninsula.* Singapore: National University of Singapore Press, 304–326.

Kemper, S., 1980. Reform and segmentation in Monastic fraternities in low country Sri Lanka. *Journal of Asian Studies,* 40 (1), 27–41.

Keyes, C.F., 1983. Merit-transference in the Kammic theory of popular Theravada Buddhism. *In:* C.F. Keyes and E.V. Daniels, eds *Karma: an anthropological inquiry.* Berkeley: University of California Press, 261–286.

Koh Beng Yan, C. and Yeoh Kia Gee. 20 September 1989. Malaysian Buddhist cultural heritage progress report, no. 3. Young Buddhist Association of Malaysia. Unpublished report.

Liow, B.W.K., 1999. K. Sri Dhammananda: in the footsteps of the Buddha. *In:* B.L.W. Khin, ed. *K. Sri Dhammananda felicitation: essays in honour of his 80th birthday.* Petaling Jaya (Malaysia): Buddhist Gem Fellowship, 25–58.

Liow, B.W.K., 1989. Buddhist temples and associations in Penang, 1845–1948. *Journal of the Malaysia Branch of the Royal Asiatic Society,* 62, 57–85.

Lothe, E., 1986. *Mission in Theravada Buddhism.* Dissertation (PhD), Institute for the History of Religions, University of Oslo.

Nagata, J., 1995. Limits to the indigenisation of Buddhism in Malaysia, with a focus on the religious community in Penang. *In:* R. Talib and T. Chee-Beng, eds *Dimensions of tradition and development in Malaysia.* Petaling Jaya, Selangor Darul Ehsan [Malaysia]: Pelanduk Publications, 307–344.

Nora, P. and Kritzman, L.D., ed., 1996. *Realms of memory: rethinking the French Past.* Vol. 1: *Conflicts and divisions.* New York: Columbia University Press.

Omar, A., 1980. An Islamic perspective. *In:* Y.K. Khoo, ed. *One God, many paths.* Penang (Malaysia): Ganesh Printing Works, 30–34.

Ong, A., Winter 1993. On the edge of empires: flexible citizenship among Chinese in diaspora. *Positions: East Asia Cultures Critique,* 1 (3), 745–778.

Ong, A., 1996. Cultural citizenship as subject-making: immigrants negotiate racial and cultural boundaries in the United States. *Current Anthropology,* 37 (5), 737–762.

Ong, A., 1999. *Flexible citizenship: the cultural logics of transnationality.* Durham, NC: Duke University Press.

Ong, Y.D., 2005. *Buddhism in Singapore – a short narrative history.* Singapore: Skylark Publications.

Rainville, L., 2008. Social memory and plantation burial grounds, a Virginian example. The African Diaspora Archaeology Newsletter.

Raja Singam, S. D., 1968. *A hundred years of Ceylonese in Malaysia and Singapore (1867–1967).* Petaling Jaya (Kuala Lumpur): Raja Singam.

Roberts, M., 1982. *Caste conflict and elite formation: the rise of a Karâva elite in Sri Lanka, 1500–1931.* Cambridge: Cambridge University Press.

Rogers, J.D., 1994. Post-Orientalism and the interpretation of premodern and modern political identities: the case of Sri Lanka. *The Journal of Asian Studies,* 53 (1), 10–23.
Samarawickrama, V., 2003. *A Buddhist reflects on Malaysian Buddhism.* Kuala Lumpur: Sasana Abhiwurdhi Wardhana Society and Sri Jayanti Association.
Samuels, J., 2007. Monastic patronage and temple building in contemporary Sri Lanka: caste, ritual performance, and merit. *Modern Asian Studies,* 41 (4), 757–794.
Samuels, J., 2010. *Attracting the heart: social relations and the aesthetics of emotion in Sri Lankan Monastic Culture.* Honolulu: University of Hawaii Press.
Tan Kim See, ed., 2010. *Seck Kia Eenh: 1920–2010. Commemorative Magazine.*

Index

Page numbers followed by n refer to notes